MW01268558

OLSAT® Preparation Guide - Levels D, E, and F

Written and published by: Bright Kids NYC

Corporate Headquarters:
Bright Kids NYC Inc.
225 Broadway, Suite 1504
New York, NY 10007
www.brightkidsnyc.com
info@brightkidsnyc.com
917-539-4575

Table of Contents

About Bright Kids NYC.. 7

Introduction.. 9

OLSAT® Overview.. 11

Content of Levels D, E, and F Tests...13

   Verbal Subtests..13

   Nonverbal Subtests..15

OLSAT® Test Structure...17

How To Use This Book..19

OLSAT® Strategies..21

OLSAT® Subtests...27

Verbal Comprehension Subtests..27

   ANTONYMS...27

      Strategies...29

      Questions...31

      Answer Key..35

   SENTENCE COMPLETION..41

      Strategies...43

      Questions...47

      Answer Key..55

   SENTENCE ARRANGEMENT...61

      Strategies...63

      Questions...65

      Answer Key..69

Verbal Reasoning Subtests..71

   ARITHMETIC REASONING...71

      Strategies...73

      Questions...75

      Answer Key..79

   LOGICAL SELECTION..83

      Strategies...85

      Questions...87

      Answer Key..91

   WORD/LETTER MATRICES..97

      Strategies...99

      Questions...101

      Answer Key..107

Table of Contents (continued)

VERBAL ANALOGIES.. 111

    Strategies.. 113

    Questions.. 115

    Answer Key.. 119

VERBAL CLASSIFICATIONS.. 125

    Strategies.. 127

    Questions.. 131

    Answer Key.. 135

INFERENCE.. 141

    Strategies.. 143

    Questions.. 145

    Answer Key.. 151

Figural Reasoning Subtests.. 159

FIGURAL CLASSIFICATIONS.. 159

    Strategies.. 161

    Questions.. 163

    Answer Key.. 169

FIGURAL ANALOGIES.. 175

    Strategies.. 177

    Questions.. 179

    Answer Key.. 187

PATTERN MATRICES.. 193

    Strategies.. 195

    Questions.. 197

    Answer Key.. 205

FIGURAL SERIES.. 211

    Strategies.. 213

    Questions.. 215

    Answer Key.. 221

Quantitative Reasoning Subtests.. 227

NUMBER SERIES.. 227

    Strategies.. 229

    Questions.. 231

    Answer Key.. 237

Table of Contents (continued)

NUMERIC INFERENCE... 243

    Strategies.. 245

    Questions.. 247

    Answer Key... 253

NUMBER MATRICES... 257

    Strategies.. 259

    Questions.. 261

    Answer Key... 267

Answer Sheets.. 273

About Bright Kids NYC

Bright Kids NYC was founded in New York City to provide language arts and math enrichment for children and to educate parents about standardized tests through workshops and consultations, as well as to prepare young children for such tests through assessments, tutoring, and publications.

At Bright Kids NYC, we strive to provide the best learning materials. Our publications are truly unique. First, all of our books have been created by qualified psychologists, learning specialists, and teachers. Second, our books have been tested by hundreds of children in our tutoring practice. Since children can make associations that many adults cannot, testing of materials by children is critical to creating successful test preparation guides. Finally, our learning specialists and teaching staff have provided practical strategies and tips so parents can best help their child prepare to compete successfully on standardized tests.

Feel free to contact us should you have any questions.

Corporate Headquarters:
Bright Kids NYC Inc.
225 Broadway, Suite 1504
New York, NY 10007
www.brightkidsnyc.com
info@brightkidsnyc.com
917-539-4575

Introduction

Bright Kids NYC created the OLSAT® Preparation Guide to familiarize students with the content and the format of the OLSAT®. Children, no matter how bright they are, do not always perform well when they are not accustomed to the format and structure of a test. Children can misunderstand the directions, may fail to consider all the answer choices, and may not always read the questions carefully. Thus, without adequate preparation and familiarization, children may not always perform to the best of their ability on standardized tests such as the OLSAT®.

The objective of the OLSAT® Preparation Guide is to help your child practice the types of questions that he or she will see on the OLSAT®. We have included 460 exercises to ensure that your child has plenty of practice material. In addition, we have included strategies on how to approach the questions, along with an answer key that has explanations to ensure that your child can learn from the practice questions.

In order to maximize the effectiveness of our OLSAT® Preparation Guide, it is important to first familiarize yourself with the test and the types of questions that will be on the test. In addition, we recommend that you utilize one of our practice tests for the appropriate level of the test that your child will be taking in order to give your child the experience of taking the real test.

Children will be taking many standardized tests throughout their school years. The best way for your child to develop his or her critical-thinking skills for these types of tests is to practice with similarly styled test questions and to utilize certain test-taking strategies. These methods will ensure that your child will perform to the best of his or her ability.

OLSAT® Preparation Guide - Levels D, E, and F

Bright Kids NYC Inc. ©

OLSAT® Overview

The Otis-Lennon School Ability Test® (OLSAT®) was discovered and published in 1918 by Dr. Arthur Otis, who was completing graduate work at Stanford University. The Otis Group Intelligence Scale was followed by the Otis Self-Administering Tests of Mental Ability, the Otis Quick-Scoring Mental Ability Tests, the Otis-Lennon Mental Ability Test, and finally the Otis-Lennon School Ability Test. As the years went by, the term *mental ability* was changed to *school ability* in order to reflect the purposes for which the test is most suitable—that is, to assess examinees' ability to cope with school learning tasks, to suggest their possible placement for school learning functions, and to evaluate their achievement in relation to the talents they bring to school learning.

The latest version of the Otis Lennon School Ability Test® is the Eighth Edition (OLSAT® 8), which is administered in education programs around the country in states such as New York, Connecticut, California, Texas, and Virginia.

OLSAT® Preparation Guide - Levels D, E, and F

Content of Level D, E, and F Tests

In order to succeed on the OLSAT®, students must perceive accurately and recall what has been perceived, understand patterns and relationships, reason abstract items, and apply generalizations to contexts both new and different. These capabilities are measured through performance on these subtests: antonyms, sentence completion, sentence arrangement, arithmetic reasoning, logical selection, word/letter matrices, verbal analogies, verbal classifications, inference, figural classifications, figural analogies, pattern matrices, figural series, number series, numeric inference, and number matrices.

Verbal Subtests

The verbal subtests are divided into two groups: verbal comprehension and verbal reasoning. The **verbal comprehension** subtests are designed to measure the student's ability to extrapolate and manipulate information from language. There is an emphasis here on the relational aspects of words and sentences and the nuances of meaning.

There are three types of questions used to test verbal comprehension skills:

1. **Antonyms:** These questions engage the student in searching for the opposite meaning of words. At the foundation of this section are a student's vocabulary skills; however, antonym questions require a high level of comprehension because students will have to understand a concept well enough to reverse it.

2. **Sentence Completion:** These questions assess a student's ability to make the logical connections necessary for sentence composition, as they will have to "fill in the blank(s)" with the word(s) necessary to create a complete and meaningful sentence.

3. **Sentence Arrangement:** Taking the form of a sentence jumble, students must look at a list of words and determine the best possible order they could go in to make a meaningful sentence. These questions measure the ability of the student to comprehend the structure of language by using parts to construct a whole.

The **verbal reasoning** subtests are designed to measure the student's ability to identify and understand patterns and relationships in writing as well as to extrapolate "clues" to aid him or her in solving a problem. The emphasis here is on skills such as necessary versus sufficient, similar versus different, and making and applying inferences.

There are six types of questions used to test verbal reasoning skills:

1. **Arithmetic Reasoning:** Arithmetic reasoning incorporates mathematical reasoning into the solving of verbal problems. This section tests basic mathematical reasoning concepts such as counting, quantity, estimation, and inequalities as well as more complex reasoning skills, including making inferences and solving basic word problems involving addition, subtraction, and simple fractions.

2. **Logical Selection:** These questions ask the student to apply logic in order to find the necessary answer—the answer that is true in every possible instance—to complete a short statement. This requires a level of focused reasoning as the student considers which answers *could* be correct versus which answer is *always* correct.

3. **Word/Letter Matrices:** In these matrices, students must be able to identify a relationship between present words or letters in order to supply the missing word or letter. These questions require students to make appropriate inferences and then practically apply them.

4. **Verbal Analogies:** Students will have to find the relationship between a pair of words and then create a second pair using the same relationship rule. Being able to infer relationships is key to success in this section.

5. **Verbal Classifications:** Here, students will be looking for the overarching principle that links a set of concepts and then identify the one that does not belong. The key to these questions is finding the relational quality and evaluating each concept against it.

6. **Inference:** Students will be given an argument and must infer an appropriate conclusion from the premises given. This skill relies heavily on the student's ability to evaluate the premises and differentiate between necessary and sufficient clauses.

Nonverbal Subtests

The nonverbal subtests are divided into two groups: figural and quantitative reasoning. The **figural reasoning** subtests are designed to measure a student's ability to reason through a visual, or non-language based, medium. The emphasis here is on inferring relationships, identifying sequences and determining next steps, and making generalizations.

There are four types of questions used to test figural reasoning skills:

1. **Figural Classifications:** Classifications require the student to figure out what does not belong among a group of items. All but one of the figures in each question share a minimum of one common trait or characteristic, requiring the student to evaluate similarities and differences among each in order to select the item that does not belong.

2. **Figural Analogies:** Students will have to find the relationship between a pair of figures and then complete a second pair using the same relationship rule. The ability to infer relationships is key to success in this section.

3. **Pattern Matrices:** Pattern matrices evaluate the ability of the student to find the next step in a geometric series, based on a set of rules. Students need to understand the rule and apply it to predict what shape would come next.

4. **Figural Series:** Figural series' assess a student's ability to evaluate a sequential series of geometric shapes and to then predict the shape that comes next.

The **quantitative reasoning** subtests measure the student's ability to infer patterns and relationships and to solve problems through utilizing numbers rather than language. In order to be successful, the student will have to be able to predict and establish outcomes based on mathematical processes.

There are three types of questions to test quantitative reasoning skills:

1. **Number Series:** In the same vein as the figural series, the student will have to extrapolate a pattern from a sequence of numbers and then apply that pattern to predict what will come next.

2. **Numeric Inference:** The student will have to reason, using computations skills and rules, why a pair or trio of numbers are related. Once the relationship is established, the student must apply it in order to create another pair or trio.

3. **Number Matrices:** The student must find an overarching principle that links numbers in a matrix and then apply that principle in order to figure out what number is missing.

OLSAT® Preparation Guide - Levels D, E, and F

OLSAT® Test Structure

The OLSAT® is a multiple-choice test. Reading skills are an important component of the Levels D, E, and F tests since the tests are entirely self-administered. They are taken in a group where students are required to mark or bubble their answers.

The OLSAT® content and structure vary for each entry level. The Level D test is 64 questions; the Levels E and F tests are 72 questions each. The number and type of questions in each section of the Levels D, E, and F tests are shown in Table 1. Students must answer all questions a group setting. They have 40 minutes to complete the test.

TABLE 1: Distribution of Types of Questions[1]

Subtest	LEVEL D Number of Questions	LEVEL E Number of Questions	LEVEL F Number of Questions
VERBAL			
Verbal Comprehension			
Antonyms	5	4	4
Sentence Completion	4	4	4
Sentence Arrangement	4	4	4
Verbal Reasoning			
Arithmetic Reasoning	4	4	4
Logical Selection	4	4	4
Word/Letter Matrices	4	4	4
Verbal Analogies	4	4	4
Verbal Classifications	4	4	4
Inferences	0	4	4
NONVERBAL			
Figural Reasoning			
Figural Classifications	8	0	0
Figural Analogies	6	6	6
Pattern Matrices	6	6	6
Figural Series	6	6	6
Quantitative Reasoning			
Number Series	6	6	6
Number Inferences	6	6	6
Number Matrices	6	6	6

[1] This may or may not represent the question mix of the actual OLSAT® test, as the mix between verbal and nonverbal questions and among different types of questions may change from year to year.

How To Use This Book

OLSAT® Levels D through F are very similar in content and style; thus we have created a workbook that helps students taking these levels of the test. While the test accelerates in difficulty, older students are required to have a higher level of accuracy in order to get a high score. The questions in each section of this workbook are designed so that they accelerate in difficulty. The number and type of questions in each section are shown in Table 2. There are a total of 460 questions, and 16 answer sheets are included at the end of this Guide.

If your child is practicing for the OLSAT® Level D test, complete all sections of the book except the Inference section. The Figural Classification section is particularly important for Level D testers, as this section is not on the Level E or Level F tests. It is important for your child to get through at least half of the questions in each section, but most of the questions on the nonverbal section of the test should be completed. If your child is advanced, you can continue to work through the rest of the questions in the other sections.

If your child is practicing for the OLSAT® Level E test, complete all sections except for Figural Classifications. Your child should be able to get through and comprehend the majority of the questions.

Finally, if your child is taking the OLSAT® Level F test, he or she needs to get through and practice all the questions in the book, except the Figural Classifications subtest. Please pay particular attention to those more advanced questions at the end of each section, as your child will be expected to master these more advanced concepts.

OLSAT® is a challenging test; thus make sure you review with your child not only the skills but also strategies for solving different types of questions on the OLSAT®. Also, go through the OLSAT® Strategy section to get a solid grasp of general test-taking skills. If you want further practice or want to give your child a sample test, we have practice tests available for all levels.

TABLE 2: OLSAT® Preparation Guide Question Distribution

Subtest	Number of Questions
VERBAL	
Verbal Comprehension	
Antonyms	30
Sentence Completion	39
Sentence Arrangement	40
Verbal Reasoning	
Arithmetic Reasoning	25
Logical Selection	25
Word/Letter Matrices	25
Verbal Analogies	37
Verbal Classifications	30
Inferences[1]	25
NONVERBAL	
Figural Reasoning	
Figural Classifications[2]	25
Figural Analogies	26
Pattern Matrices	23
Figural Series	24
Quantitative Reasoning	
Number Series	36
Number Inferences	25
Number Matrices	25
TOTAL	**460**

[1] Levels E and F only
[2] Level D only

OLSAT® Preparation Guide - Levels D, E, and F   Bright Kids NYC Inc. ©

OLSAT® Strategies

The OLSAT® is not a very long test, but it is an intense standardized test that will require you to think and reason in a variety of ways. You will encounter 15 different types of questions on the Levels D, E, and F tests of the OLSAT®. These questions are designed to test your verbal comprehension, verbal reasoning, figural reasoning, and quantitative reasoning skills. There are a total of 64 questions on the Level D test and a total of 72 questions on the Levels E and F tests. You will be given 40 minutes to complete the test using a Scantron sheet to mark your answers. Factoring in the time it will take to fill out some information on your answer sheet and listen to instructions given by the proctor, the entire administration of the test should take less than an hour.

The OLSAT® is designed to function like an IQ test; that is, its main purpose is to test you on how well you are able to think and reason. The questions on this test are quite different from any questions you would normally encounter on a school test. There is no specific level of knowledge required for this test; the OLSAT® tests you on how you think, not on how much you know. You will not need to remember fact patterns, math formulas, or anything else of that nature. All you need to remember is the best way to approach each of the 15 different types of questions that you will encounter on the test. Below are some general tips to follow when you are taking the OLSAT®. Learning and using them can only be beneficial to your score.

1. **Familiarize yourself with the types of questions you expect to encounter on the test.**

   The best way to ensure that you will feel confident before you walk in to take this test is to have had some experience with the types of questions that you will encounter on the OLSAT®. Knowing what to expect on the test can ease your mind, calm your nerves, and help you focus when the test day arrives. After going through the sections and questions in this workbook, you should be able to recognize each of the 15 different types of questions on the OLSAT® and know the best way to attack them on the actual test.

2. **Get in the habit of recognizing patterns.**

   The only way you will do well on the OLSAT® is if you are adept at recognizing and applying patterns to different types of questions. The entire test is simply testing you on whether you can discover the correct relationship between various groups of things. For the verbal comprehension subtests, you will need to look at the relationships between words and their functions in different types of sentences. For the verbal reasoning subtests, you will essentially be asked to find the patterns in different uses of letters and words. The figural reasoning questions will test you on how well you can reason and find patterns in a visual medium. Finally, the quantitative reasoning section will test you on your ability to find relationships and patterns in groups of numbers. Once you understand all of the ways that you can look for patterns in the various questions, you will be better equipped to score well on the OLSAT®.

3. **Learn to categorize. Identify the easy and hard questions on the OLSAT®.**

For some exams, the questions increase in difficulty as you progress though different sections. On the OLSAT®, the questions alternate randomly between being easy and difficult as you move through the test. So, after any given question, you're just as likely to find an easy question as a hard question. However, remember that "easy" and "difficult" are just how the questions are classified—you might actually find a question categorized as "easy" to be difficult and vice versa. Your best strategy is to focus on one question at a time and answer quickly the questions that you find easy so you can spend a little more time on the questions that you find difficult.

4. **Develop your own personal methods for each type of question.**

There are different strategies listed in this workbook for approaching each of the 15 different types of questions on the OLSAT®. However, at the end of the day, the responsibility lies with you to use methods that make the most sense to you. Feel free to use any strategy in this workbook that helps you, but don't be afraid to come up with your own strategies or methods to attack the various question types. For example, you might want to develop your own personal shorthand notation to help you keep track of a certain kind of pattern or relationship. Or, maybe you prefer to think of a question in a certain manner that is not mentioned in this workbook. As long as your reasoning is sound and leads you to the correct answer, any strategy or method you develop to help you with each question can only be beneficial. Your basic goal is to be comfortable with how you approach all of the various types of questions on the OLSAT®.

5. **Use real-world examples to help you with a question.**

Some questions in the verbal comprehension and verbal reasoning sections will require you to think about the relationships between certain words. For these questions, you may find it easier to think about how these words might operate in the real world. That is, what is their function, or what are the characteristics about the listed items that we generally associate with them in our world? Tying the words to the real world might help you in figuring out the correct answer to the question.

6. Use the "process of elimination" method.

With standardized tests, the questions and answers can sometimes work off each other to help you in finding the correct answer. If you can eliminate some of the answer choices, you immediately increase your chances of correctly guessing the answer. There will usually be one answer choice in a question that seems blatantly wrong. Eliminating just one answer choice increases your chances of correctly guessing the answer from 20% to 25% when you are given five answer choices. If you can eliminate two answer choices, your chances increase from 25% to 33%. For certain types of questions on the OLSAT®, such as the logical selection questions, the "process of elimination" method will be the key to determining the correct answer.

7. Never leave a blank answer.

Some exams penalize you for guessing incorrectly. There is no penalty for guessing on the OLSAT®. A blank answer is scored just the same as an incorrect answer. This means that you should never leave a blank answer on the OLSAT®; you should always guess on questions when you can't choose between two or more answer choices. You should also guess on a question before you move on to the next question because of the number of questions you need to get through on the OLSAT®. You probably will not have time to go back and look at the question again. Spend a little time making your best reasonable guess and then move on.

8. Get comfortable with using a Scantron sheet.

The OLSAT® is a multiple-choice test that uses a Scantron, or bubble, answer sheet. Every time you answer a question, you need to go to your answer sheet to fill in the bubble of the correct answer choice. You might find that you are not used to taking an exam in this format. While it may take some getting used to, you'll soon discover that it's not difficult to move back and forth between the test booklet and the Scantron sheet. Place your answer sheet next to the test booklet and always remember which area you are on in the Scantron sheet. Working in this manner will soon become routine for you as you progress through the test.

9. Always keep track of your time.

Before you go into your test, you should know how many questions you need to get through and how much time you will be given to complete the test. For the Level D test, you will have 40 minutes to get through 64 questions. That means you can only spend approximately 35 seconds on each question. For the Levels E and F tests, you will have 40 minutes to get through 72 questions. You shouldn't be spending more than 30 seconds on each question. Remember that this is just a general pace that you need to work at. You may answer some questions more easily than others and spend more time on certain questions that you find difficult. However, a good rule to follow is that you shouldn't spend more than 30 or 35 seconds (depending on which level of test you're taking) on a question. If you follow this rule, you will definitely have time to answer all of the questions. In any case, try to keep close track of your time so that you can finish the test.

10. Fill in the bubbles completely.

It is important to completely fill in the bubble of each of your answer choices. Even if you are in a rush, you need to make sure that your answer will be recognized by the machine that scores your test. You need to pay close attention to all of these administrative issues as you work through a standardized test. They are simple but important.

11. Only fill in a bubble when you have chosen your final answer.

You will be using a No. 2 pencil to fill in the bubbles on your answer sheet. So, if you change your mind about the answer to a question, you can erase your answer and fill in a different bubble. However, you should do your best not to do this often. No matter how well you erase, there is usually still a smudge, which could affect the machine scoring of your test. Also, it takes time to erase an answer, and every second counts on the OLSAT®. You should get in the habit of bubbling in your answer only after you are certain that you want to choose an answer choice as your final answer. Filling in the bubble should be the final thing you do before you move on to the next question. If you do fill in a bubble and realize soon after that it's the wrong answer, do your best to erase the wrong answer completely.

12. Remember to take care that you are filling in the correct bubbles on the answer sheet.

One of the most important things you need to do on a standardized multiple-choice test is to make sure that you are on the right question on your answer sheet and that you are filling in the correct bubble. If you mess up on this simple step, your entire test could be ruined. It would be a shame to do well on a test and not have that accurately reflected in your score because of a simple error in the marking of your answer sheet.

13. Don't panic.

Never panic on an exam if you're having trouble with a question. The best way to attack the OLSAT® is to think of it as a game of sorts. The goal of the game is almost always to discover and implement some kind of pattern or relationship in a question in order to identify the right answer. Being able to coolly and logically approach the various questions will be a contributing factor to your success in determining the correct patterns on this test. If you can stay calm and focused, you will be better able to identify the correct answers.

14. Get a good night's rest before the test.

The best thing you can do the day before your test is to simply relax. Do not study or cram. Eat a healthy and hearty dinner. Make sure that you get 7–8 hours of sleep the night before your test. You should feel excited that all of your hard work will soon pay off. You want to walk into your exam room relaxed and confident that you will do well on the day of your test. The only way to reach this level of calmness is to feel as though you did your best to ensure that you have mentally prepared yourself for the upcoming test. Of course, the only way to reach the level of composure that you hope to attain is to begin focusing more closely on the 15 different types of questions found in the verbal comprehension, verbal reasoning, figural reasoning, and quantitative reasoning subtests. So, let's get to work!

OLSAT® Preparation Guide - Levels D, E, and F

Antonyms

OLSAT® Preparation Guide - Levels D, E, and F

Bright Kids NYC Inc. ©

Antonym Strategies

The antonym questions in the Verbal Comprehension section of the OLSAT® will test you on whether you can identify a word that has the opposite meaning of the word you have been given. Your vocabulary skills will be tested with these types of questions; however, you will also have to use your reasoning skills in order to determine the opposite of the definition of a given word.

Example: The opposite of dirty is -

A. Heavy   B. Crazy   C. Clean   D. Mad   E. Grimy

The correct answer is (C) Clean. If something is not at all dirty, it is clean.

Remember to pick the answer choice that has the most extremely opposite definition to the given word. There might be a few answer choices that can be associated with each other in some manner. Always remember that you need to find the word that is the *complete opposite* of a given word; do not choose a word that is only associated with a *slightly* opposite meaning of the given word. The best answer will always be the word that is the polar opposite of the given word. If your given word is *big*, do not choose *short* over *small*.

Try to remember certain words that are always antonyms of each other.

Examples: *short/tall, big/small, serious/comical, heavy/light, night/day, East/West, North/South, dirty/clean, floor/ceiling, happy/sad, nice/mean, black/white*

If you cannot figure out the antonym, try imagining a real-world example. If you're able to relate the word to something in your life, you might be able to determine what the opposite definition of the word would be. First off, do not panic. Think about whether you might have encountered the word somewhere in your reading or in your life. Also, try to see if it's possible to use the word in some kind of sentence, which may jog your memory.

Example: The opposite of immobile is -

A. Tired   B. Hungry   C. Laughing   D. Jogging   E. Moving

Being immobile means being motionless and at rest. Here, it's possible to get confused with choice (D). *Jogging* is not the best choice as the antonym of *immobile* because if you're not immobile, that doesn't necessarily mean that you're jogging—you could be walking. However, if you're not immobile, you are moving in some way. The best answer is (E).

Try to remember certain words or phrases that might be related to the given word. With many antonyms, certain words appear to be naturally paired together. For example, *hard* and *soft* are antonyms that always seem to be paired together. If you come up with an opposite definition that seems to apply to more than one answer choice, try to see if one of the answer choices seems to be used more often as an antonym for the given word.

Get in the habit of immediately eliminating synonyms among the answer choices. If you're coming up with nothing, take a look at the answer choices. If you see two words that are synonymous, you can probably eliminate them because the right answer cannot have a definition too similar to another answer choice. In that same vein, if one word stands out as being quite different from the other choices, there's a chance that this might be the right answer. Every answer choice that you can eliminate will raise your chances of guessing the correct answer. Synonyms of the given word are easy eliminations in this section of the OLSAT®.

Antonyms Questions

1. **The opposite of first is -**

    A. Last   B. Beginning   C. Primary   D. Second

2. **The opposite of shallow is -**

    A. Large   B. Deep   C. Wide   D. Narrow

3. **The opposite of thick is -**

    A. Thin   B. Heavy   C. Fat   D. Jolly

4. **The opposite of grand is -**

    A. Big   B. Immense   C. Little   D. Important

5. **The opposite of worst is -**

    A. Big   B. Better   C. Little   D. Best

6. **The opposite of bought is -**

    A. Sale   B. Sold   C. Loaned   D. Give

7. **The opposite of lost is -**

    A. Found   B. Sold   C. Met   D. Invent

8. **The opposite of some is -**

    A. Sometimes   B. Many   C. Somewhere   D. Somehow

9. **The opposite of new is -**

    A. Old   B. Modern   C. Fresh   D. Plenty

10. **The opposite of sick is -**

    A. Healthy   B. Ill   C. Unwell   D. Weak

11. The opposite of mine is -

    A. Yours   B. Ours   C. Me   D. My

12. The opposite of fine is -

    A. Pure   B. Nice   C. Thin   D. Coarse

13. The opposite of cooked is -

    A. Raw   B. Stale   C. Expert   D. Fresh

14. The opposite of dawn is -

    A. Sunrise   B. Noon   C. Dusk   D. Light   E. Night

15. The opposite of southwest is -

    A. South   B. Southwest   C. Northeast   D. Northwest   E. Southeast

16. The opposite of order is -

    A. Trust   B. Confusion   C. Arrange   D. Regulate   E. Direct

17. The opposite of sweet is -

    A. Sour   B. Crumbly   C. Mild   D. Fatty   E. Loveable

18. The opposite of go is -

    A. Stay   B. Run   C. Continue   D. Depart   E. Arrive

19. The opposite of enough is -

    A. Plenty   B. Abundant   C. Real   D. Insufficient   E. Dry

20. The opposite of win is -

    A. Try   B. Lose   C. Conquer   D. Persist   E. Succed

21. **The opposite of transparent is -**

    A. Apparent   B. Real   C. Obvious   D. Clear   E. Opaque

22. **The opposite of wild is -**

    A. Animal   B. Risky   C. Tame   D. Rude   E. Violent

23. **The opposite of reject is -**

    A. Exclude   B. Refuse   C. Agree   D. Accept   E. Decline

24. **The opposite of hollow is -**

    A. Empty   B. Solid   C. Liquid   D. Transparent   E. Ice

25. **The opposite of bold is -**

    A. Brave   B. Shy   C. Arrogant   D. Fearless   E. Courageous

26. **The opposite of general is -**

    A. Great   B. Ordinary   C. Ignorant   D. Common   E. Specific

27. **The opposite of remember is -**

    A. Fame   B. Retain   C. Forget   D. Recall   E. Recollect

28. **The opposite of spend is -**

    A. Waste   B. Save   C. Gather   D. Consume   E. Buy

29. **The opposite of merciful is -**

    A. Compassionate   B. Tolerant   C. Sympathetic   D. Tender   E. Cruel

30. **The opposite of war is -**

    A. Peace   B. Tranquility   C. Agreement   D. Conflict   E. Enemy

OLSAT® Preparation Guide - Levels D, E, and F

Antonym Answer Key

1. (A) Last

To be first in something is to come before all others. The opposite of being first would be to come after all others in something. Thus, *last* is the antonym of *first*. Don't be confused by answer choice (D)—*second*. If there are more than two people, being second can never be last.

2. (B) Deep

The shallow end of the pool is the part of the pool that you can probably stand in. The other end of the pool is the deep end, where you can't stand. *Shallow* and *deep* are antonyms, so answer choice (B) is correct.

3. (A) Thin

Something that is thick has a great extent from one edge of the surface to the other; for example, a thick pizza crust has a lot of dough inside the crust, which makes it larger and softer. A thin pizza crust, however, does not have a lot of dough inside, so it is smaller and crunchier. *Thick* and *thin* have opposite meanings. Answer choice (A) is correct.

4. (C) Little

If you describe something as grand, you are saying that the thing is huge and massive. The Grand Canyon was given its name because of its immensity. The opposite of *grand* is *little*, so answer choice (C) is correct.

5. (D) Best

Being worst in something is being bad at something to the most extreme degree. If you have the worst score in your class after you take a test, it means that nobody has a lower score than you. The opposite would be to have the highest or best score in the class. Since *best* and *worst* are antonyms of each other, answer choice (D) is correct.

6. (B) Sold

If you buy something, you are paying money to receive the product or service. If you sell a product or service, you receive money for it. Thus, buying and selling are opposite actions, which makes answer choice (B) the right choice.

7. (A) Found

If you lose something, you are having trouble finding it. However, if you do happen to find the thing you were looking for, the thing is not lost anymore. *Lost* and *found* have opposite meanings.

8. (B) Many

Having 8 pennies in a jar means that you have some pennies, but not many, in that jar. But, if you had 900 pennies in a jar, it would be safe to say that you had a lot of, or many, pennies in your possession. *Some* and *many* are the two words that have opposite meanings in this group.

9. (A) Old

Something that is *new* has not been in your possession for a long time. However, something that is *old* has been in your possession, or someone else's, for a certain period of time. Thus, answer choice (A) is correct.

10. (A) Healthy

Someone who is sick is *ill* (choice B), *unwell* (choice C), or *weak* (choice D). Since we can identify all of the other answer choices as being synonymous with the given word, the correct answer must be answer choice (A)—*healthy*.

11. (A) Yours

If I own something, it's mine. If you own something, it's yours. What's mine is not yours, and what's yours is not mine, so *yours* and *mine* are opposites of each other. Answer choice (B) might trick you, but the opposite of *mine* is not *ours*; *ours* is a combination of yours and mine. Answer choice (A) is the best answer.

12. (D) Coarse

If you describe something as fine, it can be very delicate or slender. Something fine can also be good or of excellent quality. So, you should look for a word that means the opposite of *delicate* or the opposite of *good*. The best answer among the choices given is *coarse*. Something that is coarse is rough and lacking in fineness or delicacy. Sandpaper or a burlap sack could be described as having a coarse texture.

13. (A) Raw

This question is a little tricky; could the opposite of *cooked* be *stale*? Well, we generally think of something that is cooked as having just been produced, which would make it not stale. However, cooked food can certainly go stale over time, so *stale* may not be the best answer. What about *fresh*? You may initially think of fish, meat, fruits, or vegetables when you see that word. But it's also certainly possible to have a freshly cooked meal, so *fresh* is not really the opposite of *cooked*. The only other viable choice is (A)—*raw*. Unlike stale food, raw food can never be described as cooked, and vice versa. *Stale* and *raw* are complete opposites, so answer choice (A) is correct.

14. (C) Dusk

Dawn is another word for *sunrise* (choice A). So, we need to look for the word *sunset* or a synonym of *sunset* in order to find the correct answer. *Night* (choice E) is not the opposite of *dawn*; the opposite of *night* is *day*. The correct answer is *dusk* (choice C). *Dusk* is a synonym of *sunset*, so it is the best choice.

15. (C) Northeast

The best way to approach this question is to break down the word *southwest*. So, what is the opposite of *south*? It's *north*. And what is the opposite of *west*? It's *east*. Our answer must be *northeast*, which is answer choice (C).

16. (B) Confusion

If you have everything in order, everything is in its proper place. You're looking for a word that means the opposite of stability. Something that has been thrown into confusion is in a state of disorder or chaos. Answer choice (B) is correct.

17. (A) Sour

Something that is sweet has a pleasant taste to it and can't be described as being bitter or salty. Most types of candy are sweet. Something that is sour has an acid taste to it; vinegar and lemon juice are often described as being sour. *Sour* and *sweet* are antonyms of each other.

18. (A) Stay

If you go somewhere, you are traveling to another place. If you stay in a particular place, you aren't going anywhere. Don't get confused by certain common phrases that people may use, such as "going to stay in a hotel." Just remember that there is no way to stay and go at the same time—you can only do one or the other. *Stay*—answer choice (A)—is the best answer.

19. (D) Insufficient

If you have enough of something, you have an adequate amount to quench your desire or fulfill your purpose. If you have enough food in your cellar to last you over a month, you do not need to buy any more food for the next 30 days if you don't want to. The opposite of *enough*, therefore, is not having an adequate amount of something. Having an *insufficient* amount of food in your cellar to last you for a month means that you will need to buy more food before the month is over. Answer choice (D) is correct.

20. (B) Lose

If you don't win a game, you lose the game. It's impossible to both *win* and *lose* a game at the same time. Answer choice (B) is correct.

21. (E) Opaque

Something that is transparent can be easily seen through. Windows are usually transparent and clear (answer choice D). The word *transparent* can also describe someone who is apparent (answer choice A) or obvious (answer choice C) in his or her intentions, actions, or thoughts. Something that is opaque cannot easily be seen through. The word *opaque* can also describe someone who is difficult to understand or hard to fathom. Thus, *opaque* (answer choice E) is the best answer.

22. (C) Tame

Wild animals are animals that have not been domesticated and that exist in their natural state. Tame animals, on the other hand, have changed from their wild or natural state and have become domesticated and not frightened of humans. So, *wild* and *tame* have opposite meanings, which makes answer choice (C) correct.

23. (D) Accept

If you reject an offer or proposal, you have refused what has been offered or put in front of you. In other words, to reject something or someone is to refuse to accept that thing or person. If you accept something, you are not rejecting it. Thus, the opposite of *reject* is *accept* (choice D).

24. (B) Solid

Something that is hollow has an empty space inside it. So, we need to find a word that describes something that does not have an empty space inside it. We can eliminate *empty* (choice A). *Liquid* (choice C) and *ice* (choice E) don't really have empty spaces inside them, but when have you ever seen *hollow* be used in relation to liquids or ice? The word *hollow* is almost always used to describe a solid that has had its insides cleared out. Thus, to be hollow is to be not solid. *Solid* and *hollow* are opposites of each other. Answer choice (B) is correct.

25. (B) Shy

To be bold is to be brave (choice A), arrogant (choice C), fearless (choice D), or courageous (choice E). Since these answer choices are all synonymous with the given word, the correct answer must be *shy* (choice B).

26. (E) Specific

Something that happens in general is an ordinary (choice B) or common (choice D) occurrence. The word *general* can also describe something that is not limited to one person, place, or thing. Finally, *general* can also refer to something that is not definite or clear. So, we need to see if any of the word choices mean the opposite of any of these definitions. The only viable options are *great* (choice A) and *specific* (choice E). Something that is great usually isn't ordinary or common, but if someone were to ask you to give an antonym of *great* off the top of your head, would you say *general*? You'd probably instead say *small* or *little* or *unimportant*. The best answer is *specific* (choice E). Something that is specific is clear and definite. Thus, *general* and *specific* are antonyms of each other.

27. (C) Forget

To remember something is to retain (choice B), recall (choice D), or recollect (choice E) it. The only viable answer choice we have left is *forget* (choice C), which means to not be able to remember something.

28. (B) Save

If you spend money or time on something, you are expending or disbursing your money or time in a certain way. So, you want to find a word that means the opposite of *expending* or *disbursing*. The correct answer is *save* (choice B). When you save something, you are not using it in any way at the moment. Instead of spending it, you are saving it.

29. (E) Cruel

A merciful person is one who shows compassion or sympathy toward someone or something else. A cruel person refuses to show compassion or sympathy toward anyone or anything. Thus, answer choice (E) is correct.

30. (A) Peace

When two countries go to war with one another, they fight each other until some kind of victory or defeat occurs. After the war, the two countries will usually sign a peace treaty with one another. There can be no peace during a war, and there can be no war if two countries are at peace with one another. Thus, *war* and *peace* have opposite meanings. Answer choice (A) is correct.

Sentence Completion

Sentence Completion Strategies

The sentence completion questions in the Verbal Comprehension section of the OLSAT® test your knowledge of sentence structure—that is, which word or phrase among the answer choices you can insert into the sentence in order for the sentence to make sense. Most questions will contain clues that will point you toward the right answer.

There are two types of sentence completion questions in this section:

Single Blank Sentence Completion Example

John enjoyed sitting on the bench at the park on Saturdays and watching all the _____ groups of people stroll by in their various outfits.

    A. Diverse
    B. Flying
    C. Frantic
    D. Hairy

With these types of questions, you might not be able to initially tell what kind of word can be used in the blank. However, there will only be one answer choice that really makes sense, so you just need to plug in the different choices until you find the right word. Would *frantic* groups of people pass by John as he sits on a bench at the park? Perhaps, but they probably would not *stroll* by him. To *stroll* is to walk in a leisurely manner. How about *flying* groups? This cannot be right because, once again, the question mentions that these groups of people *stroll* by John. What about *diverse* groups of people? That works—especially since the question emphasizes that John enjoys watching the various outfits that people wear as they walk by the bench where he is sitting. It's possible that John enjoys watching *hairy* groups of people pass by in their various outfits, but this is certainly not the best choice given the fact that *diverse* works quite well in this sentence.

Multiple Blanks Sentence Completion Example

Bob _____ enjoyed going to the movies; he always had trouble sitting _____ for long stretches of time.

    A. Always – There
    B. Sometimes – Here
    C. Maybe – Inside
    D. Never – Still
    E. Tried – Outside

With these types of questions, you need to choose the correct answer choice that will work for both of the blanks in the question. Always focus on one blank at a time. Find the right words that could fit in the blank among the answer choices and eliminate the answer choices that do not work. Looking at the part of the sentence before the semicolon, answer choices (C) and (E) do not seem to fit. Our possible answers are (A), (B), and (D). The part of the sentence after the semicolon just doesn't work with (A) or (B), though, when you plug in the answers. How about (D)? Does it make sense that Bob would never enjoy going to the movies because he had trouble sitting still? That works grammatically and contextually in the sentence. Answer choice (D) is correct.

Read each sentence carefully. Insert the answer choices in the blanks and read the full sentence. Do not stop at the first answer choice. While the first answer choice may initially seem best, it may not be the right one after you work through all the answer choices.

Pay attention to the adjectives. Adjectives may be the clue to help you choose the correct answer choice.

Use logic to see if answer choices make sense. Ask yourself questions about each answer choice to see if it is logical.

Example: The bright student won all the _____ science awards.

    A. Big
    B. Small

Look at the adjectives first to help you determine what makes sense. A *bright,* or smart student will win big, not small, science awards. Without the adjective bright, it is impossible to choose the right answer.

Understand that multiple blanks are an opportunity. Some sentence completion questions contain multiple blanks. It will be helpful to first focus on only one of the blanks to find the answer. This strategy will help you eliminate some of the answer choices.

Beware of transitional words. Watch out for key transitional words, such as *although, but, rather,* and *except,* when they are used in the question. Any of these words usually indicate that you are looking for the opposite of the definition or key word/phrase that is used in the sentence.

Eliminate similar words. Look over the answer choices and find the words that are synonyms or that are similar. If there are any common relationships between the words, those answer choices can be eliminated.

> Example: He _____ the birds chirping in the woods.
>
>   A. Saw
>   B. Heard
>
> Would you hear the birds or see the birds? You cannot see birds chirp—you can only hear birds chirp.

Do not pick a word just because you know its meaning, are familiar with it, or simply because you recognize it. On difficult questions, you may only recognize one or two words. If you do not recognize most of the words, focus on the one that you do recognize. Try your best to determine if it fits in the sentence. However, do not force the answer; if the word you are familiar with does not fit in the sentence, do not hesitate to eliminate it.

> Example: He was _____ after he received an A on his math exam.
>
>   A. Thrilled
>   B. Disappointed
>   C. Sad
>   D. Upset
>
> In this example, the last three choices are all similar and synonyms, so *thrilled* (answer choice A) must be the correct answer.

Sentence Completion Questions

1. I will _____ forget my first teacher, as she was the best.

   A. Never
   B. Often
   C. Rarely
   D. Maybe
   E. Regardless

2. People _____ forget to put the cap back on the toothpaste.

   A. Never
   B. Often
   C. Try
   D. Maybe
   E. Only

3. The doctor tried to calm his scared _____ before the examination.

   A. Patient
   B. Nurse
   C. Sister
   D. Glasses
   E. Friend

4. We often argue because we think _____.

   A. Strangely
   B. Differently
   C. Sometimes
   D. Apart
   E. Alike

5. Once the painting is dry, you won't be able to _____ the colors.

   A. Paint
   B. Color
   C. Touch
   D. See
   E. Blend

6. It seems like yesterday that you were just a _____.

   A. Boy
   B. Man
   C. Teacher
   D. Mother
   E. Sister

7. Mary ran back to her locker as soon as she realized she had _____ her books.

   A. Remembered
   B. Forgotten
   C. Discovered
   D. Written
   E. Finished

8. The coach _____ the soccer players for their teamwork and perseverance.

   A. Dismissed
   B. Scolded
   C. Praised
   D. Ignored
   E. Helped

9. You looked so _____ that I knew by seeing your face that you got an A on your final exam.

   A. Sad
   B. Mad
   C. Happy
   D. Annoyed
   E. Indifferent

10. Joanna stored the cookies in vacuum-sealed bags in order to _____ them from going bad.

    A. Maintain
    B. Remove
    C. Create
    D. Prevent
    E. Help

11. Since Nina could hear the _____, she knew that the police were on their way.

    A. Loud
    B. Siren
    C. Yelling
    D. Lights
    E. Mirror

12. Tim was so _____ from the race that he slept for two hours before going out.

    A. Frantic
    B. Tired
    C. Dehydrated
    D. Excited
    E. Worried

13. Some people say that advice stems from recalling one's previous _____.

    A. Events
    B. Hopes
    C. Mistakes
    D. Ambitions
    E. Ideas

14. The hurricane just missed the largest city in the country; the rising sea caused by the storm could have been _____.

    A. Disastrous
    B. Fantastic
    C. Unlikely
    D. Visible
    E. Amusing

15. John was so _____ that no matter how much water he drank, he could not quench his thirst.

    A. Hungry
    B. Exhausted
    C. Tired
    D. Dehydrated
    E. Annoyed

16. It was so _____ that you could hardly even see the road in front of you.

    A. Noisy
    B. Soggy
    C. Foggy
    D. Sunny
    E. Cold

17. He never once gave up after his injury; he did not allow himself to _____.

    A. Fail
    B. Win
    C. Succeed
    D. Work
    E. Yell

18. As the sun set, the trees started _____ long shadows, finally creating some much-needed shade.

    A. Casting
    B. Making
    C. Distributing
    D. Growing
    E. Missing

19. It is _____ that the campers take a tent on their weeklong camping trip.

    A. Ridiculous
    B. Optional
    C. Essential
    D. Tough
    E. Nice

20. At _____, we settled ourselves on picnic blankets in order to watch the fireworks.

    A. Noon
    B. Sunrise
    C. Daybreak
    D. Dusk
    E. Dawn

21. The messenger must be _____ to deliver the news in time.

    A. Swift
    B. Sedate
    C. Wrong
    D. Difficult
    E. Nice

22. The workers at the construction site had to _____ their activities until the building inspector approved the work already done.

    A. Reverse
    B. Hurry
    C. Suspend
    D. Frame
    E. Continue

23. The street performer _____ the crowd by flawlessly juggling the most dangerous objects imaginable.

    A. Surprised
    B. Bored
    C. Threatened
    D. Demonstrated
    E. Enjoyed

24. When the class toured the art gallery, they found that their favorites were large landscapes painted with _____ colors.

    A. Primary
    B. Dull
    C. Eager
    D. Vivid
    E. Loud

25. When selecting a head teacher, the principal picked the one with the most _____.

    A. Experience
    B. Students
    C. Books
    D. Cars
    E. Friendly

26. She _____ expected her parents to pay for her field trip, _____ though she spent all her money at the candy store.

    A. Perhaps – Although
    B. Maybe – If
    C. Still – Even
    D. Almost – As
    E. Although – Even

27. I did not _____ to go to the party _____ I was tired from running errands all day.

    A. Cherish – Because
    B. Maybe – Even
    C. Like – Although
    D. Enjoy – Since
    E. Want – Because

28. _____ you hadn't packed your compass, we would have been _____.

    A. Perhaps – Happy
    B. If – Awake
    C. Although – Miserable
    D. If – Lost
    E. Since – Drenched

29. The teacher will _____ the class tomorrow, but please _____ her that you already paid for the field trip.

    A. Study – Remind
    B. Tell – Ignore
    C. Gather – Trust
    D. Clarify – Tell
    E. Dismiss – Notify

30. The jury _____ all the facts for days but was still unable to come up with a _____.

    A. Gathered – Solution
    B. Discussed – Juror
    C. Looked for – Idea
    D. Discussed – Verdict
    E. Gathered – Witness

31. _____ he had listened to his mother and planned ahead, he might not have been up _____ all night.

   A. Maybe – Partying
   B. If – Studying
   C. Since – Working
   D. Although – Sleeping
   E. If – Resting

32. She was very _____ when she found out her short film won first prize since she did not even go to the award ceremony.

   A. Happy
   B. Surprised
   C. Elated
   D. Upset
   E. Mad

33. The sports club _____ its membership fee for all of its old members at a discount.

   A. Reinstated
   B. Created
   C. Made
   D. Fulfilled
   E. Waived

34. His shirt was _____; his teammates were _____.

   A. Colorful – Happy
   B. Upside down – Smiling
   C. Inside out – Laughing
   D. Dirty – Crying
   E. Torn – Enjoying

35. _____ us, I knew how _____ she was about losing the basketball game.

   A. Among – Disappointed
   B. Between – Happy
   C. Along – Sad
   D. Between – Mad
   E. Like – Indifferent

36. The crops were _____ this year because there was plenty of _____.

    A. Sparse – Drizzle
    B. Abundant – Rain
    C. Stale – Rain
    D. Good – Snow
    E. Big – Wind

37. Do not _____ to lock the door behind you _____ you will be the last one leaving.

    A. Forget – Although
    B. Remember – Because
    C. Recall – Since
    D. Loose – If
    E. Forget – Since

38. Most animals are only _____ when _____.

    A. Nice – Angered
    B. Mad – Interrupted
    C. Dangerous – Provoked
    D. Fed – Attacked
    E. Mad – Petted

39. _____ I saw the invitation, I knew she was _____ a party.

    A. If – Decorating
    B. Since – Planning
    C. Although – Looking for
    D. Perhaps – Creating
    E. After – Watching

Sentence Completion Answer Key

1. (A) Never
If your teacher was the best teacher you ever had, would you forget him or her very easily? Probably not. The only possible choices you have been given are *never* (choice A) and *rarely* (choice C). People don't usually say that they will rarely forget something, do they? The most likely answer choice is *never*.

2. (B) Often
Of the given answer choices, only *never* and *often* make good grammatical sense in the sentence. Do people usually forget to put the cap back on their toothpaste? That seems to be something that people do quite often. Answer choice (B) is correct.

3. (A) Patient
Before a doctor's examination, the person most likely to be scared is probably going to be the patient. One would hope that a nurse wouldn't need to be calmed down before an examination. It's possible that the doctor could be trying to calm down his friend before he examines him or her, but the most likely and best answer is *patient*.

4. (B) Differently
If you argue often with someone, it's very likely that you think differently from that person. If you both thought alike (answer choice E), why would you argue with each other? You can't think *strangely* or *sometimes* or *apart* from each other, so you can also eliminate answer choices (A), (C), and (D). Answer choice (B) must be correct.

5. (E) Blend
When a painting is wet, the colors can be swirled or blended together. However, once it is dry, the colors will become fixed onto the painting. Thus, the only word among the given choices that makes sense in this sentence is answer choice (E)—*blend*.

6. (A) Boy
A phrase like "it seems like yesterday" implies that something has changed over time. Thus, we are looking for a word that indicates how the "you" in the sentence might have changed over time. The best choice is *boy* (choice A) because a boy will change into a man over time. A man (choice B), teacher (choice C), mother (choice D), and sister (choice E) will usually stay in those roles for a long time and not change out of them.

7. (B) Forgotten
Why would Mary be in such a hurry to get back to her locker? The best assumption is that she forgot her books in her locker and was hurrying back to retrieve them before class started. None of the other answer choices make much sense if you plug them into the sentence.

8. (C) Praised
Working as a team and persevering on the soccer field are actions that every coach should be proud of. It wouldn't make sense for a coach to scold (choice B) or ignore (choice D) his or her players for their teamwork and hustle. The only reasonable choice given to you is *praised* (choice C), and it successfully completes the sentence.

9. (C) Happy

How would you feel if you got an A on a test? Probably pretty good. Someone looking at you would be able to tell that you looked quite happy about your grade and that you didn't look sad, mad, annoyed, or indifferent.

10. (D) Prevent

If you place cookies in a vacuum-sealed bag, you want them to maintain their freshness and not go bad. Thus, by putting them in the bag, you hope to prevent them from going bad. It wouldn't make much sense to maintain, remove, create, or help the cookies from going bad; you probably wouldn't use any of those words to describe what you are trying to do. The best answer is choice (D).

11. (B) Siren

The only words listed among the answer choices that you can hear are a siren (choice B) and yelling (choice C). While there may be some yelling before and after the police arrive, it's always possible to hear yelling without the arrival of the police. However, if a police siren is approaching, you know that the police are on their way somewhere. Thus, the only thing Nina could have heard that would have indicated that the police were coming was a siren.

12. (B) Tired

How would you feel after a race? Among the answer choices, you'd probably feel either tired, dehydrated, or excited. It's not too common to feel worried or frantic after a race, although it's certainly possible. However, if you went to bed right after the race and slept for two hours, it seems safe to say that you must have felt tired. If you were excited, you wouldn't have been able to sleep, and if you were dehydrated, you would have needed to drink water. Answer choice (B) is correct.

13. (C) Mistakes

When you give advice, it's usually because you have a notion about the best course of action to take. How would you know the best course of action to take? Well, if you tried something a certain way and failed, you probably learned something from your mistakes. It's possible that you could give advice based on your previous events, hopes, ambitions, or ideas, but the best answer is *mistakes* because it makes the most sense that any advice you might offer would stem from your previous mistakes.

14. (A) Disastrous

If a hurricane just barely missed the largest city in the country, the city was lucky to have avoided a natural disaster. The implication in this sentence is that the rising waters would have been horrible for the city. The only word among the answer choices that fits in the context of the sentence is *disastrous*.

15. (D) Dehydrated

John is having a hard time quenching his thirst in this sentence. Which words among the answer choices could account for the state that John is in? The most likely choices are *exhausted, tired,* or *dehydrated*. Of these answer choices, which is closest in meaning to "having difficulty quenching a thirst for water"? The correct answer is *dehydrated* (choice D).

16. (C) Foggy

Here, we're looking for a word that describes a condition in which you can hardly see the road in front of you. The only word among the answer choices that fits that description is *foggy*, so answer choice (C) is correct.

17. (A) Fail

Someone who refuses to give up on something has in some way refused to admit defeat or failure. Thus, the best answer is (A)—*fail*. None of the other answer choices make sense in the context of the question.

18. (A) Casting

In this sentence, as the sun is setting, the trees are starting to do something with large shadows. What could that something be? Among the answer choices, the most likely words are *casting, making*, and *growing*. Do trees start *making* shadows as the sun sets? Well, they certainly can, but it doesn't sound completely right. Can trees start *growing* shadows as the sun sets? Once again, it's not wrong, but it doesn't seem like the best answer when you interpolate the word into the sentence. Do trees start *casting* shadows as the sun sets? They certainly do, and this sounds like the best answer in comparison to the other choices.

19. (C) Essential

The only two choices that initially make any sense in the sentence are *optional* and *essential*. If you were going on a weeklong camping trip, how important do you think it would be to bring a tent? You'd probably want to bring one on a camping trip of that length. Thus, the best choice for the sentence is *essential*.

20. (D) Dusk

When do you usually watch fireworks? You watch fireworks at night because it's easier to see their brilliance when the sky is dark. So, you need to find the word among the answer choices that refers to night in some way. The best choice is *dusk*, which means sunset. Fireworks usually start at the beginning of the night, not the end of the night, so *sunrise, dawn*, and *daybreak* cannot be correct. Also, those three words are synonymous, so it's impossible for one of them to be the correct answer.

21. (A) Swift

In order to deliver news on time, a messenger must be quick with his or her services. The closest synonym to *quick* among the answer choices is *swift*. The correct answer is (A).

22. (C) Suspend

Here, we are told that workers at a construction site had to do something with their activities until the building inspector approved the work they had already done. The most reasonable assumption you can make here is that the workers were ordered to stop working until their previous work had been properly inspected. The only word synonymous with *stop* among the answer choices is *suspend*. *Reverse, hurry, frame,* and *continue* do not fit in the context of the sentence.

23. (A) Surprised

Since answer choices (D) and (E) don't make grammatical sense in the sentence, we need to choose from answer choices (A), (B), and (C). A street performer is flawlessly juggling dangerous objects in front of a crowd. Would the crowd be bored by this kind of activity? Probably not. Would the crowd feel threatened? It's doubtful that they'd feel threatened since the juggler is flawlessly juggling dangerous objects. Would the crowd be surprised by a street performer who juggles the most dangerous objects imaginable? Most likely. Answer choice (A) is correct.

24. (D) Vivid

What kind of colors would a class enjoy the most in an art gallery? Probably colors that stand out in some way. Among the answer choices, *dull* and *loud* don't seem like viable choices. It's also a little odd if the class enjoyed pictures that were only painted with primary colors—that seems a little limiting. The best choices are *eager* and *vivid*. Between those two choices, *vivid* seems like the better word because it is an adjective that describes colors that stand out. *Eager* is not a word that is associated with colors as much as *vivid* is.

25. (A) Experience

The head teacher is chosen by the principal for having some sort of characteristic that would justify the principal's choice among all of the school's teachers. The best answer is *experience* (choice A). A teacher with the most experience would certainly be justified in receiving this kind of position.

26. (C) Still – Even

This question basically requires you to try each answer choice in the sentence in order to determine which choice works. Look at the first blank and see which choices work. The only two that work are *still* and *almost*. Now that you've narrowed down your answer choices to (C) and (D), you can proceed to the second blank. The only choice that works is *even*, so answer choice (C) must be correct.

27. (E) Want – Because

Remember to look at the first blank when you encounter a sentence completion question with two blanks. Hopefully, you'll be able to eliminate a number of answer choices before you move on to the second blank. With this question, you can get rid of all the answer choices except for (E) because they don't make any grammatical sense in the sentence. Therefore, answer choice (E) must be correct.

28. (D) If – Lost

Looking at the first blank, you should see that only the words *if, although,* and *since* make grammatical sense before the verb *hadn't*. So, you've narrowed down the answer choices to (B) through (E). Looking at the second blank, you'll need to find a word among the answer choices that relates to bringing a compass along on your trip. Might you get lost without a compass? Certainly, so answer (D) is correct.

29. (E) Dismiss – Notify

Reading the whole sentence, you should know that the class is going on a field trip. Looking at the answer choices, the only word that can fit in the first blank is *dismiss*. And *notify* works in the second blank since the student is being told to tell the teacher that he or she has already paid for the field trip.

30. (D) Discussed – Verdict

What do juries usually do with all the facts they have heard from the prosecution and the defense? They don't gather or look for all the facts because all the facts of the case have already been given to them. Instead, they usually discuss the case among themselves in order to come up with a proper judgment or verdict. Thus, answer choice (D) is the best answer.

31. (B) If – Studying

Looking at the first blank, the only word among the answer choices that will logically fit in the sentence is *if*. Now that you've narrowed down your answer choices to (B) and (E), plug the next two answer choices into the second blank in the sentence to see which one makes more sense. *Studying* makes a lot more sense than *resting* because if the student had planned ahead, he might not have needed to spend the whole night cramming.

32. (B) Surprised

At first glance, all of the answer choices in this sentence could be correct. At this point, you need to get rid of synonyms because it's impossible for two similar words in the answer choices to both be correct. Thus, you can get rid of *happy* and *elated*, and you can also get rid of *upset* and *mad*. That leaves you with *surprised*, which makes sense in the context of the sentence. Answer choice (B) must be correct.

33. (A) Reinstated

Looking at the answer choices, we can immediately get rid of *created* and *made* since these words are synonymous. Among the remaining answer choices, *reinstated* is the only verb that makes sense in the context of a sports club administering a discounted fee to its old members.

34. (C) Inside out – Laughing

Here, something has happened to a boy's shirt that has caused a reaction among his friends. Only *inside out* and *laughing* make any sense when put together in this sentence.

35. (D) Between – Mad

The only word among the answer choices that makes good sense in the first blank is *between*, which narrows down your answer choices to (B) and (D). Is it more likely that the person in the sentence was happy or mad about losing the basketball game? *Mad* seems like the better answer here.

36. (B) Abundant – Rain

The crops are in a certain state because there has been plenty of something to cause them to be in that state. Do crops grow well when there is plenty of rain? They certainly do, so answer choice (B) is correct. The only other choice that might make sense is *sparse* and *drizzle*, but it just doesn't sound right to say that crops were not abundant because there was a lot of drizzle; even though drizzle is a little bit of rain, plenty of drizzle probably wouldn't make crops sparse.

37. (E) Forget – Since

Do people usually tell you not to remember or recall to lock the door behind you if you're the last one leaving? Of course not. People usually say the opposite thing; thus, *forget* is the best choice for the first blank. Now that you've narrowed down the answer choices to (A) and (E), look at the second blank in the answer choices. Does *although* work in the sentence? Nope. You're looking for *since* or *because* in this sentence. Thus, the correct answer is (E).

38. (C) Dangerous – Provoked

Looking at your answer choices, you should be able to narrow down your most logical choices to (B), (C), and (E). So, do most animals only become mad when they are interrupted? Interrupted from what? Maybe from their daily activities, but the sentence isn't very clear when you use the words in answer choice (B). Do most animals only become mad after they are petted? Animals don't generally get mad if you pet them. The best answer is (C). It's common knowledge that any animal may become dangerous and defensive if you push it or provoke it in some way.

39. (B) Since – Planning

Looking at the first blank, the only answer choice that you can immediately eliminate is (D). You're going to have to look at the second blank in order to figure out the correct answer. The only answer choice that works when you plug in the words is (B). The other choices don't make much sense when you plug them into the sentence.

Sentence Arrangement

OLSAT® Preparation Guide - Levels D, E, and F

Bright Kids NYC Inc. ©

Sentence Arrangement Strategies

The sentence arrangement questions in the Verbal Comprehnsion section of the OLSAT® will test your ability to look at a sentence jumble and arrange the words in the jumble to make a coherent sentence. There is only one correct sentence that can be arranged from the jumble. If you understand the fundamental characteristics of sentence structure, you should be able to put all the pieces together to form a meaningful sentence. Questions in this section will ask you to find either the first letter of the word that begins the coherent sentence or the last letter of the word that ends the coherent sentence.

Look for the definite article. The definite article is the word *the*. You might be surprised at how many times the word *the* starts a sentence in our language. If you see the word *the* in the sentence jumble, see if it can be the first word in the sentence.

> Example: Brilliant Wrote Student The Essay A
>
> The unscrambled sentence is: The student wrote a brilliant essay.
>
> By identifying the article *the* as perhaps being at the beginning of the sentence, you can associate the word with *student* to help you figure out the sentence.

Look for pronouns. Many sentences begin with pronouns such as *he, she, it, you,* and *they*. This clue may help steer you toward unscrambling the sentence.

> Example: Ice To Loves She Cream Eat
>
> The unscrambled sentence is: She loves to eat ice cream.
>
> Noticing that the sentence could begin with *she* can help you connect to the word *loves*.

Try to associate the verb in the given sentence with the subject of the sentence. Every sentence must have a subject and a verb. If you can determine what the subject is doing, you are on a good track to figuring out the sentence.

> Example: The Is At Man Dog The Barking
>
> The unscrambled sentence is: The dog is barking at the man.
>
> In this example, determining the action (barking) and who is doing the action (the dog) will help you figure out the sentence.

Choose a few words. If you are having trouble figuring out the sentence, pick out a few random words and see if they fit together in any sort of way. If they do, write them down quickly and then choose a few different words. The key to unlocking a sentence jumble can sometimes emerge by first connecting just a few words.

Look for adjectives and the nouns that they could be describing. If you can connect an adjective to its noun, you will know the order of two words in the sentence. This can also help you figure out where the verb might be located in the sentence.

> Example: Pool His Yellow The Left At Shirt He
>
> The unscrambled sentence is: He left his yellow shirt at the pool.
>
> In this example, if you can determine that *yellow* is describing *shirt,* then you might also be able to figure out that what was *left* could have been the *yellow shirt.* Where could it have been *left?* At the *pool.* Following these steps, you should be able to unscramble the sentence.

Look for adverbs. In the same vein, if you notice an adverb (those are the words that usually end in *-ly*), it's probably modifying a verb, an adjective, or another adverb. If you can identify what word the adverb is modifying, you will know the order of two words in the jumble, which can help you to unscramble the sentence.

Sentence Arrangement Questions

1. **Find the first letter of the word that begins the sentence.**

Bed	My	Hiding	Under	The	Was	Cat

2. **Find the first letter of the word that begins the sentence.**

Corals	The	Pretty	Many	Found	Divers

3. **Find the first letter of the word that begins the sentence.**

Unusually	Pool	The	Cold	Was	Swimming

4. **Find the first letter of the word that begins the sentence.**

Early	Practice	The	Finished	Hockey

5. **Find the first letter of the word that begins the sentence.**

Gets	It	Your	Cold	Food	Eat	Before

6. **Find the first letter of the word that begins the sentence.**

Your	All	Before	Finish	Dinner	Homework

7. **Find the first letter of the word that begins the sentence.**

The	Away	He	Boats	Sail	Watched

8. **Find the first letter of the word that begins the sentence.**

Bought	Fair	He	School	Cupcakes	The	At

9. **Find the first letter of the word that begins the sentence.**

Just	Magazine	Not	The	Bought	You	Forget	Do

10. **Find the first letter of the word that begins the sentence.**

Like	Algebra	Kids	Class	Not	Do	Many

11. **Find the first letter of the word that begins the sentence.**

Kids	Finicky	None	Of	Eaters	My	Are

12. Find the last letter of the word that ends the sentence.

Closes The On Restaurant New Sundays Early

13. Find the first letter of the word that begins the sentence.

Teddy   Another   Bear   His   Lost   Kid

14. Find the last letter of the word that ends the sentence.

Others He Teasing Sister For Yelled At His

15. Find the first letter of the word that begins the sentence.

The Speeches At Parents Wedding Gave Both

16. Find the last letter of the word that ends the sentence.

Queen Girl Was The Homecoming Named Another

17. Find the last letter of the word that ends the sentence.

Again To Make Bag Your Check Sure

18. Find the first letter of the word that begins the sentence.

Specials Diner Breakfast The Pancake Offers

19. Find the first letter of the word that begins the sentence.

Lock To Bicycle Forget Do Your Not

20. Find the last letter of the word that ends the sentence.

Missing From Book Desk Another Was His

21. Find the first letter of the word that begins the sentence.

Storm Dismissed The Was Class Early Because Of

22. Find the first letter of the word that begins the sentence.

Not Was Project Happy About She Very The

23. Find the first letter of the word that begins the sentence.

| Finished | Our | Waiter | Dessert | Another | Serving |

24. Find the last letter of the word that ends the sentence.

| Latest | Bring | Sure | Make | Painting | To | Your |

25. Find the last letter of the word that ends the sentence.

| Were | South | Canada | Today | Flying | Geese |

26. Find the first letter of the word that begins the sentence.

| Home | Keys | His | Fisherman | At | Left | The |

27. Find the first letter of the word that begins the sentence.

| Pool | Many | Swimming | Cold | People | The | In | Were |

28. Find the first letter of the word that begins the sentence.

| Water | Forget | Our | Do | Not | Plants | To | Blossoming |

29. Find the first letter of the word that begins the sentence.

| Before | Feed | Dinner | Cats | The | Please |

30. Find the first letter of the word that begins the sentence.

| For | Insisted | On | Sister | Lunch | Paying | His |

31. Find the last letter of the word that ends the sentence.

| Package | The | Arrived | Late | Birthday | Very |

32. Find the last letter of the word that ends the sentence.

| My | Drenched | The | Storm | In | Brother | Was |

33. Find the last letter of the word that ends the sentence.

| Club | New | Golf | Residents | To | Offered | Memberships | The |

34. **Find the first letter of the word that begins the sentence.**

Early	Went	He	Weekends	Bed	Rarely	To	On

35. **Find the first letter of the word that begins the sentence.**

Jacket	Boutique	She	Another	Had	The	Wanted

36. **Find the last letter of the word that ends the sentence.**

From	Exhausted	Running	He	Errands	Was	Too

37. **Find the last letter of the word that ends the sentence.**

Garden	On	Brunch	The	Served	Patio	Is

38. **Find the first letter of the word that begins the sentence.**

The	She	Earrings	Happy	New	Was	About	Very

39. **Find the last letter of the word that ends the sentence.**

Combinations	Their	Students	Locker	Many	Forget

40. **Find the first letter of the word that begins the sentence.**

Exchange	Couple	To	The	Vows	Married	Forgot	Newly

Sentence Arrangement Answer Key

1. **M** (My cat was hiding under the bed.)

2. **T** (The divers found many pretty corals.)

3. **T** (The swimming pool was unusually cold.)

4. **T** (The hockey practice finished early.)

5. **E** (Eat your food before it gets cold.)

6. **F** (Finish all your homework before dinner.)

7. **H** (He watched the boats sail away.)

8. **H** (He bought cupcakes at the school fair.)

9. **D** (Do not forget the magazine you just bought.)

10. **M** (Many kids do not like algebra class.)

11. **N** (None of my kids are finicky eaters.)

12. **S** (The new restaurant closed early on Sundays.)

13. **A** (Another kid lost his teddy bear.)

14. **S** (He yelled at his sister for teasing others.)

15. **B** (Both parents gave speeches at the wedding.)

16. **N** (Another girl was named the homecoming queen.)

17. **N** (Make sure to check your bag again.)

18. **T** (The diner offers pancake breakfast specials.)

19. **D** (Do not forget to lock your bicycle.)

20. **K** (Another book was missing from his desk.)

21. **C** (Class was dismissed early because of the storm.)

22. **S** (She was not very happy about the project.)

23. **A** (Another waiter finished serving our dessert.)

24. **G** (Make sure to bring your latest painting.)

25. **Y** (Canada geese were flying south today.)

26. **T** (The fisherman left his keys at home.)

27. **M** (Many people were swimming in the cold pool.)

28. **D** (Do not forget to water our blossoming plants.)

29. **P** (Please feed the cats before dinner.)

30. **H** (His sister insisted on paying for lunch.)

31. **E** (The birthday package arrived very late.)

32. **M** (My brother was drenched in the storm.)

33. **S** (The golf club offered memberships to new residents.)

34. **H** (He rarely went to bed early on weekends.)

35. **A** (Another boutique had the jacket she wanted.)

36. **S** (He was too exhausted from running errands.)

37. **O** (Brunch is served on the garden patio.)

38. **S** (She was very happy about the new earrings.)

39. **S** (Many students forget their locker combinations.)

40. **T** (The newly married couple forgot to exchange vows.)

OLSAT® Preparation Guide - Levels D, E, and F   Bright Kids NYC Inc. ©

Arithmetic Reasoning

Arithmetic Reasoning Strategies

The arithmetic reasoning questions in the Verbal Reasoning section of the OLSAT® involve solving mathematical problems that are in written form. With these types of questions, you will need to convert the written problem to a mathematical equation of some sort in order to figure out the correct answer. You will also need to understand the sentence structure of certain questions in order to figure out the correct order of operations that you will have to use. In certain questions, you may also need to make inferences in order to figure out how to solve the problem.

Make sure you know how to use the math vocabulary correctly.

- **Addition:** If you see the words *more than* or *sum,* you will need to use addition.

- **Subtraction:** If you see the words *less than* or *difference,* you will need to use subtraction.

- **Multiplication:** If you see the words *how many times* or *product,* you will need to use multiplication.

- **Division:** If you see the words *what number is a (fraction) of (another number)* or *quotient,* you will need to use division.

Identify multiplication questions. Always be on the lookout for problems that entail multiplication. They usually show up in the form of a certain number of things in a certain number of other things. For example, if you have a DVD case that holds four DVDs to a page and there are ten pages, in order to figure out the total number of DVDs your case can hold, you will have to multiply four by ten. The mathematical equation is $4 \times 10 = 40$.

Look out for distances questions. There might be a few distance questions in this section. The trick to these questions is to find out the total distance and then find out the different distances between each part that has been given to you in the question. This may sometimes involve some calculation. In order to find the missing distance in the question, you will usually need to add together the known distances in the question and then subtract that sum from the total distance. You can also use number lines to help you figure out distance questions. Use the beginning of the line as your starting point and the end of the line as your end point. Mark all of your known points, calculate the distance of any points mentioned in the question, and then use your line to help you figure out the missing distance.

Make sure you are comfortable with fractions. Fraction questions are essentially asking you to divide the number by the denominator and then multiply your answer by the numerator. For example, 2/3 of 36 can be figured out by dividing 36 by 3 ($36/3 = 12$) and then multiplying 12 by 2 to get 24.

Break down multistep questions. Certain word problems will require you to understand sentence structure in order to figure out the correct order of operations. The best way to approach these problems is to take them one step at a time.

Example: *How many times* must eight be added to twenty to equal the difference between sixty-four and twenty?

A. 2   B. 3   C. 5   D. 10

Generally, your first step should be to figure out the total sum, difference, product, or quotient in your equation. Here, you should first figure out the difference between sixty-four and twenty: $64 - 20 = 44$. In the beginning of the sentence, the key words *how many times* are used, so multiplication is going to be involved. Eight is going to be multiplied by some number, and then that product is going to be added to twenty in order to equal 44. The mathematical equation for this is (8 x number) + 20 = 44. You can subtract 20 from both sides to get 8 x number = 24. What multiplied by 8 equals 24? The answer is 3, which is answer choice (B).

Always convert the word problem to a mathematical equation. There's a reason that math is easier to understand as numbers and equations than as word problems. These problems are specifically targeting your ability to understand mathematical concepts when they are expressed in language. If you can figure out the mathematical equation, the question becomes much easier to solve.

Arithmetic Reasoning Questions

1. Jennifer has two packages of cookies. Each package has two cookies. How many cookies will Jennifer have if she gives half away to her sister Annie?

   A.   2   B. 4   C. 1   D. 6

2. Mary has three packages of sticker sheets. Each package has four stickers. How many stickers will Mary have if she gives half away to her friends?

   A. 5   B. 8   C. 4   D. 6

3. John is a stamp collector who has four sheets of new stamps. Each sheet has four stamps on it. How many stamps will John have left if he gives one-quarter of his stamps away to his father?

   A. 4   B. 18   C. 12   D. 10

4. Caleb has three boxes of marbles. Each box has five marbles in it. How many marbles will Caleb have left if he gives one-third of his marbles away to his brother?

   A. 20   B. 15   C. 5   D. 10

5. Four cats have three kittens each. Half of the kittens are white. How many kittens are white?

   A. 12   B. 6   C. 8   D. 4

6. Five birds lay four eggs each. Half of the eggs hatch. How many do not hatch?

   A. 10   B. 8   C. 6   D. 12

7. Bill's house is 30 yards from Sandra's house. Bill's house is 10 yards from Anson's house, which is in between Sandra's house and Bill's house. How many yards is it from Anson's house to Sandra's house?

   A. 20   B. 15   C. 10   D. 14

8. The grocery store is 50 yards from the pet store. The grocery store is 20 yards from the hardware store, which is in between the grocery store and the pet store. How many yards is it from the hardware store to the pet store?

   A. 50   B. 20   C. 30   D. 70

9. Cathy's tent is 80 feet from Mary's tent. Cathy's tent is 50 feet from Joanna's tent, which is in between Cathy's tent and Mary's tent. How many feet is it from Joanna's tent to Mary's tent?

    A. 54   B. 50   C. 30   D. 70

10. What number is eight more than five times one?

    A. 10   B. 9   C. 12   D. 14   E. 13

11. What number is two more than five times two?

    A. 10   B. 9   C. 12   D. 14   E. 16

12. What number is three less than nine times three?

    A. 25   B. 17   C. 16   D. 24   E. 30

13. What number is five more than six times seven?

    A. 49   B. 47   C. 37   D. 42   E. 40

14. What number is half the sum of ten and six?

    A. 12   B. 16   C. 8   D. 10   E. 5

15. What number is half the sum of thirteen and nine?

    A. 11   B. 12   C. 14   D. 22   E. 10

16. What number is half the sum of eight and twelve?

    A. 10   B. 4   C. 14   D. 7   E. 8

17. What number is half the difference between nineteen and seven?

    A. 9   B. 4   C. 6   D. 16   E. 8

18. What number is one-third of the sum of eighteen and twenty-four?

    A. 18   B. 12   C. 14   D. 16   E. 20

19. How many times must six be added to equal the sum of twenty-four and thirty?

  A. 9   B. 8   C. 6   D. 10   E. 7

20. How many times must four be added to ten to equal the sum of twenty-four and eighteen?

  A. 10   B. 8   C. 4   D. 9   E. 7

21. How many times must six be added to twenty to equal the sum of forty-six and twenty-two?

  A. 9   B. 5   C. 6   D. 8   E. 7

22. Allentown is 900 miles from Joe's office. On a trip to Allentown, Joe drove one-third of the total distance one day, one-half of the total distance the second day, and the remaining distance the third day. How many miles did Joe drive the last day?

  A. 100   B. 150   C. 200   D. 250   E. 300

23. Peter's house is 800 miles from New York City. On a trip to New York City, Peter drove one-fourth of the total distance one day, one-half of the total distance the second day, and the remaining distance the third day. How many miles did Peter drive on the last day?

  A. 250   B. 150   C. 200   D. 100   E. 600

24. A bicyclist wants to ride in a 400-mile bike race that lasts four days. The first day, he rides 80 miles, the next day he rides twice as much as the first day, the third day he rides one-fourth of the total distance, and he rides the remaining distance on the last day. How many miles does the bicyclist ride on the last day?

  A. 80   B. 100   C. 60   D. 120   E. 200

25. Mary's plane arrived 40 minutes late. If Mary was at the terminal one hour early, how long did she wait for her plane to arrive?

  A. 60 minutes   B. 40 minutes   C. 80 minutes   D. 30 minutes   E. 100 minutes

OLSAT® Preparation Guide - Levels D, E, and F

Arithmetic Reasoning Answer Key

1. (A) 2

If Jennifer has 2 packages of cookies and each package has 2 cookies, Jennifer has a total of 4 cookies since 2 x 2 = 4. If she were to give half of her cookies away, she would only have 2 cookies left because $\frac{4}{2}$ = 2.

2. (D) 6

Mary has 3 packages of sticker sheets, and each package has 4 stickers. So, you're going to have to multiply 3 by 4 in order to get the total number of Mary's stickers. 3 x 4 = 12. To find out how many stickers she will have left after she gives half of her stickers away, you will need to divide 12 by 2. $\frac{12}{2}$ = 6. The correct answer is (D).

3. (C) 12

Here, we need to multiply the number of sheets of stamps by the number of stamps on each sheet in order to get the correct answer. 4 x 4 = 16. So, John has 16 stamps. He then decides to give one-quarter of his stamps away. What is one-quarter of 16? $\frac{1}{4}$ x 16 = $\frac{16}{4}$ = 4. So, how many stamps does John have after he has given away 4 stamps? 16 – 4 = 12. The correct answer is (C).

4. (D) 10

Caleb has 3 boxes of marbles, and each box contains 5 marbles. So, he has a total of 15 marbles because 3 x 5 = 15. He then gives one-third of his marbles away to his brother. 15 x $\frac{1}{3}$ = $\frac{15}{3}$ = 5. So, $\frac{1}{3}$ of 15 is 5. So, after giving 5 marbles to his brother, Caleb will only have 10 (choice D) marbles left.

5. (B) 6

Four cats have three kittens each. That means that there are 12 kittens total because 4 x 3 = 12. Half of the kittens are white. What is half of 12? $\frac{1}{2}$ x 12 is the same as $\frac{12}{2}$, and both equations give you 6 as the answer. Since 6 kittens are white, answer choice (B) is correct.

6. (A) 10

Because 5 birds lay 4 eggs each, there must be a total of 20 eggs since 5 x 4 = 20. If half of the eggs hatch, that means that half of the eggs do not hatch. So, to find out how many eggs don't hatch, you just need to divide 20 by 2. $\frac{20}{2}$ = 10. So, answer choice (A) is correct.

7. (A) 20

Bill's and Sandra's houses are 30 yards apart from each other. Anson's house is in between Bill's and Sandra's houses. Bill's house and Anson's house are 10 yards apart from each other. So, how far is Anson's house from Sandra's house? If you were to draw this out, you could represent Bill's house with a "B," Anson's house with an "A," and Sandra's house with an "S." The order of the houses is BAS, with the distance between B and A being 10 yards and the distance between B and S being 30 yards. To find the distance between A and S, you need to subtract the distance between B and A from the total distance between B and S. So, 30 yards – 10 yards = 20 yards. Answer choice (A) is correct.

8. (C) 30

The order of the stores is the grocery store (represented by "G"), the hardware store (represented by "H"), and then the pet store (represented by "P"). So, the order of the stores is GHP. The total distance from G to P is 50 yards. The distance from G to H is 20 yards, and you are being asked to find the distance from H to P. You need to subtract the distance between G and H from the total distance between G and P. 50 yards – 20 yards = 30 yards. The correct answer is (C).

9. (C) 30

The order of the tents is Cathy (represented by "C"), Joanna (represented by "J"), and Mary (represented by "M"). Written out, the order is CJM, with the total distance between C and M being 80 feet and the distance between C and J being 50 feet. You need to subtract the shorter distance (CJ) from the total distance (CM) in order to find the distance between Joanna's tent and Mary's tent (JM). 80 ft. – 50 ft. = 30 ft. The correct answer is (C).

10. (E) 13

What is five times one? Converted to an equation, that is 5 x 1, which of course equals 5. What is eight more than five? Converted to an equation, that is 8 + 5 = 13. Answer choice (E) is correct.

11. (C) 12

You are being asked to find the number that is two more than five times two. Let's first figure out what "five times two" is. "Five times two" = 5 x 2 = 10. "Two more than ten" = 10 + 2 = 12. The correct answer is (C).

12. (D) 24

What number is three less than nine times three? "Nine times three" = 9 x 3 = 27. You now need to find the number that is "three less than" 27. That sentence can be converted to the equation 27 – 3 = 24, which is answer choice (D).

13. (B) 47

"What number is five more than six times seven" = 5 + (6 x 7) = 5 + (42) = 47. So, the correct answer is (B).

14. (C) 8

What number is half the sum of ten and six? "The sum of ten and six" = 10 + 6 = 16. What number is half of 16? $^{16}/_{2}$ = 8. Answer choice (C) is correct.

15. (A) 11

You're being asked to find the number that is half the sum of thirteen and nine. What is the sum of thirteen and nine? That sentence can be converted to the equation 13 + 9 = 22. "Half the sum of thirteen and nine" is $^{22}/_{2}$ = 11, making answer choice (A) correct.

16. (A) 10

"What number is half the sum of eight and twelve" = $(8 + 12)/2 = {}^{20}\!/_2 = 10$. Answer choice (A) is correct.

17. (C) 6

What number is half the difference between nineteen and seven? The difference between nineteen and seven can be converted to $19 - 7 = 12$. What is half of 12? ${}^{12}\!/_2 = 6$. The correct answer is (C).

18. (C) 14

What number is one-third of the sum of eighteen and twenty-four? First, you should find the sum of eighteen and twenty-four. That sentence can be converted to the equation $18 + 24 = 42$. Now, you need to find out what one-third of 42 equals. Your equation is $\frac{1}{3} \times 42$, which also equals ${}^{42}\!/_3$. If you're having trouble calculating this equation in your head, just break it down. You know that $3 \times 10 = 30$, and 42 is 12 more than 30. How many times does 3 go into 12? ${}^{12}\!/_3 = 4$. Adding 10 and 4 together, you should be able to figure out that ${}^{42}\!/_3 = 14$. Double-check by multiplying 14 by 3 to get 42. Answer choice (C) is correct.

19. (A) 9

How many times must six be added to equal the sum of twenty-four and thirty? Let's first figure out the sum of twenty-four and thirty. That can be converted to $24 + 30 = 54$. How many times must six be added in order to equal 54? This question is essentially asking you to find out how many times 6 goes into 54. In order to find this out, you need to divide 54 by 6. $54/6 = 9$, which makes answer choice (A) correct.

20. (B) 8

How many times must four be added to ten to equal the sum of twenty-four and eighteen? Let's break the question down. "The sum of twenty-four and eighteen" = $24 + 18 = 42$. Now you need to find out how many times four must be added to ten in order to equal 42. You should subtract ten from 42. $42 - 10 = 32$. How many times can 4 go into 32? ${}^{4}\!/_{32} = 8$. Does 4 have to be added 8 times to 10 in order to equal 42? In other words, does $(4 \times 8) + 10 = 42$? The equation works, so answer choice (B) is correct.

21. (D) 8

How many times must six be added to twenty to equal the sum of forty-six and twenty-two? Let's find the sum first. "The sum of forty-six and twenty-two" = $46 + 22 = 68$. How many times does six have to be added to twenty in order to equal 68? First, subtract twenty from 68. $68 - 20 = 48$. How many sixes go into 48? ${}^{48}\!/_6 = 8$. Let's double-check and see if this works. Does 6 have to be added 8 times to 20 in order to equal 68? In other words, does $(6 \times 8) + 20 = 68$? The equation works, so answer choice (D) is correct.

22. (B) 150

    The total distance from Allentown to Joe's office is 900 miles. On the first day, Joe drives one-third of the total distance. One-third of 900 is $\frac{1}{3} \times 900 = \frac{900}{3} = 300$ miles driven on the first day. On the second day, Joe drives half of the total distance. One-half of 900 is $\frac{1}{2} \times 900 = \frac{900}{2} = 450$. On the first and second days, Joe has driven 300 miles + 450 miles = 750 miles. To figure out the remaining miles that he must drive on the third day, you need to subtract 750 from 900. 900 miles – 750 miles = 150 miles. The correct answer is (B).

23. (C) 200

    There is a total distance of 800 miles between Peter's house and New York City. On the first day, Peter travels one-fourth of the total distance. $800 \times \frac{1}{4} = \frac{800}{4} = 200$ miles. On the second day, Peter travels one-half of the total distance. $800 \times \frac{1}{2} = \frac{800}{2} = 400$ miles. The distance traveled on the first and second days is 200 miles + 400 miles = 600 miles. To find the distance that Peter traveled on the third day, you need to subtract 600 from 800. 800 miles – 600 miles = 200 miles, which is answer choice (C).

24. (C) 60

    A 400-mile bike race lasts four days. On the first day, the bicyclist rides 80 miles. On the second day, he rides twice the distance traveled on the first day, which is 80 x 2 = 160 miles. On the third day, he rides one-fourth of the total distance, which is 400/4 = 100 miles. On days 1–3, he rides 80 miles + 160 miles + 100 miles = 340 miles. To find out how many miles the bicyclist rides on the fourth day, you need to subtract 340 miles from the total distance that the bicyclist rides. 400 – 340 = 60 miles. The bicyclist rides 60 miles on the fourth day, so answer choice (C) is correct.

25. (E) 100 minutes

    Mary was at the terminal an hour before her flight was supposed to arrive, so she was there 60 minutes early. Her plane, however, was late and didn't arrive until 40 minutes later. 60 minutes + 40 minutes = 100 minutes. So, Mary had to wait 100 minutes for her plane to arrive.

Logical Selection

OLSAT® Preparation Guide - Levels D, E, and F

Bright Kids NYC Inc. ©

Logical Selection Strategies

The logical selection questions in the Verbal Reasoning section of the OLSAT® are tough. The questions will ask you to peel away at a word until you can discover its core definition—that is, the fundamental element of the word that makes it what it is. Sounds a bit tough, doesn't it? The best way to approach these questions is to think of examples or ways that the given word could do without some of the given answer choices. In other words, without the things mentioned in the answer choices, can the word maintain its core definition and still mean the same thing? Most of the questions will be in one of these two formats:

> *Every _____ has -*
> *There can be no _____ without -*

Try to think of the best definition of the given word. The key to success in this section is determining the fundamental characteristic of the given word. In other words, what could be taken away from the word that would ultimately affect its purpose or the way we think of the word in our daily life?

Think of real-life examples. It will be necessary to think of examples in the real world in this section. Always look at each answer choice and try to think if it's possible for the word to exist in this world without the answer choice.

Reverse the question in your mind. If you're given the question format *There can be no _____ without -,* try to consider whether the meaning of the given word would still be preserved if one of the answer choices was not associated with it. If the given word would still retain its essential characteristics and/or definition, you can eliminate the answer choice.

Use process of elimination. For each of these questions, you are probably going to have to eliminate some answer choices in order to see which answer is correct. Eliminating answer choices will help you narrow down the core definition and fundamental characteristics of the given word.

Let's go through an example before you begin the practice questions.

Example: There can be no music without -

A. Instruments   B. Music sheets   C. Fingers   D. Musical pitches   E. Drums

What is a fundamental characteristic of music? What is necessary for music to exist? You can approach this question by asking yourself if music could still exist if you did not have one of the answer choices. So, could there be music without instruments? There certainly could; a cappella groups can sing great songs just by using their combined voices. This means you can eliminate answer choice (A). You can also eliminate answer choice (E) because a drum is a type of instrument. Can there be music without music sheets? Most bands go on stage at concerts and play their music from memory, so answer choice (B) can be eliminated. Could there be music without fingers? It might be tough, but some people can play instruments with their feet or other parts of their bodies. Also, we would still be able to sing without fingers. Therefore, eliminate answer choice (C). We are left with answer choice (D). Could there be music without musical notes? All of the music we hear is a variation of different musical pitches or sound frequencies that we call musical notes. Without these pitches, there would be no way to make all the different sounds that we associate with music. Answer choice (D) is the best answer.

Logical Selection Questions

1. **Every zoo has -**

   A. Birds   B. Seals   C. Animals   D. A garden   E. A rainforest

2. **Every restaurant has -**

   A. Cooks   B. Kids   C. Magazines   D. Music   E. Waiters

3. **Every school has -**

   A. Teachers   B. A library   C. A playground   D. Bells   E. An art room

4. **Every house has -**

   A. Walls   B. A garden   C. Flowers   D. Residents   E. Stairs

5. **Every bread has -**

   A. Corn   B. Butter   C. Slices   D. Jam   E. Crust

6. **There can be no paintings without -**

   A. Painters   B. Pencils   C. Ink   D. Paper   E. Brushes

7. **There can be no public libraries without -**

   A. Magazines   B. Newspapers   C. Computers   D. Books   E. Students

8. **There can be no swimming without -**

   A. Pools   B. Water   C. Oceans   D. Lifeguards   E. Instructors

9. **There can be no lightning without -**

   A. Rain   B. Clouds   C. Electricity   D. Sun   E. Tornados

10. **There can be no poems without -**

    A. Books   B. Pencils   C. Metaphors   D. Notes   E. Words

11. **There can be no deserts without -**

    A. Cactuses   B. Aridity   C. Oases   D. Camels   E. Mirages

12. There can be no flowers without -

    A. Grass   B. Gardens   C. Seeds   D. Bees   E. Trees

13. There can be no recipe without -

    A. Instructions   B. A cookbook   C. Fruit   D. A cook   E. Utensils

14. There can be no town without a -

    A. Fire station   B. Library   C. Hospital   D. Resident   E. Park

15. There can be no forest without -

    A. Streams   B. Flowers   C. Animals   D. Trees   E. Birds

16. There can be no vegetables without -

    A. Lunch   B. Rabbits   C. Carrots   D. Fruit   E. Plants

17. There can be no TV repairmen without -

    A. Wrenches   B. Electricity   C. Cars   D. Colleges   E. Teeth

18. There can be no guitars without -

    A. Bands   B. Musicians   C. Teachers   D. Musical notes   E. Picks

19. There can be no written words without -

    A. Sentences   B. Pencils   C. Pens   D. Lectures   E. Symbols

20. There can be no baseball team without -

    A. Uniforms   B. Players   C. Hats   D. Gloves   E. Shoes

21. There can be no airplane without -

    A. Wings   B. Passengers   C. Parachutes   D. Seats   E. Seat belts

22. There can be no sandwich without -

    A. Lettuce   B. Tomatoes   C. Cheese   D. Ingredients   E. Meat

23. **There can be no contracts without -**

    A. Documents   B. Lawyers   C. Agreements   D. Licenses   E. Pens

24. **There could be no purchases without -**

    A. Trade   B. Gift cards   C. Gifts   D. Banks   E. Credit cards

25. **There can be no effects without -**

    A. People   B. Animals   C. Choices   D. Causes   E. Desires

Logical Selection Answer Key

1. (C) Animals

In this section, you want to try to get down to the core definition of the word that you have been given. Here, the word is *zoo*. What does every zoo need to have? That is, it would be impossible to call a zoo a zoo without which one element? A zoo doesn't necessarily have to have birds (choice A), seals (choice B), a garden (choice D), or a rainforest (choice E). However, a zoo must have animals (choice C). Without animals, there could not possiblybe a zoo.

2. (A) Cooks

What do you do in a restaurant? You usually eat a meal. Does a restaurant need magazines (choice C) or music (choice D) in order to be considered a restaurant? No, plenty of restaurants have neither of these. A restaurant also certainly doesn't need kids (choice B). Does a restaurant need waiters (choice E)? Not necessarily, because some restaurants are strictly buffets. However, every restaurant serves some kind of prepared food, so there must be cooks (choice A) who prepare that food.

3. (A) Teachers

What does every school need to have? Many schools in the world are not lucky enough to have a library (choice B), playground (choice C), or an art room (choice E), yet those places are still considered schools. What about bells (choice D)? If all the bells in your school broke, your school wouldn't stop being a school. However, if there were no teachers (choice A), who would teach you? What would be the point of going to school without any teachers to educate you? Thus, every school needs teachers, so answer (A) is correct.

4. (A) Walls

What does every house need to have to be called a house? Many houses don't have a garden (choice B) or flowers (choice C), so you can eliminate those choices. Does a house need stairs (choice E)? Nope, because there are plenty of one-story houses. Does a house need residents (choice D)? Well, when your family goes on vacation, does your house stop being a house? It may not be a full or lively house, but your house still exists as a house when you are not there. There are plenty of empty houses that don't have residents. The best answer is *walls* (choice A). A house can only be considered a house if it has walls and the means to support a roof over your head.

5. (E) Crust

What is a fundamental characteristic of bread? What does every piece of bread need to have in order for it to be called bread? You certainly don't need to have corn (choice A) in order to make bread. Does every bread have butter (choice B)? Nope, you need to add butter if you want to eat your bread with butter. The same goes for jam (choice D). Does every bread have slices (choice C)? Most of the bread you buy in stores is presliced, but you can also buy whole loaves of bread that are unsliced in some stores. Or you could own a bread maker, which allows you to make whole loaves of bread at home. So, every bread does not need to have slices. However, every bread must have a crust (choice E). Bread only becomes bread by baking dough. Bread crust is always formed in one way or another by this baking process. You might cut off the crust or buy crustless bread at the grocery store, but every loaf of bread has a crust when it is first formed. Thus, answer choice (E) is correct.

6. (A) Painters

Can there be a painting that is not done with pencils (choice B) or ink (choice C)? Certainly, so we can immediately eliminate those two choices. Can there be a painting that doesn't involve the use of brushes (choice E)? Sure, because a painter can finger paint if he or she wants to. Can there be a painting without paper (choice D)? You could paint on canvas or another type of fabric if you wanted to, and frescos are paintings done on plaster walls or ceilings. Is it possible to have paintings without painters (choice A)? Who would do the painting? In order for there to be a painting, there always has to be a painter, so answer choice (A) is correct.

7. (D) Books

What truly makes a public library a library? Does a public library need magazines (choice A) or newspapers (choice B) in order to be considered a library? Having those items does not make a library a library; public libraries existed before they started carrying magazines and newspapers. The same reasoning can be applied to computers (choice C). Are students (choice E) needed in order for a public library to exist? Of course not, since many other types of people also use a public library. The choice you are left with is *books* (choice D). Every public library needs to offer books to the public in some form.

8. (B) Water

Looking at the answer choices, we can get rid of pools (choice A) and oceans (choice C) since they can't both be right because it's possible to swim in one without the other. If there were no pools, you could still swim in the ocean and vice versa. You can also swim without a lifeguard (choice D) or an instructor (choice E) looking out for you. However, without water (choice B), what would you swim in? If there were no water, there wouldn't be any other liquid that you could swim in since most liquids are at least partially comprised of water in some form. There also wouldn't be human life without water. So, there could definitely be no swimming without water.

9. (C) Electricity

Lightning is an electrical spark that is discharged in clouds and that can occur during a thunderstorm. So, there can be no lightning without electricity (choice C). Heat lightning can occur when there is no rain (choice A). While lightning does occur in clouds (choice B), it's possible for scientists to create lightning in laboratories, so clouds do not need to be present for lightning to occur. Lightning is a universal phenomenon because it involves electricity. Thus, it can happen anywhere in the universe, even in a place without our sun (choice D). Finally, you don't need tornados (choice E) for lightning to occur.

10. (E) Words

What is the main component of a poem? Books (choice A) can't be right because there were poems and poetry before printing was invented. How about pencils (choice B)? Well, in ancient Greece, long heroic poems were passed down from generation to generation through singing. Also, if you have a pen or a computer, you can write a poem, so *pencils* can't be the correct answer. There are also plenty of poems that don't use metaphors (choice C) or notes (choice D). The only answer choice left is *words* (choice E). Is it possible to have a poem without words? Nope. Even the shortest poems in the world have a few words. The best answer is (E).

11. (B) Aridity

You could certainly have a desert without cactuses (choice A), oases (choice C), camels (choice D), or mirages (choice E). Would it be possible to have a desert without aridity (choice B)? *Aridity* means extreme dryness, or a lack of moisture. If you took away the aridity, a desert really wouldn't be a desert anymore. The correct answer is (B).

12. (C) Seeds

What does a flower have to have in order to be considered a flower? Does a flower have to grow in grass (choice A) or in a garden (choice B)? No. You can grow flowers in pots in your home. Do flowers need bees (choice D) in order to be considered flowers? Although pollination is important, flowers can get pollinated through other means. Do flowers need trees (choice E) to make them flowers? Nope. However, flowers do need seeds (choice C). Without seeds, germination wouldn't occur, so flowers would never be able to grow and develop.

13. (A) Instructions

What do you need in order to have a recipe? You certainly don't need fruit (choice C) because plenty of recipes don't require fruit. Utensils (choice E) are also not required because it's possible to make some recipes just with your hands. You also don't need a cook (choice D) because a recipe is still a recipe even if there is no one to prepare it. You can also have a recipe without having a cookbook (choice B) that the recipe is published in. But how would you have a recipe without any instructions (choice A)? A recipe's main purpose is to provide step-by-step instructions on how to prepare a certain kind of dish.

14. (D) Resident

What does a town need in order for it to be considered a town? While it's a good idea for a town to have a fire station (choice A) and a hospital (choice C), many smaller towns cannot afford to fund these types of services. The same can be said for libraries (choice B) and parks (choice E). But can there be a town without residents (choice D)? A town is defined as a town because it has some kind of population, no matter how small. So, the best answer choice is (D).

15. (D) Trees

What is the first thing that comes to mind when you think about a forest? In other words, what is a forest? A forest is a collection of trees (choice D). It's possible to have a forest without streams (choice A), flowers (choice B), animals (choice C), or birds (choice E). However, there really is no way to have a forest without trees.

16. (E) Plants

What is a fundamental characteristic of vegetables? What do vegetables need in order to be vegetables? Could there be vegetables without lunch (choice A)? Of course there could still be vegetables if human beings didn't eat lunch. How about rabbits (choice B) or carrots (choice C)? If rabbits became extinct, there would still be vegetables growing all over the world. If there were no carrots, there would still be a multitude of other types of vegetables. Is fruit (choice D) necessary for the cultivation of vegetables? Fruits and vegetables are grown independently of one another, so answer choice (D) is incorrect. But could there be vegetables without plants (choice E)? Nope. Vegetables are produced by plants, so plants are necessary for vegetables to exist.

17. (B) Electricity

How could there be no TV repairmen? Could there still be TV repairmen if there were no wrenches (choice A)? Probably, since TV repairmen could use—or invent—other types of tools to use on your television. What about cars (choice C)? Even if we didn't have cars, it seems likely that TV repairmen would be able to get around in some way in order to get to your house to fix your TV. There certainly could be TV repairmen without the institution of college (choice D) since TV repairmen don't need to go to college to learn the skills to do their job. Without teeth (choice E), the human race would have a tough time eating certain types of foods, but that wouldn't necessarily stop TV repairmen from doing their job. However, if there were no electricity (choice B), there couldn't be electronics of any kind. There actually wouldn't be any electromagnetic force in the universe without electricity, which means that the universe as we know it couldn't exist without electricity. So, there would also be no TV repairmen without electricity. Answer choice (B) is correct.

18. (D) Musical notes

Could there be guitars without bands (choice A)? Many solo guitarists play without a band, so the answer is yes. You can eliminate answer choice (A). Do you need musicians (choice B) in order for a guitar to exist? Not necessarily. It's possible that the guitar could have been invented by someone who wasn't a musician or by someone who didn't really understand the mechanics of music. There could also be guitars without teachers (choice C). People could just learn to play the guitar on their own if they wanted to. Guitars can be strummed with your fingers, so there could certainly be guitars if there were no picks (choice E). How about notes (choice D)? How could there be guitars, or any musical instruments, if there weren't any musical notes? A fundamental characteristic of a guitar is that it can be used to play a variety of musical notes on a number of strings. Answer (D) is correct.

19. (E) Symbols

What does a word need to have in order for it to be a word? There were certainly written words before sentences (choice A) were ever developed, so answer choice (A) is wrong. There could be no sentences without words, but at some point in time, there were written words without sentences. That also must mean that people could have written words without there being lectures (choice D). Early civilizations used crude tools such as styluses to create written words, so it was possible to have words without pencils (choice B) or pens (choice C). Could you have written words without symbols? Every letter in every language is just a symbol for a sound. Those sounds are what form different words in different languages. The Egyptians used hieroglyphics, or pictures, as symbols to convey certain words. If we were unable to use symbols to convey our thoughts to one another or to label things, it would be impossible to have written words. Words are symbols that people who speak a certain language use.

20. (B) Players

What is the fundamental characteristic of a baseball team? Can there be a baseball team without uniforms (choice A)? Of course there can be. You may get together with your friends and play baseball without any clothing denoting who is on which team. There could be baseball teams in poor countries that play without hats (choice C) or shoes (choice E). Do you need gloves (choice D) in order for there to be a baseball team? It's probably a good idea, but you could form a baseball team without gloves. However, you must have players (choice B) in order for there to be a baseball team. Without any players, there can be no baseball team.

21. (A) Wings

What does an airplane need to have in order for it to be an airplane? You could have an airplane without passengers (choice B) since a plane can be piloted by one person. While it might not be a good idea, you could also have a plane without parachutes (choice C). All airplanes have seats (choice D), but if there were no seats, could there still be airplanes? Seats aren't really a fundamental characteristic of airplanes because an airplane could still fly if it didn't have seats. The same goes for seat belts (choice E). How about wings (choice A)? Have you ever seen an airplane without wings? Wings are necessary to lift an airplane into the sky and to help steer the airplane once it is airborne. Without wings, an airplane couldn't fly. Answer choice (A) is correct.

22. (D) Ingredients

What is the essential thing that makes a sandwich a sandwich? Is lettuce (choice A), tomatoes (choice B), cheese (choice C), or meat (choice E) a type of food that is necessary in a sandwich? Nope. You could have a sandwich with all, some, or none of these types of food. However, you cannot have a sandwich without ingredients (choice D). The ingredients can be anything you want, but without them, it would be impossible to make a sandwich.

23. (C) Agreements

What is the fundamental nature of a contract? Do you need documents (choice A) in order to make a contract with another person? Most contracts involve documents, but there can also be oral contracts. Some people just shake hands to indicate that a contract has been formed; this is how many contracts were made out on the frontier during the early history of the United States, when many people were illiterate and documents were scarce. In the same vein, contracts can certainly be formed without the existence of lawyers (choice B) and without the invention of pens (choice E). You also don't need licenses (choice D) in order to make a contract with another person. You do need the notion of agreements (choice C), though. Contracts can only be formed when two or more parties can broadly agree on the terms binding each party to the other party. If there were no such thing as an agreement, there could not possibly be a contract. Of course, sometimes people will argue that they didn't agree to this or that term in a contract. But fundamentally, without agreements, it would be impossible to ever form a contract.

24. (A) Trade

Could there be purchases without gift cards (choice B) or gifts (choice C)? There certainly were purchases before gift cards came into existence. If no one understood the nature of a gift, everything would have to be a purchase of some sort. So, you can eliminate answer choices (B) and (C). People were also purchasing items before the invention of banks (choice D) and credit cards (choice E). In fact, before there was printed money or coins, people purchased items by bartering and trading with other people. Even today, selling and purchasing are just another form of trade. You trade goods or services to someone else in order to receive money. Or, you trade money in order to receive goods or services. So, there couldn't be purchases if we didn't understand the concept of trade.

25. (D) Causes

Could there be effects without people (choice A) or animals (choice B)? There certainly could be. Effects, like solar flares and asteroid collisions and whatnot, are taking place all over the universe all the time, so this concept couldn't just be limited to people or animals. Could there be effects without choices (choice C) or desires (choice E)? Most reactions that occur in our world are not volitional; a cloud doesn't choose or desire to start raining. However, for an effect to occur, there must be a cause (choice D). For every reaction or effect in the world, something caused it to react in that manner. So, in order for there to be an effect, there must have been some sort of cause. Answer choice (D) is correct.

Word/Letter Matrices

OLSAT® Preparation Guide - Levels D, E, and F Bright Kids NYC Inc. ©

Word/Letter Matrices Strategies

The word/letter matrix questions in the Verbal Reasoning section of the OLSAT® ask you to find the pattern or relationship between different letters or words in a box. There will be a top row that establishes the pattern and a bottom row with a missing letter or word. Once you have determined the correct relationship, you need to apply the same pattern to the bottom row in order to determine the correct answer. An example of a question is shown below:

AC   **DF**

HJ   **?**

What is the pattern in the example above? The first pair of letters in the first row is "AC," so you can see that the second letter moves up two letters from the first letter. Another way to look at it is that you need to skip a letter in order to get the second letter. What happens with the second pair of letters in the first row? The first letter of the second pair is sequentially the next letter after the second letter in the first pair. The pattern of skipping a letter also occurs with the second pair of letters. Looking at the second row, you know that the first letter of the missing pair of letters has to be "K." Moving two letters ahead, or skipping a letter, the second letter will be "M." The missing pair of letters in the second row is "KM."

Be careful with the alphabet. Some of the word/letter matrix questions are going to involve finding patterns in the movements between letters. That is, you will need to discover how many letters are skipped between two letters in a pair or between two pairs, and then you will have to apply this pattern to another pair of letters. Make sure that you count correctly the number of letters skipped and that you do not accidentally skip or forget a letter when you apply the pattern to the bottom row. If you have trouble thinking of what letter comes after another letter in the alphabet, writing out the entire alphabet may be very helpful.

Get used to going backward in the alphabet. Some questions may require you to go backward in the alphabet. If you have a hard time doing this, you should go through the alphabet from the beginning and slow down as you reach the letter. Writing out the entire alphabet may also be very helpful. This should help you determine the letters that come before a letter in the alphabet.

Beware of a mix of letters and words. Some questions will use different pairs of letters to form a word. You will need to discover the pattern of how the letters are being placed to form the word. For example, your first pair of letters might be "ar," the second pair of letters might be "eb," and the word might be *bear*. The pattern is that the second pair of letters are reversed and then placed in front of the first pair of letters to form the word. Once you figure out the pattern, you will need to apply it to the bottom row of letters in order to find the missing word.

Make sure you have the correct pattern/relationship. Once again, identifying the correct answer choice will solely depend upon whether you have determined the correct relationship or pattern. Write down the pattern/relationship if you are having trouble keeping it in your head. You can use shorthand notation to help you, such as "S2" to mean "skip 2 letters." A good method is to constantly look back at the top row and mimic its changes as you try to figure out the correct answer for the bottom row.

Visualize the movement of letters. You might find that you can visualize some of the movements of letters. It might be easier to imagine invisible letters in between some of the pairs of letters. Or, for missing words, maybe you can visualize the different pairs of letters coming together in the correct pattern to form the missing word. In any case, with these questions you need to discover the method you are most comfortable with so you can quickly and accurately answer these questions.

Look out for the relationship questions. Some questions might test you on the relationships between the definitions of certain words. You will need to look at the first word and see how it is related to the second word. Then, you will have to look at the third word and see how it is related to the second word. The relationships between each of the words will be duplicated in the bottom row. If you're having trouble determining the relationships, try to think of real-life examples. It's also likely that the relationships will involve either one word being a type of another word or some kind of movement in the words from the specific to the general or vice versa.

Use process of elimination. With many of these questions, you can use a process of elimination to narrow down your answer choices. For example, if you are given two pairs of letters and you need to find the missing word, you can immediately eliminate the answer choices that do not contain any of the letters. Or, if you know the first letter in a word or a pair of letters, you can eliminate all the answer choices that do not start with that letter.

Word/Letter Matrices Questions

1.

The letters in the box go together in a certain way.
Choose the letters that goes where you see the question mark.

AB	BAC
KL	?

A. LKM   B. MLK   C. KML   D. MLN   E. LMN

2.

The letters in the box go together in a certain way.
Choose the letter that goes where you see the question mark.

A	B
C	?

A. D   B. F   C. A   D. C

3.

The letters in the box go together in a certain way.
Choose the letter that goes where you see the question mark.

B	D	F
M	O	?

A. P   B. Q   C. R   D. S

4.

The letters in the box go together in a certain way.
Choose the letter that goes where you see the question mark.

A	B	C
R	S	?

A. W   B. T   C. X   D. R

5.

The letters in the box go together in a certain way.
Choose the letters that goes where you see the question mark.

AB	CD	EF
OP	QR	?

A. RS   B. TV   C. SU   D. ST

6.

The letters in the box go together in a certain way.
Choose the letter that goes where you see the question mark.

A	D	G
B	E	?

A. H   B. D   C. F   D. A

7.

The letters in the box go together in a certain way.
Choose the letters that goes where you see the question mark.

AA	AB	BAC
LL	LM	?

A. LMN   B. MLN   C. MNL   D. NOP   E. PON

8.

The letters in the box go together in a certain way.
Choose the letters that goes where you see the question mark.

AZ	BY
CX	?

A. AB   B. CZ   C. DW   D. DY   E. WD

9.

The letters in the box go together in a certain way.
Choose the letters that goes where you see the question mark.

ACD	EGH	IKL
NPQ	RTU	?

A. UST   B. VXY   C. VWL   D. VWX   E. STW

10.

The letters in the box go together in a certain way.
Choose the letters that goes where you see the question mark.

EGI	IKM	MOQ
BDF	FHJ	?

A. KMO   B. KMN   C. JKM   D. JLN   E. KJN

11.

The letters/words in the box go together in a certain way.
Choose the word that goes where you see the question mark.

am	tr	tram
at	br	?

A. brat   B. tar   C. part   D. bram

12.

The letters/words in the box go together in a certain way.
Choose the word that goes where you see the question mark.

ea	bt	beat
oa	ct	?

A. cat   B. coat   C. boat   D. boar

13.

The letters/words in the box go together in a certain way.
Choose the word that goes where you see the question mark.

ta	tr	tear
pe	pl	?

A. pear   B. peal   C. peer   D. peel

14.

The letters/words in the box go together in a certain way.
Choose the word that goes where you see the question mark.

me	it	time
re	if	?

A. reef   B. fire   C. tire   D. ifer

15.

The letters/words in the box go together in a certain way.
Choose the word that goes where you see the question mark.

rf	now	frown
rb	kin	?

A. brown   B. break   C. brink   D. brake   E. braun

16.

The letters/words in the box go together in a certain way.
Choose the word that goes where you see the question mark.

oa	td	toad
ea	pr	?

A. pear   B. tear   C. peer   D. pare   E. prea

17.

The letters/words in the box go together in a certain way.
Choose the word that goes where you see the question mark.

ef	li	life
ta	be	?

A. beat   B. bate   C. tab   D. bile   E. beta

18.

The letters/words in the box go together in a certain way.
Choose the word that goes where you see the question mark.

ai	fl	fail
ea	dr	?

A. dere   B. dear   C. read   D. fear

19.

The letters/words in the box go together in a certain way.
Choose the word that goes where you see the question mark.

fiend	fin	fed
faint	fan	?

A. fit   B. fin   C. fat   D. fai   E. fad

20.

The words in the box go together in a certain way.
Choose the word that goes where you see the question mark.

frank	ran	fan
steak	tea	?

A. seat   B. tear   C. far   D. sea   E. teal

21.

The words in the box go together in a certain way.
Choose the word that goes where you see the question mark.

table	wood	pine
dress	?	silk

A. wool   B. closet   C. cloth   D. sew   E. tree

22.

The words in the box go together in a certain way.
Choose the word that goes where you see the question mark.

rose	flower	plant
cottage	house	?

A. forest   B. skyscraper   C. building   D. city   E. garden

23.

The words in the box go together in a certain way.
Choose the word that goes where you see the question mark.

candle	lamp	fluorescent
cottage	house	?

A. skyscraper   B. shack   C. tent   D. home   E. city

24.

The words in the box go together in a certain way.
Choose the word that goes where you see the question mark.

branch	tree	forest
petal	?	garden

A. rose   B. petal   C. flower   D. bee   E. pollen

25.

The words in the box go together in a certain way.
Choose the word that goes where you see the question mark.

orange	cow	ice
juice	?	liquid

A. ice cream   B. fruit   C. milk   D. cheese   E. dairy

OLSAT® Preparation Guide - Levels D, E, and F

Word/Letter Matrices Answer Key

1. **A) LKM**

   In the first row, you're given the pattern "AB" changes to "BAC." It looks as though the A and B change positions, and then the next letter after B is placed third in the set. In the second row, you have "KL" changes to ?, so you know that your answer will be LK-something. What comes after L? The letter M. The answer is "LKM," which is answer choice (A).

2. **(A) D**

   In the first row, the letters are moving sequentially through the alphabet. So, what comes after C? The letter D must be our answer. Answer choice (A) is correct.

3. **(B) Q**

   The pattern in the first row is to move up two letters, or skip a letter, as you move from left to right. In the second row, you have "MO," and you need to find the third letter in the sequence. Moving up two letters, or skipping the letter after O, your answer should be "Q," which is answer choice (B).

4. **(B) T**

   The letters are moving up sequentially in the first row. What comes after S in the alphabet? The letter T. Answer choice (B) is correct.

5. **(D) ST**

   In the first row, the letters are moving up sequentially in pairs. So, after QR, you should expect to see ST. The correct answer is (D).

6. **(A) H**

   The pattern is that next letter is moving up three letters from the previous letter. Or, you could think of the pattern as skipping two letters each time. In the bottom row, you have BE, and you are being asked to find the next letter in the sequence. Moving three letters up from E, or skipping two letters, you should get "H," answer choice (A), as your answer.

7. **(B) MLN**

   A simple way to solve this problem is to notice that, in the third pair of letters in the first row, the first two letters from the second pair are flipped. Looking at the bottom row, the second pair of letters is LM. So, your answer is going to be ML-something. The only answer choice with "ML" as the first two letters is answer choice (B). Does it work? Yep, because the last letter in the third pair is supposed to be the next letter after M, which is N. "MLN" is the right answer.

8. **(C) DW**

   Here, the pattern seems to be that each letter in a pair is moving away from the other one sequentially. In the first row, AZ changes to BY. The second row begins with CX. So, what comes after C? Our answer choice must contain the letter D, so we can narrow down our answer choices to (C) and (D). What comes before X? The letter W. The correct answer is "DW," which is answer choice (C).

9. **(B) VXY**

The first set of letters in the first row is ACD. So, the pattern is: use a letter, then move up two letters (skip a letter) and use the next two letters sequentially. The next set of letters in the row moves sequentially up the alphabet from the last letter in the first set, and it has the same pattern. So does the third set of letters in the first row. In the second row, the second set of letters is RTU. So, your answer is going to be V-something since V comes after U. Our viable answer choices are (B), (C), and (D). If you move up two letters from V (skip a letter), the next letter is X, and the letter after that is Y. So, the correct answer is "VXY," which is answer choice (B).

10. **(D) JLN**

The first set of letters is EGI. The pattern is to move up or skip a letter after each letter in the set. Looking at the second set in the first row, you can see that the last letter from the first set is repeated. The pattern is also the same for the second set of letters. The second set of letters in the second row is FHJ. So, J has to be the first letter in the third set. Our possible answer choices are narrowed down to (C) and (D). Moving up two letters from J, the next letter in the sequence is going to be L and then N. The answer is "JLN," which is answer choice (D).

11. **(A) brat**

In the first row, the second pair of letters is being placed before the first pair of letters to get the third item. Using the same process in the second row, the answer must be *brat*. *Brat* is also the only answer choice that uses all the letters from both pairs in the question. Answer choice (A) is correct.

12. **(B) coat**

Here, the first pair of letters is being placed in between the second pair of letters. Employing the same pattern for the second row, the answer must be *coat*, which is answer choice (B). You could also easily get rid of answer choices (A), (C), and (D) because they either don't have enough letters or include the letter "B."

13. **(D) peel**

This pattern is a little tricky. The pattern is to take the first letter being used in both pairs, put an E after that letter, then use the last letter from the first pair, and finally use the last letter from the second pair. If you follow this pattern in the bottom row, you'll find that the missing word is *peel*. Answer choice (D) is correct.

14. **(B) fire**

The pattern here is to reverse the letters in the second pair and then add the letters from the first pair. So, "me" and "it" becomes *time*. Therefore, "re" and "if" must become *fire*. Answer choice (B) is correct. You should also notice that answer choices (A) and (C) could easily be eliminated because they don't contain the letters from the second row that need to be used in this question to get the missing word.

15. **(C) brink**

Here, you need to take the first pair of letters and reverse them to get the first two letters in your missing word. So, your missing word is going to be "br"-something.

That doesn't really help us with our answer choices. The next step is, in order, to place the second letter, the third letter, and the first letter from the second pair after the "br." Placing "ink" after "br" gets you the word *brink*.

16. (A) pear

The pattern is to place the first pair of letters in between the second pair of letters to get the missing word. Employing this pattern for the second row, your answer should be *pear*, which is answer choice (A).

17. (A) beat

To find the missing word, you need to reverse the first pair of letters and place them after the second pair of letters. Following this pattern, your answer should be *beat*. Answer choice (A) is correct.

18. (B) dear

To find the missing word, you need to place the first pair of letters in between the second pair of letters. The correct answer is *dear*, which is answer choice (B).

19. (A) fit

Here, we are given a word as our first set of letters. The second set of letters is another word. This word uses the first two letters and then the fourth letter from the first word. The third set of letters is another word, which uses the first, third, and fifth letters from the first word. Since we need to find the third word in the second row, this is our pattern. Using the pattern, the missing word is *fit*, which is answer choice (A).

20. (D) sea

There are two ways that you can solve this question. One way is to notice that the third word in the row uses, in order, the first, third, and fourth letters from the first word. The other way is to notice that you only need to place the first letter from the first word before the second and third letters from the second word in order to get the third word. In either case, the answer is *sea*, which is answer choice (D).

21. (C) cloth

This is a different type of question from the other questions you have encountered in this section. In this question, you need to look at the definitions of the words in the row in order to figure out the relationships between the words. So, in the first row, you have *table*, *wood*, and *pine*. How are these words related? Well, a table can be made from wood, and pine is a type of wood. Now you need to apply this relationship to the words in the second row. Looking at the second row, what is a dress made from? You might think that *wool*, answer choice (A), could be correct, but you need to look at both relationships in the row. So, is silk a type of wool? Nope. Does *cloth* work? A dress can be made from cloth, and silk is a type of cloth. Answer choice (C) is correct.

22. (C) building

Once again, you're looking at the relationships between the definitions of the words in the row. When you have found the correct types of relationships, you need to apply these relationships to the words in the second row. The words in the top row are *rose*, *flower*, and *plant*. These words appear to be types of each other; that is, a rose is a type of flower, and a flower is a type of plant. So, you are moving from the specific to the general. Applying this relationship to the bottom row, can you see that a cottage is a type of house? What is more general than a house? Or, what is a house an example of? Looking at the answer choices, the best choice seems to be *building*. Is a house a type of building? It sure is. There are numerous types of buildings, and a house is an example of a building.

23. (B) shack

Here's another question that involves looking at the relationships between different types of things. The three words in the first row are *candle, lamp,* and *fluorescent*. How are these words related? Well, a candle is a type of lamp, and a fluorescent lamp is another type of lamp. In the second row, you can see that a cottage is a type of house. So, you need to look for an answer choice that is another type of house. A skyscraper and a tent are not commonly considered houses, so we can eliminate those answer choices. A house could be a type of home, like a skyscraper could be a type of home, but a home is not a type of house. A city, of course, is not a house. The best answer is *shack*. A shack, although it might not be the best place to live, is a type of house. Answer choice (B) is correct.

24. (C) flower

How are *branch, tree,* and *forest* related to one another? A branch is one of the fixtures or characteristics of a tree. Where can a number of trees be found? In a forest. Looking at the second row, we need to find a word for which a petal is a common characteristic and the word can be commonly found in a garden. Our two best choices are (A) and (C), *rose* and *flower*. Both fit the relationships that we found in the first row, so how do we choose between them? Well, looking back at the second word in the top row, *tree* is a very general type of word. There are many different kinds of trees, just as there are many different kinds of flowers. While there are a few types of roses, a rose is really a specific kind of flower. Since we're looking for the more general word, *flower* is the better choice. The correct answer is (C).

25. (C) milk

In this question, the clearest relationship we can find between the words comes from looking at the different columns of words instead of the rows. So, how are *orange* and *juice* related? You can get juice from an orange. Can you get *liquid* from *ice?* You can if you let the ice melt. What can you get from a cow? Our best answer choices are *ice cream* (choice A), *milk* (choice C), and *cheese* (choice D). Looking back at the relationships, you should hopefully notice that the bottom word can come directly from the top word in some way. Juice can be squeezed from an orange, and you can get liquid after the ice has melted. Can you get ice cream or cheese directly from a cow? No, other ingredients and processes are needed to make ice cream and cheese. The best answer is *milk*, which is answer choice (C).

Verbal Analogies

OLSAT® Preparation Guide - Levels D, E, and F Bright Kids NYC Inc. ©

Verbal Analogies Strategies

The verbal analogy questions in the Verbal Reasoning section of the OLSAT® aret designed to test your knowledge of the relationship between two words. While the definitions of the words in the analogy may not be similar, the two words can be classified together in some way. It will be your job to determine the type of relationship between the two words. Once you determine the relationship, you will need to turn to the second analogy in the question. There will be a question mark for the second word in this pair. Using the relationship you identified between the first analogy, you will need to figure out the correct word to complete the second analogy. Below is an example of the type of questions you will see in this section of the exam.

Example: **In is to Out as Left is to ?**

A. Right   B. Side   C. In   D. Direction   E. Between

The first two words are *in* and *out*. These words are related in a certain way. *In* is the opposite of *out*. Now look at the third word. The answer we are looking for must have the same relationship with *left* that the first two words, *in* and *out*, have with each other. Hence, we are looking for the opposite of *left*, which is *right*. The correct answer is A.

Always ask yourself this question: In the first analogy, how is the first word related to the second word? The most important step in answering an analogy question correctly is figuring out the correct relationship that the two analogies are going for. If you can discover the relationship, finding the correct answer among the choices for the second analogy is quite simple.

Look for analogy categories. Many analogies fall into a number of categories. If the first analogy falls into one of these categories, it shouldn't be too tough to figure out the missing word in the second analogy. Remember that the list on the next page is not exhaustive; it is simply a helpful guide to recognizing some of the more common analogy categories. Also, each category on the list can easily be reversed in order on a question.

Word → Opposite Word: The relationship in the analogy might be that the two words have opposite meanings.
Example: **Love is to Hate as Big is to Small**

Word → Similar Word: This is similar to the above category, except for the fact that the two words are synonymous.
Example: **Beverage is to Drink as Story is to Tale**

Outer Part → Inner Part: The relationship here is that some part of an object or thing is inside another object or thing.
Example: **Shoes are to Shoebox as DVD is to DVD case**

Bigger → Smaller: The relationship is that one thing starts off one way and then becomes larger or smaller.
Example: **Baby is to Adult as Calf is to Cow**

Whole → Parts: The relationship is that one word is a whole thing, and the other word is a part of that whole thing.
Example: **Tire is to Car as Wing is to Airplane**

Single → Group: Here, one word is a single object or being, and the other word is a group of those objects or beings.
Example: **Traveler is to Caravan as Bird is to Flock**

Item → Use of Item: The relationship between the two words might be that one item is used to do something to another item.
Example: **Hammer is to Nail as Tennis racket is to Tennis ball**

Intense Version → Less Intense Version: The relationship here is that one word refers to something that happens frequently or intensely, and the other word refers to something that happens less frequently or less intensely.
Example: **Blizzard is to Snow as Heavy Fog is to Mist**

Category → Specific Example: Here, one word is a category or a type of thing, and the other word is a specific example of that type of thing.
Example: **Fall is to Season as Football is to Sport**

Beware of association tricks. Do not ever choose an answer just because it is somehow associated with the word in the second analogy. The important thing is applying the relationship in the first analogy to the second analogy—not the fact that the word in the question and the word in the answer choice can be used together.

Verbal Analogy Questions

1. **North is to South as East is to ?**

   A. South   B. Compass   C. West   D. Leg   E. Nail

2. **Finger is to Hand as Toe is to ?**

   A. Finger   B. Foot   C. Bone   D. Leg   E. Nail

3. **Shell is to Egg as Peel is to ?**

   A. Fruit   B. Bread   C. Knife   D. Strawberry   E. Bread

4. **Theater is to Play as Stadium is to ?**

   A. Peanuts   B. Grass   C. Athletes   D. Sports   E. Fun

5. **Up is to Down as Above is to ?**

   A. Below   B. Around   C. Beside   D. Outside   E. Near

6. **Cat is to Kitten as Goat is to ?**

   A. Kid   B. Fawn   C. Chick   D. Animal   E. Milk

7. **Car is to Garage as Ship is to ?**

   A. Water   B. Station   C. Dock   D. Sail   E. Engine

8. **Feather is to Bird as Scale is to ?**

   A. Octopus   B. Weight   C. Measurement   D. Fish   E. Animal

9. **Clock is to Time as Scale is to ?**

   A. Vegetables   B. Fruits   C. Balance   D. Distance   E. Weight

10. **Pillowcase is to Pillow as Envelope is to ?**

    A. Stamp   B. Letter   C. Postage   D. Mail   E. Buy

11. **Bow is to Arrow as Bat is to ?**

    A. Base   B. Hat   C. Mammal   D. Animal   E. Ball

12. Month is to February as Day is to ?

    A. Calendar   B. Cold   C. Time   D. Tuesday   E. Week

13. Flock is to Geese as Herd is to ?

    A. Goats   B. Wolf   C. Shepherd   D. Pasture   E. Graze

14. Painter is to Palette as Sculptor is to ?

    A. Sculpture   B. Painting   C. Museum   D. Chisel   E. Brush

15. Tease is to Cry as Joke is to ?

    A. Cry   B. Laugh   C. Clown   D. Comedian   E. Play

16. Plum is to Prune as Grape is to ?

    A. Eat   B. Fruit   C. Raisin   D. Juice   E. Strawberry

17. Pen is to Poet as Needle is to ?

    A. Yarn   B. Sew   C. Tailor   D. Sewing machine   E. Thread

18. Exercise is to Gym as Graze is to ?

    A. Cow   B. Eat   C. Pasture   D. Hay   E. Nibble

19. Propeller is to Airplane as Wick is to ?

    A. Burn   B. Candle   C. Wicker   D. Flame   E. Light

20. Person is to Talk as Bird is to ?

    A. Birdhouse   B. Chirp   C. Cry   D. Eat   E. Hunt

21. s is to Microscope as Star is to ?

    A. Comet   B. Sun   C. Constellation   D. Telescope   E. Gaze

22. Fish is to School as Person is to ?

    A. Concert   B. Play   C. Crowd   D. Men   E. Family

23. Banana is to Peel as Corn is to ?

    A. Cob   B. Husk   C. Kernel   D. Vegetable   E. Eat

24. Sapphire is to Gem as Shorts are to ?

    A. Clothes   B. Pair   C. Laundry   D. Wear   E. Hands

25. Run is to Jog as Rain is to ?

    A. Pour   B. Hurricane   C. Umbrella   D. Wet   E. Drizzle

26. Fin is to Fish as Rudder is to ?

    A. Oar   B. Sail   C. Schooner   D. Boat   E. Mast

27. Scold is to Reprimand as Persevere is to ?

    A. Coast   B. Disregard   C. Linger   D. Persist   E. Determine

28. Saw is to Carpenter as Microscope is to ?

    A. Telescope   B. Scientist   C. Measure   D. Look   E. Lens

29. Mare is to Stallion as Doe is to ?

    A. Buck   B. Horse   C. Deer   D. Fawn   E. Calf

30. Clock is to Hand as Wheel is to ?

    A. Wheelbarrow B. Road   C. Spoke   D. Car   E. Tire

31. Sponge is to Porous as Rubber is to ?

    A. Elastic   B. Inflexible   C. Tire   D. Massive   E. Solid

32. Ingredients are to Recipe as Pictures are to ?

    A. Paint   B. Write   C. Collage   D. Pen   E. Tree

33. Embarrassed is to Humiliated as Frightened is to ?

    A. Annoyed   B. Agitated   C. Terrified   D. Courageous   E. Fearless

34. Elated is to Despondent as Enlightened is to ?

    A. Annoyed   B. Cherished   C. Tolerant   D. Courageous   E. Ignorant

35. Depressed is to Sad as Exhausted is to ?

    A. Gloomy   B. Tired   C. Happy   D. Energetic   E. Moody

36. Analogy is to Comparison as Metaphor is to ?

    A. Symbol   B. Language   C. Poetry   D. Rhythm   E. Literal

37. Interest is to Obsession as Dream is to?

    A. Awake   B. Night   C. Sleep   D. Fantasy   E. Remember

Verbal Analogy Answer Key

1. (C) West

Most analogies fit into a certain kind of category. Here, we are given the initial analogy *North is to South.* So, how are *North* and *South* related? They are antonyms, or the opposite of each other. Thus, you are dealing with an opposite analogy. The opposite of *East* is *West*, so answer choice (C) is correct.

2. (B) Foot

The first analogy you have been given is *Finger is to Hand.* How is a finger related to a hand? Well, a finger is one of several jointed parts of a hand. The category here is going from a part to a whole. The next analogy gives you the word *toe.* What is a toe a jointed part of? The correct answer is (B). A toe is a jointed part of a foot.

3. (A) Fruit

How is a shell related to an egg? The shell is the outer part that contains and protects the soft inner parts. The category is outer part to inner part. A peel is the outer part of what kind of thing? The only answer that makes sense is *fruit* (choice A). A peel contains and protects the soft, fleshy part of many types of fruits, such as bananas.

4. (D) Sports

How is a theater related to a play? Well, a theater is a place where people can go to watch plays. The category is location/event. What usually happens in a stadium? People usually go to a stadium to watch a sporting event. So, the best answer is *sports* (choice D).

5. (A) Below

This question is an opposite analogy because you've been given the analogy *Up is to Down.* What's the opposite of *above?* The correct answer is (A)—*below.*

6. (A) Kid

A kitten grows up to become a cat. So, the category here is essentially larger to smaller. The second analogy is *Goat is to _____.* What grows up to become a goat? The name for a baby goat is a kid. The correct answer is (A).

7. (C) Dock

What's the relationship between a car and a garage? People often park their car in their garage after they are done driving for the day. Where does a ship usually go after it has been out at sea? Captains usually tie their ship to a dock. Thus, the best analogy is *Ship is to Dock* (choice C).

8. (D) Fish

The analogy you've been given is *Feather is to Bird.* It looks as though the category of the relationship here is a part to a whole since a feather is one part of a whole bird. What is a scale a part of? A scale is one part of a whole fish. The correct answer is (D).

9. (E) Weight

How are a clock and time related? You use a clock to find out the time. What do you use a scale for? You use a scale to measure your weight or the weight of a thing, such as apples in a supermarket. The best answer is *weight* (choice E).

10. (D) Mail

The category here is outer part/covering to inner part/covering since a pillowcase holds a pillow inside it and covers the pillow to protect it from getting dirty. What does an envelope usually hold inside it? You may be tempted by *letter* (choice B), but an envelope doesn't always hold a letter. It might hold a birthday card, a postcard, a coupon, or something else. The better answer is *mail* (choice D). Generally, mail is enclosed in an envelope in order to protect the mail while it travels from one place to another.

11. (E) Ball

The analogy given is *Bow is to Arrow*. A bow is used to shoot or propel an arrow a certain distance. This is an object/instrument type of analogy. So, what does a bat usually hit a certain distance? A bat usually hits a ball. The correct answer is (E).

12. (D) Tuesday

Here, we have a category/example type of analogy. You are given a category *(month)* and then given an example of an item in that category *(February)*. The next analogy says *Day is to ____*. What is a specific example of a day? The best answer is *Tuesday*, which is answer choice (D).

13. (A) Goats

The analogy given is *Flock is to Geese*. How are *flock* and *geese* related? Well, geese usually fly in a flock. The second analogy is *Herd is to ____*. So, what usually walks around in a herd? Among the answer choices, the only animal listed that walks in a herd is goats (choice A). Remember not to get fooled by other answer choices, such as *shepherd, wolf,* and *pasture*, which seem associated with the idea of a herd. You need to focus on the relationship between the words in the analogies. Here, the relationship is clearly a group of animals in comparison to the type of animal in that group.

14. (D) Chisel

How are a painter and a palette related? A palette is a tray or board that holds the colors that a painter will use to help him or her paint a picture. So, a palette is a type of tool that a painter uses to create a painting. What kind of tool does a sculptor use to carry out his or her work? Sculptors usually use a chisel to sculpt their creations out of marble or another type of rock. The correct answer is (D).

15. (B) Laugh

If you tease someone, a plausible reaction on the part of the other person might be crying. If you tell a joke, what's a plausible reaction on the part of the other person? While it's possible that he or she may start crying at your joke, the best answer among the choices is that the person will probably (hopefully) laugh. The best answer choice is (B).

16. (C) Raisin

How are a plum and a prune related? A prune is a dried plum. So, what is a dried grape called? A dried grape is called a raisin. Answer choice (C) is correct.

17. (C) Tailor

Here, the category of the analogy is instrument/user of the instrument because a pen can be used by a poet to write poetry. The second analogy is *Needle is to* ____. Who uses a needle in his or her line of work? The only two options are a tailor and a sewing machine since both use needles to do their job. *Tailor* is the better choice because a poet is a person, not a machine. Answer choice (C) is correct.

18. (C) Pasture

The first analogy is *Exercise is to Gym,* and the second analogy is *Graze is to* ____. So, how is exercise related to the gym? Well, people usually go to the gym in order to exercise. The word *graze* usually refers to animals. So, where do animals usually go in order to graze? *Pasture* is the best answer among the choices you have been given.

19. (B) Candle

The category of the analogy is parts/whole because a propeller is a part of an airplane. What is a wick a part of? A wick is a braid of threads in a candle; lighting the wick keeps the candle burning. So, a wick is a part of a candle (choice B).

20. (B) Chirp

How is a person related to the verb *talk?* People usually communicate by using their mouths to talk to other people. The second analogy is *Bird is to* ____. How do birds usually use their mouths to communicate? They generally chirp (choice B) in order to communicate with other birds.

21. (C) Constellation

The first analogy is *Lens is to Microscope.* How are a lens and a microscope related? A microscope has many different types of lenses that are used to look at an object under different magnifications. The second analogy is *Star is to* ____. What has many different types of stars in it? The correct answer is *constellation* (choice C). If you confused a lens with a slide (the object you place under a microscope to look at), you may have incorrectly chosen *telescope* (choice D).

22. (C) Crowd

Here, we have another analogy that deals with a single thing and then a group of those things. So, in the first analogy, we have a fish, and we know that a group of fish is called a school. In the second analogy, we have a person. What can a group of people be called? The best answer is *crowd* (choice C). It's true that a group of people can also be a family (choice E), but a school of fish is usually a large number of fish. Thus, *crowd* is the best answer.

23. (B) Husk

The category here is once again an outer part that covers an inner part. The first analogy is *Banana is to Peel.* You know that a peel is the outer covering of a banana. So, in the second analogy, you should be looking for an answer choice that reflects the outer covering of corn. A husk is the dry external covering of an ear of corn, so answer choice (B) is correct.

24. (A) Clothes

The first analogy is *Sapphire is to Gem.* A sapphire is a type of gem. The category of the analogy here is an example of a type of thing and then the type of thing. So, shorts are a type of what? Among the answer choices, you can narrow down the answers to either *clothes* (choice A) or *laundry* (choice C). Regarding *laundry,* shorts may be something found in the laundry, but are shorts really a type of laundry? The more likely answer choice is *clothes.* Shorts are certainly a type of clothes, so answer choice (A) is correct.

25. (E) Drizzle

Running is usually considered to be a faster version of jogging. The category of the analogy here is an intense version of something and then a less intense version of the same thing. The second analogy is *Rain is to _____.* Since *running* was the first word in the first analogy, you should know that the more intense version of the action comes first. Thus, you need to find a word among the answer choices that refers to a less intense version of rain. The correct answer is *drizzle* (choice E).

26. (D) Boat

The first analogy in this question is *Fin is to Fish.* How are a fish and a fin related? A fish uses a fin to direct itself through the water. So, what can a rudder direct through the water? The two best choices are *schooner* (choice C) and *boat* (choice D). A schooner is a specific type of sailing vessel. In the first analogy, we weren't given a specific type of fish. So, the best choice is a more general answer—*boat* (choice D).

27. (D) Persist

Here is an example of an analogy that is a synonym—that is, the two words in the analogy are related because they have similar definitions. *Scold* is synonymous with *reprimand.* What is *persevere* synonymous with? The correct answer among the choices given is *persist* (choice D). You might have had a tough time choosing between *persist* and *linger* (choice C). *Persist* is the better choice of the two because it better reflects the definition of *persevere,* which is to be determined to continue a course of action and work hard.

28. (B) Scientist

The category is an instrument and the person who uses that instrument. A saw is used by a carpenter. Who uses a microscope? The best answer is *scientist* (choice B).

29. (A) Buck

How are a mare and a stallion related? A mare is a fully mature female horse, and a stallion is a fully mature male horse. So, it looks as though the category of the analogy is an adult female and an adult male of a certain kind of animal. In the second analogy, we have *Doe is to _____*. A doe is a female deer. So, we need to find an answer choice that is a male deer. A male deer is a buck, which makes answer choice (A) correct.

30. (C) Spoke

The category of the analogy is a whole and then a part of the whole. A hand is a part of a clock. What is a part of a wheel? The best answer choices are *spoke* (choice C) and *tire* (choice E). Of these choices, which one do you think is the better choice when you compare each of them to the hand of a clock. *Spoke* is the better choice because, like the hand of a clock, it extends outward from the middle. Therefore, answer choice (C) is the correct answer.

31. (A) Elastic

How is a sponge related to the adjective *porous*? Well, a sponge is able to collect water because it is full of pores. So, its porous quality enables it to soak up water. What are the qualities of rubber? You know that rubber bands can stretch, so what is a quality of rubber that allows it to stretch? Rubber can stretch because it is elastic (choice A). The correct answer to the analogy is *elastic*.

32. (C) Collage

How are ingredients and a recipe related? Well, you can find many different types of ingredients in a recipe. What contains many different types of pictures? The correct answer is *collage* (choice C). A collage is a work of art in which many different types of pictures are pasted on a single surface.

33. (C) Terrified

Here's another analogy that involves synonyms. *Embarrassed* and *humiliated* are synonymous. So, you need to find a word among the answer choices that is synonymous with *frightened*. The only viable choice is *terrified* (choice C).

34. (E) Ignorant

If you are feeling elated about something, you are feeling happy. If you are feeling despondent about something, you are feeling depressed or unhappy. So, in the first analogy, we are dealing with words that are antonyms of each other. In the second analogy, we have *Enlightened is to _____*. You need to figure out which word among the choices you have been given is an antonym of *enlightened*. To be enlightened is to have a sudden realization about something. The opposite of that definition would be to have no sort of realization about anything at all. The best answer is *ignorant* (choice E).

35. (B) Tired

Depressed and *sad* are synonymous. What word is synonymous with *exhausted?* The correct answer is *tired* (choice B).

36. (A) Symbol

By this point, you should know that an analogy is a type of comparison between two things. What is a metaphor? A metaphor is a figure of speech in which someone uses something to represent another thing. A metaphor is basically a type of symbol (choice A). We use metaphors in our language (choice B) all the time, but a metaphor is not really a type of language; it's more a function of language. A type of language would be English or Spanish. Metaphors can be used in all types of languages. Metaphors are also used in poetry (choice C), but a metaphor is not a type of poetry. Rhythm (choice D) is also used in poetry, but rhythm and metaphor are not similar in any way.

37. (D) Fantasy

Here, the category of the analogy is a less intense thing and then a more intense thing. For example, you may develop an *interest* in collecting stamps. But, if all you start caring about is stamp collecting and you can't think about anything else, it might be said that you have become *obsessed* with collecting stamps. In the second analogy, you have *Dream is to ____*. Let's say you have a dream of becoming a baseball player. What is a more intense version of a dream? Imagine that you actually start believing that you have become a baseball player. That would be called a *fantasy* (choice D). None of the other choices represent a more intense version of a dream.

Verbal Classifications

OLSAT® Preparation Guide - Levels D, E, and F Bright Kids NYC Inc. ©

Verbal Classifications Strategies

The verbal classification questions in the Verbal Reasoning section of the OLSAT® mainly test you on how to group different words together. Essentially, all of the questions will ask you to find the one word that doesn't belong in the group of answer choices that you have been given. In order to find the correct answer, you will have to find a characteristic that exists among four of the five words. If you are able to find that characteristic, you will be able to eliminate the odd word out of the group. Note that the odd word out of the group is the correct answer.

Become used to recognizing a verbal classification question. There is a particular format to this type of question. It is:

> *Which word does not go with the other four?*

There are four different types of classifications:

1. **Classification of objects:** Generally, you are going to look for the one type of broad or essential characteristic that most of the words in the given group share. Ask yourself what the purpose is of each word in the group and see if you can detect an overall pattern to these purposes.

> Example: Which word does not go with the other four?
>
> A. Plate   B. Fork   C. Meat   D. Spoon   E. Knife
>
> You can classify a plate, a fork, a spoon, and a knife as utensils. A piece of meat is not a utensil. You may use all of these objects to eat a piece of meat, but they are in a different verbal classification from meat.

2. **Classification of animals:** Try to think in broad terms when you encounter a question involving an animal classification. Ask yourself questions like:

    - To which animal group do these animals belong (mammals, birds, reptiles, invertebrates, etc.)?
    - How do the animals generally move around?
    - Where can you find these animals?
    - Does age or size matter with these animals?
    - Are these animals considered dangerous/wild or docile/domesticated?

3. **Classification of words and their meanings:** These types of classifications will basically test your vocabulary. If you can reasonably understand the definitions of the words in the group, you should be able to pick the odd word out of the group.

> Example: Which word does not go with the other four?
>
> A. Deny   B. Disclaim   C. Renounce   D. Affirm   E. Refute
>
> *Deny, disclaim, renounce,* and *refute* are all verbs that express an action of disagreement or a refusal to accept something. *Affirm* actually means to confirm or to assert something as being true. The odd word out is *affirm.*

4. **Classification of words with phonics:** These types of classifications will involve a similar type of spelling of the words in the answer choices. You will usually discover that there is probably a phonics classification when you realize that there is no possible relationship between the definitions of the different words. There are generally two types of phonics classifications:

- A similar spelling of the first few letters in four of the answer choices
- A similar spelling of the last few letters in four of the answer choices

> Example: Which word does not go with the other four?
>
> A. Tree   B. Bee   C. Knee   D. Free   E. Feet
>
> The last two letters of four of the words are "ee." The odd word out is *beet.* Notice that answer choices (A) and (D) try to fool you by being two words that end in "ree".

Use the following strategies to find the correct answer to classification questions.

Beware of association tricks. Watch out for a word that is associated with some of the words in the group but does not share a fundamental characteristic with the rest of the words.

Break down the group of words to find their core definition. Looking at all the words in the group as a whole, can you see what most of the words generally do? That is, can you see a core purpose to most of the words that will help to exclude one of the words? In many respects, you are trying to take a step back with each new question to see some broad connection between four of the five words in the answer choices.

> Example: Which word does not go with the other four?
>
> A. Hammer   B. Baseball Bat   C. Nail   D. Club   E. Mallet
>
> The classification here is items that hit other items. The odd word out is *nail*. The association trick is that you may think that *nail* belongs because it is usually associated with a hammer.

Look out for antonyms/synonyms. Always be on the lookout for words that have similar definitions or two words that are the opposite of each other. If you find an antonym pair, you know that one of those two words will be the odd word out (unless it's a phonics classification question). If you find two synonyms, you know that you have discovered some kind of pattern or classification among the words (unless it's a phonics classification question).

Always remember that the classification must work for four out of the five words. If it doesn't, you will know you are on the wrong path.

If all else fails, look for a similarity in phonics. You may find that you notice the phonics classifications right off the bat. That's great! But if you do not, and if you can see no possible connections between the words, start looking at the first and last letters in the answer choices. You most probably have encountered a phonics classification question.

OLSAT® Preparation Guide - Levels D, E, and F

Bright Kids NYC Inc. ©

Verbal Classifications Questions

1. **Which word does not go with the other four?**

    A. Fly   B. Bee   C. Mosquito   D. Ladybug   E. Robin

2. **Which word does not go with the other four?**

    A. Snowboard   B. Skis   C. Skateboard   D. Bicycle   E. Helmet

3. **Which word does not go with the other four?**

    A. Crocodile   B. Lizard   C. Iguana   D. Lion   E. Snake

4. **Which word does not go with the other four?**

    A. Pencil   B. Molasses   C. Gum   D. Glue   E. Tape

5. **Which word does not go with the other four?**

    A. Parrot   B. Finch   C. Toucan   D. Crow   E. Butterfly

6. **Which word does not go with the other four?**

    A. Weed   B. Lilac   C. Tulip   D. Daffodil   E. Rose

7. **Which word does not go with the other four?**

    A. Shrimp   B. Crab   C. Octopus   D. Crayfish   E. Lobster

8. **Which word does not go with the other four?**

    A. Shore   B. Beach   C. Atlantic   D. Cape   E. Bay

9. **Which word does not go with the other four?**

    A. Jog   B. Sit   C. Run   D. Stroll   E. Walk

10. **Which word does not go with the other four?**

    A. Typhoon   B. Hurricane   C. Earthquake   D. Tornado   E. Rain

11. Which word does not go with the other four?

    A. Mimic   B. Copy   C. Repeat   D. Misrepresent   E. Imitate

12. Which word does not go with the other four?

    A. Urge   B. Perceive   C. Command   D. Insist   E. Demand

13. Which word does not go with the other four?

    A. Timid   B. Pompous   C. Arrogant   D. Boastful   E. Lofty

14. Which word does not go with the other four?

    A. Argue   B. Discuss   C. Persuade   D. Reason   E. Dictate

15. Which word does not go with the other four?

    A. Discard   B. Scatter   C. Disperse   D. Dissipate   E. Distribute

16. Which word does not go with the other four?

    A. Funny   B. Personality   C. Attitude   D. Temper   E. Mood

17. Which word does not go with the other four?

    A. Ordinary   B. Primary   C. Chief   D. Principal   E. Main

18. Which word does not go with the other four?

    A. Stubborn   B. Tough   C. Hard   D. Insecure   E. Inflexible

19. Which word does not go with the other four?

    A. Immense   B. Colossal   C. Grand   D. Huge   E. Slight

20. Which word does not go with the other four?

    A. Renew   B. Wear   C. Restore   D. Polish   E. Furbish

21. Which word does not go with the other four?

A. Hat   B. Lit   C. Fat   D. Cat   E. Mat

22. Which word does not go with the other four?

A. Melt   B. Bolt   C. Colt   D. Jolt   E. Volt

23. Which word does not go with the other four?

A. Spoil   B. Spill   C. Spear   D. Split   E. Score

24. Which word does not go with the other four?

A. Drive   B. Drink   C. Brink   D. Dream   E. Dread

25. Which word does not go with the other four?

A. Posh   B. Fish   C. Leash   D. Polish   E. Least

26. Which word does not go with the other four?

A. Stain   B. Stair   C. Steep   D. Stale   E. Sweat

27. Which word does not go with the other four?

A. Bread   B. Bride   C. Bring   D. Barter   E. Brink

28. Which word does not go with the other four?

A. Sail   B. Pale   C. Fail   D. Hail   E. Mail

29. Which word does not go with the other four?

A. Crane   B. Cramp   C. Swamp   D. Trump   E. Clump

30. Which word does not go with the other four?

A. Fight   B. Height   C. Flaunt   D. Right   E. Plight

OLSAT® Preparation Guide - Levels D, E, and F

Verbal Classifications Answer Key

1. (E) Robin

A fly, a bee, a mosquito, and a ladybug are all types of insects or bugs. Generally, they are smaller than most other animals. You probably have swatted or stepped on a few insects or bugs in your lifetime. A robin, however, is a type of bird. It's doubtful that you have ever swatted or stepped on a robin because they have a level of awareness of the world around them, which allows them to fly away and stay safe from close encounters. Like most birds, robins are often found in high places and fly at relatively high altitudes in comparison to most insects or bugs.

2. (E) Helmet

Snowboards, skis, skateboards, and bicycles are all modes of transportation. You could use any of these items to get from one place to another. Can you use a helmet to get from one place to another? Nope. You may need to wear a helmet whenever you use these types of transportation, but a helmet is not a type of transportation. Remember to break down every word to its core definition and/or use. Also, watch out for the association trick used here.

3. (D) Lion

Crocodiles, lizards, iguanas, and snakes are all types of reptiles. They all have scales and are cold-blooded. A lion is a mammal that has hair and is warm-blooded. The lion is the animal that doesn't belong in this group.

4. (A) Pencil

Molasses, gum, glue, and tape are all sticky items. A pencil is not sticky and, therefore, it does not fit in this classification of items. You may have gotten a little confused since you may sometimes use glue, tape, or a pencil on paper in school. But you usually don't use molasses or gum on paper in school, so that can't be the right type of classification. Just remember to look for the core definition—what do molasses, gum, glue, and tape all have in common? They can stick to other items.

5. (E) Butterfly

A parrot, a finch, a toucan, and a crow are all types of birds. A butterfly is an insect. It's true that every animal listed here can fly, but you need to go one step further and determine what other type of classification can separate four of these animals from the other animal. You could also determine that a parrot, a finch, a toucan, and a crow stay as those types of animals throughout their lives, whereas a butterfly starts its life as a caterpillar and later becomes a butterfly.

6. (A) Weed

A weed is something that is usually harmful to grass and flowers. Lilacs, tulips, daffodils, and roses are different types of flowers. You may have seen these types of flowers growing in a garden or being sold in a store. Even if you didn't know that the right classification was types of flowers, you might have guessed that the weed was the only word in the group that has a negative connotation—nobody wants weeds in their garden or lawn.

7. (C) Octopus

Here is another animal classification question. At first glance, you can tell that all of the choices are marine animals, or animals that live in the sea, so you are going to have to work a little harder to distinguish the odd word out. Shrimps, crabs, crayfish, and lobsters are all crustaceans. An octopus is a mollusk; it has a soft body and does not have an exoskeleton.

8. (C) Atlantic

A shore, a beach, a cape, and a bay are all places where water meets land. They are also generic names for certain types of geographic features. *Atlantic* is the name of a large ocean between North America and Europe. It's a specific body of water, which makes it different from the other four nouns, which are generic geographic terms.

9. (B) Sit

If you jog, run, stroll, or walk somewhere, you are actually moving to a different location—you are traveling, however quickly, from one place to another. If you sit down, you aren't moving to a different location. Answer choice (B) is the word that doesn't fit with the other words.

10. (E) Rain

A typhoon, a hurricane, an earthquake, and a tornado are types of natural disasters that may or may not cause damage or destruction to certain areas. It's possible that a lot of rain could cause flooding—another type of natural disaster—but rain on its own is usually not considered dangerous or a cause for alarm for most people.

11. (D) Misrepresent

If you misrepresent something, you are portraying it differently from the way it should be presented. For example, you may misrepresent a past event to someone by adding in a number of things that never actually happened. However, if you mimic, copy, repeat, or imitate something else, you are trying to produce an exact replication of the original thing. Thus, you would not want to misrepresent anything in your mimicry, copy, repetition, or imitation. Answer choice (D) is correct.

12. (B) Perceive

If you urge, command, insist, or demand something from somebody, you want an action from that person that will result in getting you the thing you originally wanted. These types of verbs require an action to be done or a result to be achieved by somebody else. When you perceive something, you usually have a sense in your mind of how something looked or appeared. You may also come to some kind of realization through your perception. However, perceiving is not the same as urging, commanding, insisting, or demanding something from another person, so it doesn't belong in this group.

13. (A) Timid

A timid person is someone who is shy or insecure in his or her interactions with another person. A pompous, arrogant, boastful, or lofty person is someone who is not shy at all—instead, he or she enjoys bragging about his or her accomplishments to other people. *Timid* is the odd adjective among all the other adjectives listed in this group.

14. (E) Dictate

If you dictate something to someone else, you are commanding someone to do a particular thing. There is no room for interpretation or argument with a dictation or a command. The act of arguing, discussing, persuading, or reasoning with another person involves trying to convince the person that your opinion is right. You are using these methods to bring someone around to your side instead of simply imposing your will onto the other person. Answer choice (E) is correct.

15. (B) Scatter

Looking at these five words, you may initially realize that they all seem to have similar definitions, so it may be hard to find the right classification to single out a word from the rest of the words in the group. At this point, you should look at the phonics of each word or compare the spellings of all the words. *Discard, dissipate, disperse,* and *distribute* all begin with the three letters "dis." Thus, the odd word out must be *scatter.*

16. (A) Funny

Personality, attitude, temper, and *mood* are all nouns that reflect the behavior or character of an individual. Different people can have a wide range of personalities, attitudes, tempers, or moods. *Funny* is an adjective that describes a person as being humorous or causing amusement; it's a single trait or a single characteristic of a person. Thus, *funny* doesn't fit with the other four words.

17. (A) Ordinary

Something that is described as being the primary, chief, principal, or main thing in a group is the most important thing among all the other things listed in the group. Something that is ordinary is common and occurs on a daily basis. So, something that is an ordinary occurrence usually isn't described as being important since it seems to happen often. Answer choice (A) is correct.

18. (D) Insecure

If you are acting in a stubborn, tough, hard, or inflexible manner, you are refusing to budge on a certain issue. However, if you are insecure in your beliefs, you might be more easily persuaded to take one side or the other. Answer choice (D) is correct.

19. (E) Slight

Things that are immense, colossal, grand, or huge are massive and large. The Pacific Ocean is a colossal or huge body of water. Something that is slight is frail, not heavy or sturdy. A structure made out of cardboard boxes might be described as being slight. Something that is immense, colossal, grand, or huge could not also be described as being slight.

20. (B) Wear

If you renew, restore, polish, or furbish an object, you are trying to bring back the original appearance or condition of the object. You essentially want the object or thing to look like new again. However, if you wear something down, you are removing the newness from the object and making it appear more deteriorated. Using *wear* in this context makes the verb an antonym of *renew, restore, polish,* and *furbish.*

21. (B) Lit

Looking at the given words, it's difficult to see any connection at all in their definitions. So, it's time to look at their spellings. *Hat, fat, cat,* and *mat* all have the letters "at" at the end. *Lit* ends with the letters "it," so answer choice (B) must be correct.

22. (A) Melt

At first, you may see some connection between *bolt, jolt,* and *volt,* but *colt* doesn't fit with that group of words. *Melt* has some connection with those three words, as a bolt, jolt, or volt of electricity could melt something. But, you really wouldn't place the verb *melt* in the same classification as *bolt, jolt,* and *volt* since those verbs describe actions that usually happen quite quickly. Besides, any time you see four words spelled similarly in a group, the odd word out is going to be the one that is spelled differently. So, here you have four words that end in "olt" and one word that ends in "elt." The odd word in the group is answer choice (A)—*melt.*

23. (E) Score

Once again, it's hard to see any connection between the definitions of the given words. Looking at the spellings, we can see that four of the words begin with "sp." The correct answer must be the word that starts with "sc," so answer choice (E) is correct.

24. (C) Brink

At first glance, you might think that the letters "rink" or "rea" might be a potential similarity in spelling among the words in the group. Remember, though, that you need to identify a spelling that works for four out of the five words. Here, you should see that *drive, drink, dream,* and *dread* all start with "dr." *Brink* starts with "br," so it must be the correct answer.

25. (E) Least

Posh, fish, leash, and *polish* all end with "sh." *Least,* which ends with "st," is the correct answer.

26. (E) Sweat

Initially, you can probably see some kind of relationship between *stair* and *steep.* It's possible that you could *sweat* going up stairs or that there could be a *stain* on some stairs. But you should also notice that these are all different types of words—*stair* is a noun, *steep* is an adjective, and *sweat* can be a noun or a verb. Generally, if you see a number of different types of words, you should look at the spellings. Here, *stain, stair, steep,* and *stale* all begin with the letters "st." The odd word out is *sweat.*

27. (D) Barter

Bread, bride, bring, and *brink* all begin with the letters "br." *Barter,* which begins with the letters "ba," is the correct answer.

28. (B) Pale

Sail, fail, hail, and *mail* all end with the letters "ail." *Pale* ends with "ale," so it is the correct answer.

29. (A) Crane

Looking at the words, you should see no similarity in their definitions. So, it's time to look at the beginning and ending of each word to see if you can find some connection there. *Crane* and *cramp* both start with "cr," but you need to find a spelling similarity in four of the words if you want to find the odd word in the group. *Cramp, swamp, trump,* and *clump* all end with the letters "mp." Only *crane* ends with "ne." Answer choice (A) is correct.

30. (C) Flaunt

Fight, height, right, and *plight* all end with "ght." *Flaunt* ends with "unt," so it is the correct answer.

Inferences

Inferences Strategies

The inference questions on the OLSAT®, like the logical selection questions, can sometimes be quite tricky. The key to these questions is to never assume something that hasn't been explicitly stated or that can be logically deduced from the statements you have been given. You will need to pay very close attention to the words that are used to describe different things. The use of one word or another can completely determine how to approach and solve the problem. Essentially, you are given a number of rules, and from those rules you must determine what you do and do not know. There may also be some ordering questions that will require the use of inference to figure out the correct order of a number of items.

Inference questions will usually end with one of these phrases:

> We know that -
>
> What is the order of ____?

Watch out for these words:

- *All* = This will indicate that everything can be classified under the word at the end of the sentence. If all dogs have tails, that means every dog in this question has a tail. It would be impossible for a dog not to have a tail in this question.

- *Some* = This will indicate that only a certain number of things can be classified under the word at the end of the sentence. If some dogs are brown, there must be other dogs that have a different color or colors, depending on the question.

- *Fewer than/More than* = Don't get confused by questions that use these words. Keep each relationship that is determined by these words straight in your head.

Combinations: The main trick with inference questions is to be able to determine the relationships in questions that use *all/some* and *fewer than/more than.* If you can keep the relationships between the words straight, and if you do not make unnecessary assumptions, you should be able to figure out the correct answer. However, sometimes you will also have to make some logical deductions based on the rules given to you.

Example: All dogs have tails. All tails can wag. Some dogs are brown. Some masters enjoy watching their dogs chase their tail. We know that -

A. Some dogs are black
B. All masters enjoy watching their dogs
C. Most dogs are not brown
D. Some brown dogs wag their tail
E. All brown dogs wag their tail

We have four rules listed in this question. So, could some dogs be black? We are given no information in this question that some dogs are black. We only know that some dogs are brown. There must be other dogs that have colors other than brown, but we are given no information as to what those colors are. You can eliminate answer choice (A). You can also eliminate answer choice (B) because it is in direct violation of one of the rules we have been given. You also have no idea whether most dogs are not brown; you only know that some dogs are brown. You can eliminate answer choice (C). Do only some brown dogs wag their tail? Well, we're told that all dogs wag their tail. That means that all brown dogs must wag their tail. Answer choice (E) is correct.

Use process of elimination. As you can tell, you'll need to employ a process of elimination on these types of questions. You will usually have to get rid of the impossible answers in order to correctly discover the one answer that works. You must constantly refer back to the premises, or rules, that you have been given to figure out if a certain answer choice adheres to these premises. Eliminate answer choices that have no relation to the premises given. Then, logically approach each remaining answer choice and see if it works according to the rules.

Make sure you order the questions correctly. You can approach ordering questions in a couple of ways.

1. One way is to use shorthand notation to order your items from left to right or up to down, according to the rules you have been given. Just remember whether you are going from tallest to shortest, largest to smallest, and so on, in your ordering. If you are using shorthand, make sure you clearly recognize what stands for what in your ordering.

2. You can also use "greater than" and "less than" signs to indicate whether one thing is bigger or smaller than another thing. You will usually have to make some kind of deduction, like: If $X > Y$ and $Y > Z$, then X must be $> Z$.

Beware of non-comparisons in ordering questions. There will usually be two people or items that will not be compared at all in a question. Sometimes you cannot logically deduce any comparison between these two people or things. Do not get tricked by answer choices that try to compare them. Always stick to the premises you have been given.

Inferences Questions

1. Melanie has four children. Two of the children have green eyes, and two of the children have brown eyes. Half the children are girls. We know that -

   A. At least one girl has green eyes
   B. Two of the children are boys
   C. The boys have brown eyes
   D. All children are girls
   E. The girls have green eyes

2. All chickens are birds, and some chickens are hens. Female birds lay eggs. We know that -

   A. All birds lay eggs
   B. Hens are birds
   C. All chickens lay eggs
   D. All chickens are hens
   E. Hens are not birds

3. Pictures can tell a story. All storybooks have pictures. Some storybooks have words. We know that -

   A. Pictures can tell a better story
   B. Storybooks are very simple
   C. Some storybooks have both pictures and words
   D. Most storybooks do not have words
   E. Children like storybooks without words

4. Islands are surrounded by water. St. Lucia is an island. A volcano formed St. Lucia. We know that -

   A. St. Lucia is surrounded by water
   B. St. Lucia is a big island
   C. All islands are formed by volcanoes
   D. There are volcanoes on all islands
   E. St. Lucia is only one of two islands formed by volcanoes

5. All drink mixes are beverages. All non-mixed drinks are beverages. All beverages are drinkable. Some beverages are brown. We know that -

   A. People like drinking brown beverages
   B. Some drink mixes are not drinkable
   C. Some drink mixes are brown
   D. People do not like drink mixes that are brown
   E. Not all beverages are drink mixes

6. John has six cats. Three of the cats are black and white, and three of them are striped. Half the cats are male. We know that -

    A. At least one male cat is striped
    B. Half the cats are female
    C. All female cats are black and white
    D. Most male cats are striped
    E. All male cats are black and white

7. All dogs like to play fetch. Some dogs like to swim. Some dogs look like their masters. We know that -

    A. All dogs that like to play fetch like to swim
    B. All dogs that like to play fetch look like their masters
    C. Dogs that like to swim also like to play fetch
    D. Dogs that like to play fetch do not look like their masters
    E. All masters like dogs that like to swim

8. Kyle is taller than Mark but shorter than Jack. If Jack and Alex are the same height, which one of these is also true?

    A. Kyle is the tallest
    B. Jack is shorter than Kyle
    C. Jack and Alex are the tallest
    D. Alex is shorter than Mark
    E. Mark and Jack are the same height

9. James is younger than Kate but older than Nina. If Nina and Jennifer are the same age, which of these is also true?

    A. Jennifer is younger than James
    B. Nina is older than Kate
    C. Nina and Kate are in the same grade
    D. James is the oldest
    E. Kate and Jennifer are the same age

10. Carrie has fewer fish than Mike or Alex, but more fish than Karen. If Karen has ten fish, we know that -

    A. Karen wants to buy more fish
    B. Carrie has the biggest fish tank
    C. Mike and Alex have the same number of fish
    D. Carrie has more than ten fish
    E. Mike and Alex have at least twenty fish

11. **Katherine has more dolls than Madeline or Alexandra, but fewer dolls than Kendra. If Kendra has six dolls, we know that -**

   A. Kendra like dolls the best
   B. Madeline and Alexandra have the same number of dolls
   C. Katherine has the most dolls
   D. Alexandra has the most dolls
   E. Madeline does not have six dolls

12. **William bought more balloons than Mary or Caleb, but fewer balloons than Ellen. If William bought three red balloons and two green balloons, we know that -**

   A. William likes red balloons more than green ones
   B. Ellen bought more than five balloons
   C. Ellen's balloons are bigger than Mary's
   D. Mary spent the least amount of money on balloons
   E. Caleb and Mary bought the same number of balloons

13. **Olga is taller than Martin, who is taller than Peter but shorter than Elizabeth. We know that -**

   A. Olga is taller than Elizabeth
   B. There are only four children in this family
   C. Martin is the youngest
   D. Peter is the shortest
   E. Olga and Elizabeth are the same height

14. **Oscar is older than Mina, who is older than Paola but younger than Erin. We know that -**

   A. There are only four children in the class
   B. Mina is the youngest
   C. Erin is the oldest
   D. Oscar is the middle child
   E. Paola is the youngest

15. **Jennifer has fewer cats than Peter but more cats than Isabella. If Isabella has eight cats, we know that -**

   A. Peter likes cats
   B. Peter has the least number of cats
   C. Jennifer has at least nine cats
   D. Peter and Jennifer have the same number of cats
   E. Jennifer and Isabella have the same number of cats

16. Last week, Tara visited the gym and discovered that she had gone to the gym less often that week than Sandra. Sandra later discovered that she had gone less often than Tom during that week. If Tom went to the gym last Tuesday, Thursday, and Friday, we know that -

    A. Sandra was not at the gym on Monday or Wednesday of last week
    B. Sandra went to the gym on one or two days
    C. Tara usually goes to the gym in the morning
    D. Tara went to the gym only one day last week
    E. Sandra went to the gym on Monday and Wednesday of last week

17. In a school lunch line, Amy is ahead of Maureen, who is in between Lily and Sam. If Sam is next to Amy and behind James, who is first in line?

    A. Lily
    B. Amy
    C. James
    D. Maureen
    E. Sam

18. If A is one-third the size of B, and B is more than C but less than D, which one of these statements is true?

    A. C is less than A
    B. B is more than D
    C. D is three times the size of C
    D. A is less than C
    E. D is more than A

19. If X is twice the size of Y, which is more than W but less than Z, which one of these statements is true?

    A. X is the same size as Z
    B. Z is the biggest
    C. X is more than Z
    D. Y is more than X
    E. W is less than X

20. If Jane does not have swimming practice on Thursdays, she either goes to Ashley's house to play or helps her sister with her homework. Today is Thursday, and Jane is helping her sister with her homework. We know that -

    A. There was no swimming practice today for Jane
    B. Ashley likes swimming the best
    C. Ashley is not home today
    D. Jane likes to help her sister with her homework
    E. Jane only swims on Thursdays

21. Finn has afterschool on Tuesdays and Fridays. When he does not have afterschool, Finn enjoys going to soccer practice two days a week. He also enjoys playing with his Legos at home. Today is Wednesday, and Finn is at home playing with his Legos.
    We know that -

    A. Finn likes playing with his Legos the most
    B. There was no soccer practice today
    C. There was no afterschool today for Finn
    D. Finn only plays with his Legos on Wednesdays
    E. Finn does not like afterschool

22. When Heather does not have volleyball practice on Sundays, she either goes to art class or plays video games. Today is Sunday, and Heather is playing video games.
    We know that -

    A. Heather's favorite activity is playing video games
    B. Heather does not always like volleyball practice
    C. Heather does not have volleyball practice today
    D. Heather only has volleyball practice on Sundays
    E. Heather likes video games better than art class

23. At a bake sale, cakes are next to cupcakes, which are in the middle. If the cookies are to the far right and the croissants are next to the donuts, which are on the far left, what is the order of items from right to left?

    A. Cookies, cakes, cupcakes, croissants, donuts
    B. Cakes, cookies, cupcakes, croissants, donuts
    C. Donuts, croissants, cupcakes, cakes, cookies
    D. Cupcakes, croissants, donuts, cookies, cakes
    E. Cookies, cakes, cupcakes, donuts, croissants

24. At a department store, the children's clothing section is above the grocery store. If the toys are in the middle, below the home appliances, which is below the café, what is the order of the merchandise sold on each floor from top to bottom?

    A. Children's clothing, grocery store, toys, home appliances, café
    B. Café, home appliances, toys, children's clothing, grocery store
    C. Grocery store, children's clothing, toys, home appliances, café
    D. Grocery store, toys, children's clothing, café, home appliances
    E. Children's clothing, toys, grocery store, home appliances, café

25. At the balloon store, the red balloons are next to the blue balloons, which are on the far right, and the white balloons on the far left. The green balloons are in the middle of black balloons and white balloons. What is the order of the balloons from left to right?

    A. Blue, red, black, green, white
    B. Red, blue, green, black, white
    C. White, green, black, red, blue
    D. Green, black, white, red, blue
    E. White, black, green, red, blue

Inferences Answer Key

1. (B) Two of the children are boys

We know that there are a total of four children and that two of the children have green eyes and two of the children have brown eyes. We also know that two of the children are girls. Does one of the girls necessarily have green eyes? No, because according to what we've been told, any two children could have green or brown eyes. You could have two girls with green eyes, one girl with green eyes, or no girls with green eyes. So, we can get rid of answer choices (A) and (E). Similarly, we can also get rid of answer choice (C) because it's just as possible that both girls have brown eyes and the two boys have green eyes. Answer choice (D) can't be right because only two of the children are girls. Since there are a total of four children and two of the children are girls, two of the children must be boys. Answer choice (B) is correct.

2. (B) Hens are birds

We are told that all chickens are birds and that some chickens are hens. We are also told that female birds lay eggs. Looking at answer choice (A), do all birds lay eggs? Nope, because only female birds lay eggs. What about answer choice (C)? Do all chickens lay eggs? Well, all chickens are birds, but only female birds lay eggs. That means that only female chickens lay eggs, so answer choice (C) cannot be correct. Answer choice (D) isn't correct since only some chickens are hens, according to our rules. Finally, hens must be birds because a hen is a chicken, and all chickens are birds. The correct answer is (B).

3. (C) Some storybooks have both pictures and words

Our rules for this question are that pictures can tell a story, all storybooks have pictures, and some storybooks have words. You can get rid of answer choice (A) because nothing is mentioned in the question about how pictures tell a better story. You can also eliminate answer choices (B) and (E) because the question doesn't inform us about the simplicity of storybooks or whether children like storybooks that don't have words. Answer choice (D) can also be eliminated because you are never told that most storybooks don't have words; you only know that some storybooks have words. Answer choice (C) is correct. If all storybooks have pictures and only some storybooks have words, there must be some storybooks that have both pictures and words.

4. (A) St. Lucia is surrounded by water

You are told that islands are surrounded by water, that St. Lucia is an island, and that a volcano formed St. Lucia. You can immediately get rid of answer choice (B) because nothing is mentioned in the question about the size of St. Lucia. Are all islands formed by volcanoes? You are only told that St. Lucia was formed by a volcano; there is no indication in the three statements you were given that all islands are formed by volcanoes. Answer choices (C) and (E) can be eliminated. Similarly, you have only been told that there is a volcano on St. Lucia; this doesn't mean that there are volcanoes on every other island in the world. You can eliminate answer choice (D). Is St. Lucia surrounded by water? Well, according to the rules in the question, all islands are surrounded by water, and St. Lucia is an island. Therefore, since St. Lucia is an island, it must be surrounded by water. Answer choice (A) is correct.

5. (E) Not all beverages are drink mixes

The rules in this question are: all drink mixes are beverages, all non-mixed drinks are beverages, all beverages are drinkable, and some beverages are brown. You can get rid of answer choices (A) and (D) because there is nothing in our rules to indicate that people like or dislike drinking brown beverages or drink mixes. Are some drink mixes not drinkable? Well, if all drink mixes are beverages, and all beverages are drinkable, all drink mixes must be drinkable. You can eliminate answer choice (B). So, now it's between (C) and (E). Are some drink mixes brown? You know that all drink mixes are beverages and that some beverages are brown, but you don't necessarily know that some drink mixes are brown. According to our rules, it's possible that none, some, most, or even all drink mixes are brown. Thus, we have no way of knowing whether some drink mixes are brown. The correct answer must be (E). You know that both drink mixes and non-mixed drinks are beverages. Thus, not all beverages are drink mixes because some beverages are non-mixed drinks.

6. (B) Half the cats are female

You know that there are six cats, three of the cats are striped, three of the cats are black and white, and half the cats are male. Looking at your rules, you should notice that the only definite things you know in this question are the number of cats, how many of the cats are male, and how many of the cats are striped or black and white. You should have no idea how many male cats are striped or black and white. The same goes for the female cats. The only possible answer choice is (B); since half the cats are male, the other half must be female.

7. (C) Dogs that like to swim also like to play fetch

You are told that all dogs like to play fetch, some dogs like to swim, and some dogs look like their masters. Do all dogs that like to play fetch also like to swim? That can't be true because only some dogs like to swim. That means that some dogs don't like to swim. Since all dogs like to play fetch, some of those dogs must not like to swim. Using the same logic, you can also deduce that there must be some dogs that like to play fetch and don't look like their masters. Conversely, since all dogs play fetch and only some dogs look like their masters, there must also be dogs that like to play fetch and that look like their masters. Answer choices (A), (B), and (D) can be eliminated. You can also get rid of answer choice (E) because there is nothing in our rules that tells us whether all masters like dogs that enjoy swimming. Answer choice (C) is correct. If all dogs like to play fetch and some dogs like to swim, there must be dogs that both like to swim and play fetch.

8. (C) Jack and Alex are the tallest

For this question, you should write the order of the heights of all the people. The order of heights, from tallest to shortest, is Jack/Alex, Kyle, and then Mark. Looking at your answer choices, the only choice that fits with this order is (C). Jack and Alex, since they are the same height, are the tallest in the group.

9. (A) Jennifer is younger than James

You should write out the order of ages in this question. We'll go from oldest to youngest. You know that James (represented by "J") is younger than Kate (represented by "K"), so K will come before J. However, James is older than Nina (represented by "N"), so the order so far is KJN. Then, you are told that Jennifer (represented by "JF") is the same age as Nina. Our order is K J N/JF. Out of all your answer choices, the only one that works is (A); Jennifer is younger than James. Remember to somehow distinguish between two names or objects that start with the same letter when you are attempting to order the names or objects. Otherwise, you could make a mistake and think that Jennifer is older than James when you look at your ordering.

10. (D) Carrie has more than ten fish

Carrie has fewer fish than Mike or Alex, but she has more fish than Karen. Karen has ten fish. You can immediately get rid of answer choices (A) and (B) because, according to the question, you should have no idea whether Karen wants to buy more fish or whether Carrie has the biggest fish tank. You also don't know whether Mike and Alex have the same number of fish; all you know is that Carrie has fewer fish than both of them. It's certainly possible that Mike has more fish than Alex or vice versa. Likewise, both Alex and Mike could have fewer than or more than twenty fish. Nothing is mentioned in this question about the number of fish they have, so answer choices (C) and (E) can be eliminated. You only know the exact number of fish that Karen has (ten). However, you also know that Carrie has more fish than Karen. Thus, Carrie must have more than ten fish. Answer choice (D) is correct.

11. (E) Madeline does not have six dolls

Katherine has more dolls than Madeline and Alexandra, but fewer dolls than Kendra. Kendra only has six dolls, but she owns the most dolls in the group. This means that Katherine, Madeline, and Alexandra must own fewer than six dolls. You can immediately eliminate answer choices (C) and (D) because you know that neither Katherine nor Alexandra has the most dolls in the group. You can also eliminate answer choice (A) because there is no mention in the question of who likes dolls the best. Do Madeline and Alexandra have the same number of dolls? Who knows? All you know is that Katherine has more dolls than both of them. You can eliminate answer choice (B). The correct answer is (E). If Kendra has the most dolls in the group and she owns six dolls, Madeline certainly cannot have six dolls.

12. (B) Ellen bought more than five balloons

William bought more balloons than Mary or Caleb, but fewer balloons than Ellen. William bought three red balloons and two green balloons. So, he bought five balloons in total. This means that Ellen bought more than five balloons, and both Mary and Caleb bought fewer than five balloons. Looking at your answer choices, you should see that answer choice (B) states one of these facts, so it must be the correct answer. Looking at the other answer choices, you should notice that (A), (C), and (D) contain information that was never mentioned in the question. We are also given no information on the actual number of balloons that Mary and Caleb bought, so there is no way to know if they bought the same number of balloons. Answer choice (E) can be eliminated. The correct answer is (B).

13. (D) Peter is the shortest

Olga (represented by "O") is taller than Martin (represented by "M"), and Martin is taller than Peter (represented by "P") but shorter than Elizabeth (represented by "E"). Is Olga taller than Elizabeth? Well, we have no idea who is taller between Olga and Elizabeth. All we know is that both are taller than Martin, or O > M and E > M. So, you can eliminate answer choice (A). You also don't know that there are only four children in this family. In fact, you don't even know whether the four people listed in this question are related (or children). Answer choice (B) can be eliminated. There is nothing about age mentioned in this question, which means that you can get rid of answer choice (C). Are Olga and Elizabeth the same height? Since there is no comparison of Olga's and Elizabeth's heights in the question, you can eliminate answer choice (E). Is Peter the shortest in the group? Well, you know that O > M and E > M. You are also told that M > P, which necessarily means that O > P and E > P. Thus, Peter must be the shortest in the group. Answer choice (D) is correct.

14. (E) Paola is the youngest

Oscar (represented by "O") is older than Mina (represented by "M"), and Mina is older than Paola (represented by "P"), but younger than Erin (represented by "E"). You can immediately get rid of answer choice (A) because there is no mention of a class in the question. Is Mina the youngest? The question tells us that M > P, so you can eliminate answer choice (B). Is Erin the oldest? Well, you know that O > M and E > M, but there's no mention of who is older between Olga and Erin. It's possible that Olga is the oldest. Thus, you can eliminate answer choice (C). There is also no mention of whether these people are related, so there's no way to know whether Oscar is a middle child. Eliminate answer choice (D). Is Paola the youngest? O > M, E > M, and M > P, so Paola has to be the youngest in the group. Answer choice (E) is correct.

15. (C) Jennifer has at least nine cats

Jennifer has fewer cats than Peter but more cats than Isabella. Isabella has eight cats. You can easily eliminate answer choice (A) since, even though Peter has the most cats, nothing in the question tells us that Peter likes cats. You can also get rid of answer choice (B) because the question tells us that Peter has the most cats in the group. Peter and Jennifer can't have the same number of cats because the question informs us that Jennifer has fewer cats than Peter. Eliminate answer choice (D). Similarly, Jennifer and Isabella cannot have the same number of cats. The only answer choice left is (C). Does Jennifer have to have at least nine cats? Since Jennifer has more cats than Isabella, and Isabella owns eight cats, Jennifer must have at least nine cats. Answer choice (C) is correct.

16. (D) Tara went to the gym only one day last week

The question informs us that last week, Tara went to the gym less often than Sandra, and Sandra went less often than Tom. Tom went to the gym on Tuesday, Thursday, and Friday. So, Sandra went to the gym twice last week, and Tara went once. Was Sandra not at the gym on Monday or Wednesday? You actually have no idea when Sandra went to the gym. You only know that she went on two days. You can get rid of answer choices (A) and (E). Answer choice (B) could fool you. Is it possible that Sandra went to the gym on one day and Tara never went to the gym? Looking back at the question, you should be able to see that it's quite clear that Tara visited the gym one day last week. This means that Sandra had to go to the gym two days last week. Therefore, answer choice (B) can't be right. There is no mention of the time of day when Tara went to the gym, so answer choice (C) can be eliminated. The correct answer is (D). Tara only went to the gym one day last week.

17. (C) James

In the school lunch line, Amy (represented by "A") is ahead of Maureen (represented by "M"). Maureen is in between Lily (represented by "L") and Sam (represented by "S"). Sam is behind James (represented by "J") and next to Amy. You are being asked to figure out who is first in line. You know that part of the order has to be JSA. Amy is ahead of Maureen, and Maureen is in between Lily and Sam. Our order has to be JSAML. This fits all of our rules. The first person in line is James, and answer choice (C) is correct.

18. (E) D is more than A

A is one-third the size of B, B is more than C, and B is less than D. So, could C be less than A? Well, you don't really have any information about how C is related to A. All you know is that both C and A are less than B. Answer choice (A) can be eliminated. B is not more than D, so answer choice (B) can be eliminated. Is D three times the size of C? There's no mention of this in the question, so the right answer cannot be (C). Is A less than C? Just as you saw above, there's no way to know how A and C are related; all we know is that both of them are less than B. Is D more than A? You know that A is one-third of B and that D is larger than B. Therefore, A must be less than D, so D is more than A. Answer choice (E) is correct.

19. (E) W is less than X

    X is twice the size of Y, Y is more than W, and Z is more than Y. So, could X be the same size as Z? Well, both Z and X are larger than Y, but we don't know whether X is smaller, larger, or the same size as Z. So, answer choices (A) and (C) cannot be correct. Likewise, we don't know if Z is the biggest, so answer choice (B) must be wrong as well. Y can't be more than X because we know that X is twice the size of Y. Answer choice (D) can be eliminated. The correct answer is (E). Is W less than X? X > Y and Y > W, so X > W, which means that
W is less than X.

20. (A) There was no swimming practice today for Jane

    If Jane doesn't go to swimming practice on Thursdays, she either plays at Ashley's house or helps her sister with her homework. So, if it's a Thursday and Jane is at home helping her sister with her homework, there must have been no swimming practice for her that day. Answer choice (A) is correct. None of the other answer choices make sense in light of the rules that you have been given.

21. (C) There was no afterschool today for Finn

    Finn has afterschool on Tuesdays and Fridays. When he doesn't have afterschool, Finn has soccer practice two days a week. Finn also enjoys playing with his Legos whenever he is home. Today is Wednesday, and Finn is at home playing with his Legos. We can get rid of answer choices (A) and (E) because the question does not mention whether Finn likes playing with his Legos the most or whether he doesn't like afterschool. Was there no soccer practice today? Actually, you don't know if Finn has soccer practice on Wednesdays. Finn could have had soccer practice and then come home to play with his Legos. Or maybe he didn't have soccer practice. In any case, you don't know for sure that Finn didn't have soccer practice today. So, you can eliminate answer choice (B). Does Finn only play with his Legos on Wednesdays? The question tells us that Finn enjoys playing with his Legos whenever he is home, so he must play with his Legos on other days in addition to Wednesdays. The only thing you know for sure is that there was no afterschool today for Finn because it is a Wednesday, and he has afterschool on Tuesdays and Fridays. The correct answer is (C).

22. (C) Heather does not have volleyball practice today

    When Heather doesn't have volleyball practice on Sundays, she either goes to art class or plays video games. Today is Sunday, and Heather is playing a video game. You can eliminate answer choices (A), (B), and (E) because you are given no information about whether any of the information in these answer choices could possibly be true. Does Heather only have volleyball practice on Sundays? You don't know that, either. You know that she sometimes has volleyball practice on Sundays, but she could also have volleyball practice on other days of the week. All you do know is that since Heather is playing video games on a Sunday, she must not have had volleyball practice today. Answer choice (C) is correct.

23. (A) Cookies, cakes, cupcakes, croissants, donuts

Here is an ordering question that will probably require you to write the order out in some kind of shorthand. So, the cakes (represented by "C") are next to the cupcakes (represented by "CK"), and the cupcakes are in the middle. The cookies (represented by "CO") are to the far right, and the croissants (represented by "CR") are next to the donuts (represented by "D"). The donuts are on the far left. So, left to right, you should have D CR CK C CO. Looking back at the rules that were given to you, this order works with everything that you were told in the question. However, remember that the question is asking for the order of the items from right to left. The correct order from right to left is cookies, cakes, cupcakes, croissants, and donuts. In this question, if you use shorthand to write down the order, you're going to want to make sure you remember what each shorthand notation represents. Four out of the five items start with "C," so you need to make sure that you don't confuse yourself with what means what. Also, always pay attention to the order in which the question is asking you to list the items.

24. (B) Café, home appliances, toys, children's clothing, grocery store

The question tells us that the toy section is in the middle of the department store and is under the home appliances section. The home appliances section is under the café. Since there are only five sections listed, you know that the café is at the top, home appliances is underneath it, and then comes the toy section. The other two sections must be below the toy section. The children's clothing section is above the grocery store. So, your final order, from top to bottom, should be the café, home appliances, toys, children's clothing, and finally the grocery store. The correct answer is (B).

25. (C) White, green, black, red, blue

The blue balloons are to the far right, and the red balloons are next to them. The white balloons are to the far left. The green balloons are in the middle of the white balloons and the black balloons. Following these rules, the order of balloons from left to right must be white, green, black, red, and blue. Answer choice (C) is correct.

OLSAT® Preparation Guide - Levels D, E, and F

Figural Classifications

(Level D Only)

OLSAT® Preparation Guide - Levels D, E, and F

Figural Classifications Strategies

The figural classifications questions in the Figural Reasoning section of the OLSAT® are just like the verbal classification questions that you encountered earlier in the workbook. The only difference is that, instead of words, you're dealing with the characteristics of shapes and images. You will be given five figures and asked to find the one figure that doesn't belong with the other four figures. Thus, you will need to identify one characteristic that exists for four out of the five figures. If the characteristic exists for all of the figures or two or three of the figures, you are not looking in the right direction. The characteristic must be so distinguishable that it would be impossible to include one of the figures with the other four figures.

Note different shapes in each of the figures. You should get in the habit of noting the different shapes in each of the figures. Do the same shapes keep reappearing in the figures? Is there a repetition of shapes in one of the figures? Make sure to count the number of shapes in certain figures; sometimes the number of shapes will be the distinguishing characteristic. Also pay close attention to when shapes get larger or smaller. These changes could clue you in to a certain kind of pattern that is occurring with each figure. Finally, be aware of how certain shapes are aligned with one another. The position of one shape relative to another might be the distinguishing characteristic that you are looking for.

Look for patterns in shading. You should look for how many different areas or shapes are shaded or unshaded in different figures. If one figure does not have as many shaded areas as four of the other figures, you have found your distinguishing characteristic. Once again, though, remember that the characteristic must hold for four out of the five figures.

Beware of lines of symmetry. A line of symmetry is a line that can go through a shape or a figure and cut it in two so that one half perfectly reflects the other half. In other words, you could take one half of the figure and perfectly fold it over the other half. Lines of symmetry might be used as a distinguishing characteristic on these questions.

Watch out for rotations. You might encounter a question in which four out of five figures are the same shape that are just rotated to various degrees. Try to mentally visualize the shape and eliminate the answer choices in which the shape has simply been rotated around. This will help you find the shape that is different from the other four shapes.

Look for relationships when numbers and letters are used. Some questions might use numbers or letters instead of shapes. Try to notice if there's something about the numbers or letters themselves, such as whether they are right side up, in a different font, capitalized, and so on. If you cannot identify anything obvious, you may have to delve deeper to see if there's any connection between the content of the numbers or letters. Try to see how the numbers or letters relate to each other sequentially and whether there is a pattern to the number of numbers or letters skipped within each figure.

Take a step back and look at all of the figures at once. The best way to approach these problems is to take a step back and look at all of the figures at once. What is a common characteristic that most of the figures have in common? Can you see a certain trend in the figures? Does one just seem "off" for some reason? These types of queries can help you narrow down the characteristic that binds four of the five figures together.

Figural Classifications Questions

1.

Which figure does *not* go with the others?

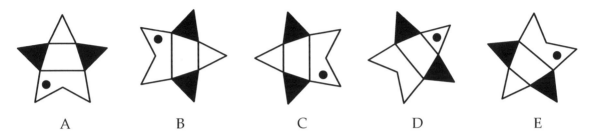

2.

Which figure does *not* go with the others?

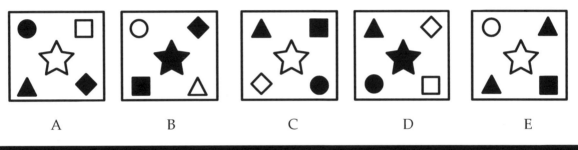

3.

Which figure does *not* go with the others?

4.

Which figure does *not* go with the others?

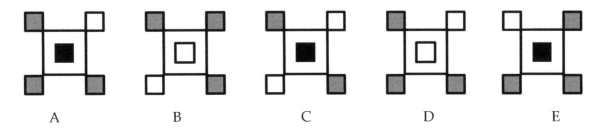

5.

Which figure does *not* go with the others?

| A | B | C | D | E |

6.

Which figure does *not* go with the others?

| A | B | C | D | E |

7.

Which figure does *not* go with the others?

| A | B | C | D | E |

8.

Which figure does *not* go with the others?

| A | B | C | D | E |

9.

Which figure does *not* go with the others?

   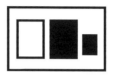 

A   B   C   D   E

10.

Which figure does *not* go with the others?

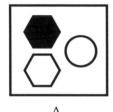   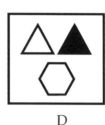 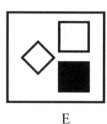

A   B   C   D   E

11.

Which figure does *not* go with the others?

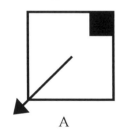 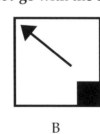 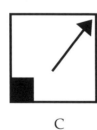  

A   B   C   D   E

12.

Which figure does *not* go with the others?

GGＧ FℲF ƧZZ RRR EƎE

A   B   C   D   E

13.

Which figure does *not* go with the others?

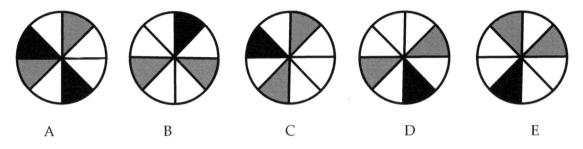

A   B   C   D   E

14.

Which figure does *not* go with the others?

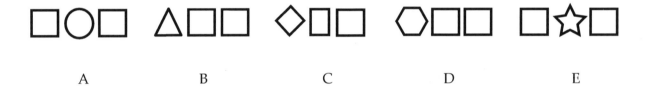

A   B   C   D   E

15.

Which figure does *not* go with the others?

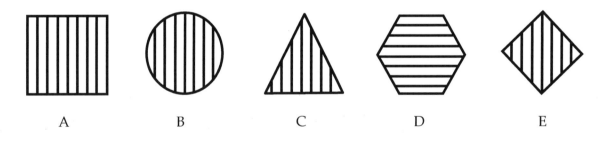

A   B   C   D   E

16.

Which figure does *not* go with the others?

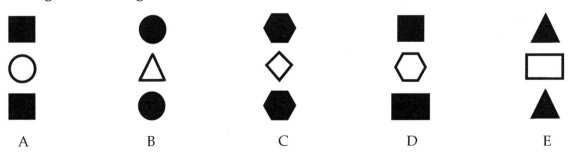

A   B   C   D   E

17

Which figure does *not* go with the others?

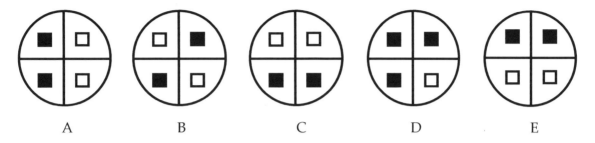

| A | B | C | D | E |

18.

Which figure does *not* go with the others?

| A | B | C | D | E |

19.

Which figure does *not* go with the others?

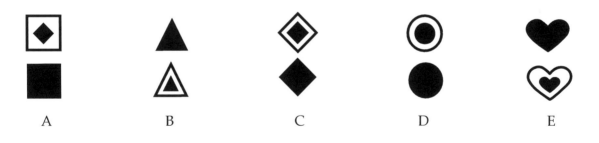

| A | B | C | D | E |

20.

Which figure does *not* go with the others?

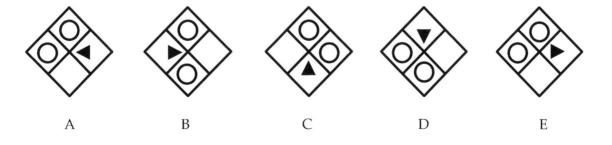

| A | B | C | D | E |

21.

Which figure does not go with the others?

LOOO   QTTT   CFFF   NPPP   HKKK

   A   B   C   D   E

22.

Which figure does not go with the others?

   A   B   C   D   E

23.

Which figure does not go with the others?

   A   B   C   D   E

24.

Which figure does not go with the others?

   A   B   C   D   E

25.

Which figure does not go with the others?

6G5   9H8   2N3   2R1   7J6

   A   B   C   D   E

Figural Classifications Answer Key

1. (D)

Four of the figures in this series are the same—they've just been rotated around in various positions. Locating the dot on the figure will help you to distinguish which figure does not belong with the rest. In four of the figures, the dot is on the bottom left-hand corner of the star when the two black tips of the star are pointing to the left and right, as in answer choice (A). In answer choices (B), (C), and (E), the dot is in the exact same location; the star has just been rotated around in these answer choices. In answer choice (D), however, the dot would be at the top of the star if you were to rotate the star so the two black tips pointed to the left and right. Answer choice (D) is the odd figure out of this group, so it is the correct answer.

2. (E)

Here, you have a star in the middle of a square and four smaller shapes at the corners of the square. In four of the five figures, the smaller shapes do not repeat themselves—there is a circle, a square, a diamond, and a triangle in the corners of each large square. In answer choice (E), there are two triangles, a circle, and a square in the corners of the large square. Answer choice (E) is the figure that doesn't belong with the other four. You may have gotten confused if you tried to find some kind of pattern with the shading in these answer choices. There is no pattern with the shading that exists for four out of the five figures, though. Remember that the characteristic that binds these figures into a group must exist for four out of the five figures—if it doesn't, then you haven't found the right characteristic.

3. (E)

In these figures, you have a line dividing the figures, with one side of each figure being black and the other side being white. What characteristic do four of the figures share? Well, for four of them, the shapes seem to be divided into mirror images of one another, with one half being the reflection of the other half. You could take the white or black side of the figure and fold it perfectly onto the other side. In geometry, you would say that these four figures all have a line of symmetry drawn through them. The figure in answer choice (E) does not have a line of symmetry drawn through it, so it doesn't belong in this group. Answer choice (E) is correct.

4. (C)

In this question, you have a smaller square inside a larger square that has four smaller squares at the corners. There is no pattern for four of the figures involving the shading of the center square. How about the smaller squares at the corners? In answer choices (A), (B), (D), and (E), three of the four smaller squares are shaded gray. In answer choice (C), only two squares are shaded gray. The correct answer is (C).

5. (C)

In these figures, you have a whole bunch of different shapes inside one another. What characteristic exists for most of these figures? Each figure has a large shape, a midsized shape inside the large shape, and a small shape inside the midsized shape. Different shapes are used in each of the answer choices, so there's no pattern in the use of specific shapes. But what about the number of different shapes? Four of the figures each use three different shapes. But in answer choice (C), only two different shapes are used—a hexagon for the large shape and a diamond for both the midsized and small shapes. Answer choice (C) is the odd figure out of this group.

6. (B)

Each answer choice has five bars, so the number of bars cannot be the distinguishing characteristic that we are looking for. What about the number of bars that are darkened? In answer choices (A), (C), (D), and (E), three of the bars are black, and two of the bars are white. In answer choice (B), three of the bars are white, and two of the bars are black. Answer choice (B) is correct.

7. (C)

This is another question with a bunch of shapes inside one another. Here, however, the same shape is repeated inside itself in all of the answer choices. Also, for every answer choice, the smaller shapes have light outlines, while the largest shape has a bold outline. Let's look at the number of similar shapes in each answer choice. For four of the figures, you can count three white shapes inside the bold outline. In answer choice (C), there are only two white stars inside the bold outline. Answer choice (C) is the correct answer.

8. (B)

The distinguishing characteristic in this question might have been a little difficult to notice at first. For four of the figures, there are four squares connected to an outer circle. In answer choice (B), only three of the squares are connected to the outer circle. You may have tried focusing on the shading of the squares first, which is fine—hopefully, though, you noticed that nothing involving the shading could distinguish one figure from the other four. Don't get discouraged after you focus on one characteristic that doesn't end up helping you solve the question. Just take a step back and choose a different characteristic to focus on that might exist for four out of the five figures.

9. (D)

In each figure, you have three similar shapes inside a rectangles. As you move from left to right, the shapes are getting smaller for four of the answer choices. In answer choice (D), the first and second rectangle are the same size. This must be your distinguishing characteristic. Answer choice (D) is correct.

10. (C)

     In this question, you have three shapes inside a rectangle in each answer choice. For every answer choice, there are also two similar shapes (one white and the other black) and a different shape. What could be the distinguishing characteristic that separates one of these figures from the other four? What about the placement of the shapes? In four of the figures, the similar shapes are either directly vertical or horizontal to each other. In answer choice (C), the two stars are diagonal to each other. Answer choice (C) is the odd figure out of the group.

11. (A)

     Hopefully the distinguishing characteristic in this question was easy to catch. Four of the figures have arrows inside the square pointing to a corner of the square. In answer choice (A), the arrow pointing to the corner of the square goes outside of the square.

12. (D)

     In four of the figures, two capital letters are normal, while one of the capital letters has been reversed. Answer choice (D) has three normal capital letters next to each other—none are reversed. Answer choice (D) is correct.

13. (A)

     In each of the figures, you have a circle that has been divided into eight slices. Answer choices (B), (C), (D), and (E) all have five white slices, two gray slices, and one black slice. Answer choice (A) has four white slices, two gray slices, and two black slices. The circle in answer choice (A) is the odd figure in this group.

14. (C)

     Each of the figures has three shapes next to one another. For four of the figures, there are two squares and a different shape in each figure. The figure in answer choice (C) has a diamond, a rectangle, and a square. Answer choice (C) is correct.

15. (D)

     In four of the figures in this question, you have a shape containing vertical lines. In answer choice (D), the figure instead has horizontal lines. The figure in answer choice (D) doesn't belong with the other four figures.

16. (D)

     Here, you have three shapes in each figure that are lined up vertically. In each answer choice, the top and bottom shapes are black, and the middle shape is white. In four out of the five figures, the top and bottom shapes are identical. However, in answer choice (D), the top shape is a square, and the bottom shape is a rectangle. Thus, answer choice (D) is correct since it is the odd figure out of the group.

17. (D)

     Each answer choice has a circle divided into four slices, each of which contains a square. In four of the figures, two of the squares are black, and two of the squares are white. In answer choice (D), three of the squares are black, and one of the squares is white. Answer choice (D) is the correct answer.

18. (B)

There are two shapes and a letter inside a rectangle in four of the figures. The odd figure out is the figure with two shapes and a number inside of a rectangle. That figure can be found in answer choice (B), which makes it the correct answer.

19. (A)

Answer choices (B), (C), (D), and (E) each have a black shape and a smaller version of the black shape inside a similar white shape. For example, answer choice (B) has a black triangle and, below it, a smaller black triangle inside a white triangle. This pattern does not hold for the figure in answer choice (A). In that figure, there is a black square and a black diamond inside a white square. The figure in answer choice (A) doesn't belong with the other figures in this group.

20. (E)

In this question, each of the answer choices has a large diamond divided into four smaller diamonds. Two of the smaller diamonds in each answer choice contain a circle, and one of the smaller diamonds contains a triangle. In four of the figures, the triangle is pointing toward the center of the large diamond. In answer choice (E), however, the triangle is pointing toward one of the corners of the large square. Answer choice (E) is correct.

21. (D)

Each answer choice has a letter and then three repeating letters. So, there must be something involving the letters themselves that can help you to discover which group of letters doesn't belong here. Looking at the letters "LOOO," you can see that to get from "L" to "O," you need to skip ahead three letters. The same pattern occurs in answer choices (B), (C), and (E). In answer choice (D), looking at "NPPP," you only need to skip ahead two letters to get from "N" to "P." The group of letters in answer choice (D) doesn't belong with the other groups of letters.

22. (A)

Here, in four of the figures, you have two similar shapes that overlap. In answer choice (A), you have two hearts that touch but don't overlap. Answer choice (A) is the correct answer. You may have gotten a little confused as to what the distinguishing characteristic could be if you looked at answer choice (D) and saw three rectangles. Of course, instead of three rectangles, you could also be looking at two squares that overlap—the overlapping squares just happen to form three rectangles.

23. (B)

In this question, you have the top part of a triangle at various angles in each answer choice, with a number of lines inside the triangle. In answer choices (A), (C), (D), and (E), there are two lines inside of the triangle. In answer choice (B), there are three lines inside of the triangle, which makes it the correct answer.

24. (E)

Here, each answer choice has two smaller, similar shapes inside a different larger shape. Since both of the shapes are shaded in only three of the five figures, the distinguishing characteristic you're looking for cannot be the shading of the smaller shapes. There are also two lines outside each larger shape in these figures. In four of the figures, the two lines are on different sides of the larger shape. In answer choice (E), the two lines are right next to each other on the same side of the diamond. Answer choice (E) is correct.

25. (C)

Every answer choice has a number, a capital letter, and then a number. Looking at the numbers, in four of the answer choices, the numbers decrease sequentially from left to right. In answer choice (C), the numbers increase sequentially from left to right. Answer choice (C) is the correct answer.

OLSAT® Preparation Guide - Levels D, E, and F

Figural Analogies

OLSAT® Preparation Guide - Levels D, E, and F

Figural Analogies Strategies

The figural analogy questions in the Figural Reasoning section of the OLSAT® essentially require you to find out what is being done to a certain figure or shape from one picture to the next. As in the verbal analogy section, the key to success on these questions lies in determining the correct relationship between one thing and another thing. Once you discover the correct relationship, all you need to do is apply it to the figure in the question. In each question, you will be given an example. In the example, you will be shown a figure and an arrow that points to the changed figure. You will need to find out what was done to the first figure to change it to the second figure. Once you discover what was done, you need to apply this change to the figure in the question and choose from among the answer choices the correct figure that belongs after the arrow.

Look out for rotational movement. There will be questions in which the change that occurs from one figure to the next is a rotational movement. You will have to notice whether the figure is rotated 45 degrees, 90 degrees, or 180 degrees. You will also need to see whether the movement is clockwise or counterclockwise. It might help to visualize rotating the shape with your hand and placing it after the arrow.

Identify color changes. Color changes are very important in the figural analogy questions. You will specifically need to recognize certain parts of the figure that change colors and remember to change the colors on the correlating parts of the figure after the arrow in the question. It's the change that matters; if a small black circle on top of a trapezoid changes to white after the arrow, then the small white triangle on top of a parallelogram must change to black after the arrow.

Beware of the placement of dots and small shapes. Dots and small shapes tend to move around after the arrow. Note their placement and ask yourself what's important about the placement. For example, did the dots or small shapes move outside or inside a larger shape? Did they rotate around a larger shape? Did some of the dots or small shapes disappear or increase in number?

Recognize shape transformations. Sometimes shapes on one side of the arrow will be enlarged to various degrees and placed inside one another. You will need to recognize which shapes were enlarged and apply the same pattern to the figures in the question.

Beware of pattern reversals. You may encounter a question that, at first, looks like your typical analogy question. However, once you get past the example, you might recognize that the pattern is being reversed in the question itself. Remember that the same principle applies; you just need to look at the figures on the right in the example and notice that the pattern of the figures on the left is being changed into the same pattern of the figures on the right.

Identify shapes within shapes. There might be a question that involves a number of shapes within another shape; after the arrow, the shapes might exchange places with one another. The easiest way to figure out the pattern is to quickly note what size each shape becomes after the arrow. For example, using shorthand, you may want to write down L → S to indicate that the large shape becomes a small shape or M → L to indicate that the midsized shape becomes a large shape. Once you have figured out what happens to each shape, all you have to do is apply the changes to the figure in the question.

Beware of shapes that switch places. Sometimes all that will happen with shapes is that they will switch places with one another after the arrow. In a similar vein, some shapes might just replace each other after the arrow. Be on the lookout for these types of patterns in figural analogy questions.

Figural Analogies Questions

1.

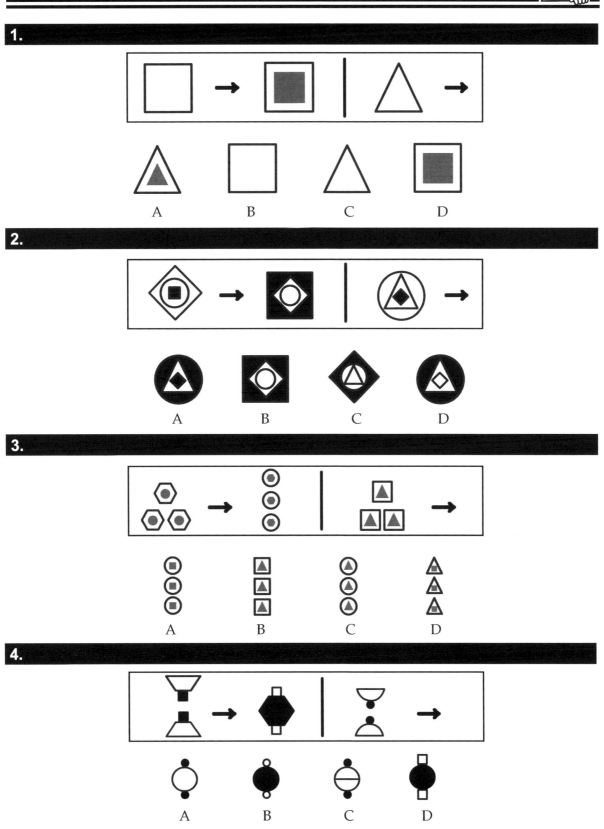

2.

3.

4.

5.

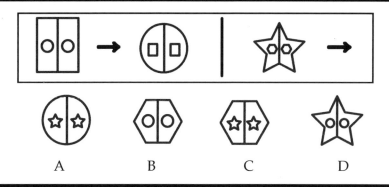

6.

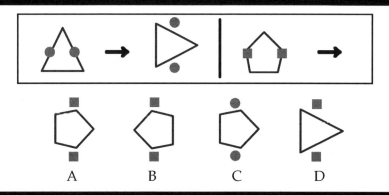

7.

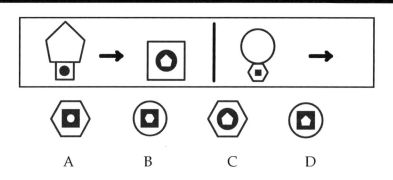

8.

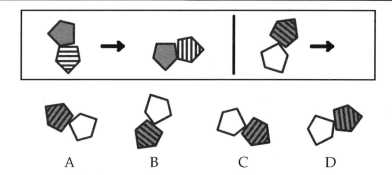

9.

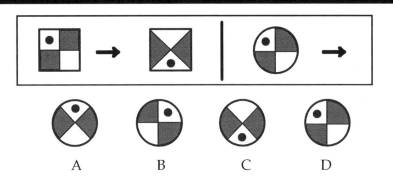

10.

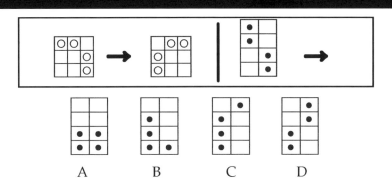

11.

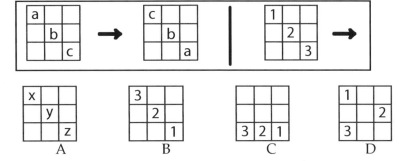

12.

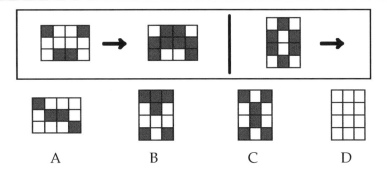

Figural Analogies

13.

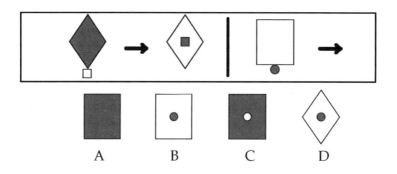

14.

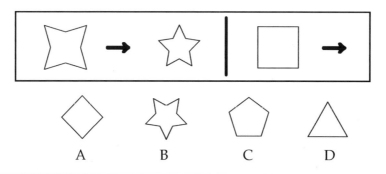

15.

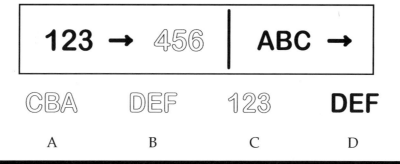

16.

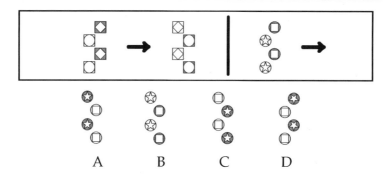

OLSAT® Preparation Guide - Levels D, E, and F   Bright Kids NYC Inc. ©

17.

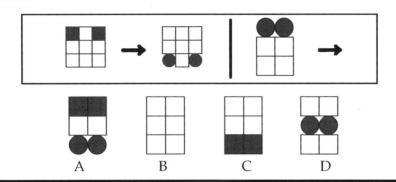

18.

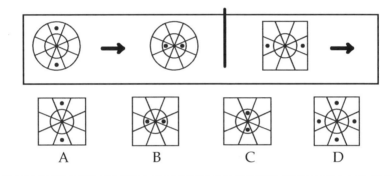

19.

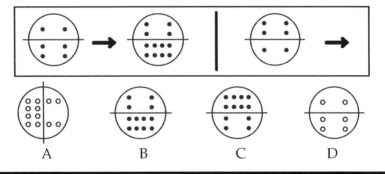

20.

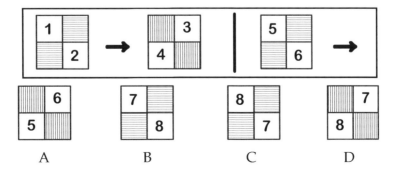

21.

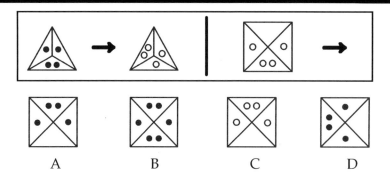

22.

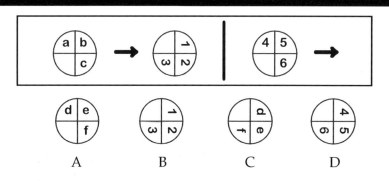

23.

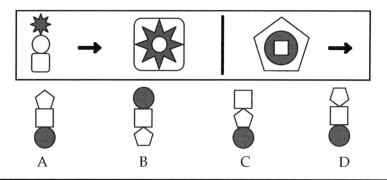

24.

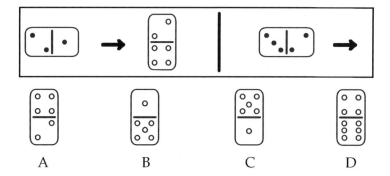

25.

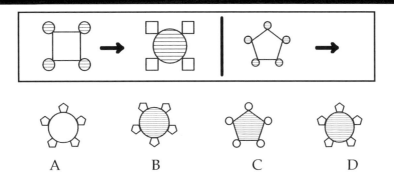

A   B   C   D

26.

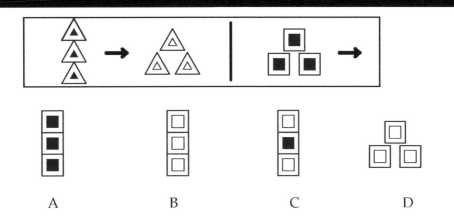

A   B   C   D

OLSAT® Preparation Guide - Levels D, E, and F

Figural Analogies Answer Key

1. (A)

In the first set of figures, there is a shape, and after the arrow the same shape has a similar gray shape inside it. So, if you're given a triangle, after the arrow you should have a triangle with a small gray triangle inside it. This is the figure in answer choice (A), so it is the correct answer.

2. (C)

Here, you have three shapes inside one another that trade places after the arrow. In the example given to you, the small shape becomes the large shape, the middle shape becomes the small shape, and the large shape becomes the middle shape. So, after the arrow in the second set of figures, you should look for a figure in which the small diamond is now a large diamond, the middle triangle is now a small triangle, and the large circle is now a midsized circle. The figure in answer choice (C) has these characteristics, so it is the correct answer.

3. (D)

The example given to you has three identical shapes with a different type of gray shape inside each one. The three shapes are arranged in a triangle. After the arrow, the larger and smaller shapes have exchanged places; the gray shapes are now larger and white, and the larger shapes have become smaller and gray. These three new shapes are arranged vertically. Looking at the question, you should look for an answer choice that has three white triangles arranged vertically with a gray square inside of each one. Answer choice (D) is correct.

4. (B)

The first set of figures has two similar figures that would be mirror images of each other if you were to draw a horizontal line between them. After the arrow, each figure is rotated 180 degrees, and the two are placed together to form a new shape. The colors also reverse; whatever was white is now black and vice versa. If you were to draw a horizontal line through the center of the new figure, the top and bottom of the figure would be mirror images of each other. So, in this question, you need to imagine taking the shapes before the arrow and rotating them 180 degrees so that the two semicircles come together to form a circle with a small circle at the top and a small circle at the bottom. The colors will also reverse, so you should be looking for white circles at the top and bottom of a larger black circle. Answer choice (B) shows this figure, so it is the correct answer.

5. (C)

In the example here, there are two connected rectangles, each with a small circle inside it. After the arrow, there is a large circle divided into two, with a small rectangle in each half of the circle. So, what seems to happen is that one of the smaller shapes becomes a larger shape after the arrow; that shape is divided into two, and the two larger shapes become two smaller shapes inside this divided shape. Looking at the figure in the question and following this pattern, you should look for an answer choice that contains a large hexagon divided into two, with a small star in each half. Answer choice (C) is correct.

6. **(A)**

   The first set of figures has a triangle with gray circles on two of its sides. After the arrow, the triangle is rotated 90 degrees to the right, and the gray circles are now outside of the sides that they used to be on. You are given a pentagon with squares on two of its sides. After the arrow, you should expect the pentagon to rotate 90 degrees to the right, and the squares should be outside the sides that they used to rest on. This figure can be seen in answer choice (A), so it is the correct answer.

7. **(A)**

   Here is another example of shapes exchanging places with one another in some way. In the example, the large shape becomes much smaller, and the small shape is enlarged. The now-small shape is placed in the middle of the enlarged shape. In addition, the midsized shape from the first figure is greatly enlarged and placed around the other two shapes. Looking at the question, you are hoping to find an answer choice that shows a white circle in the center surrounded by a medium-sized black square inside a white hexagon. Answer choice (A) is correct.

8. **(A)**

   This is a question that will require you to visualize rotating a shape around to get the correct answer. The two shapes in this example remain the same shape and size after the arrow; they even remain in the same relative position to each other. The only thing that is different about the two shapes is that they have been rotated 90 degrees counterclockwise. So, looking at the two shapes in the question, you just need to imagine using your hand to rotate them 90 degrees counterclockwise, or to the left. If you visualized correctly, you should see that the shapes in answer choice (A) represent the correct rotation.

9. **(C)**

   In this question, after the arrow, the vertical and horizontal lines in the shape become diagonal lines with gray shading on the left and right sides. Also, the black dot moves to the bottom white section of the shape. In the question, you are given a circle containing a horizontal line and a vertical line, with the upper right and lower left sections shaded. The upper left section contains a black dot. After the arrow, you should look for a circle with two diagonal lines that divide the circle into four sections, the left and right sections will be shaded, and the black dot will be in the bottom white section of the circle. Answer choice (C) is correct.

10. **(D)**

   In the first set of figures, the circles inside the squares in each figure form mirror images of one another. The circles in the first figure sort of form a backward lowercase "r," while the circles in the second figure form a normal lowercase "r." If you were to draw a vertical line between the two figures, they would reflect the image of each other. So, looking at the question, you want to find an answer choice that reflects the black dots in the first figure in a perfect mirror image. The correct answer is (D). If you were to place the figure in answer choice (D) next to the first figure, all the dots would be symmetrical if you drew a vertical line between the two figures.

11. (B)

     Here's a question in which the only changes in the figure involve certain things replacing other things. So, in the example, after the arrow, the "a" and "c" switch places. In the question, you are given the numbers "1 2 3" going down diagonally in the squares. Following the same pattern, the "1" and "3" should switch places. So, you are looking for a figure with the numbers "3 2 1" going down diagonally to the right. Answer choice (B) is correct.

12. (C)

     After the arrow, all the gray squares in the figure have become white, and all the white squares have become gray. Following this pattern in the question, you should get answer choice (C) as the correct answer.

13. (C)

     In the first set of figures, the large shape after the arrow changes color to become the color of the small shape, the small shape changes color to become the color of the large shape, and the small shape moves from the bottom of the large shape to the center of the large shape. Following this pattern for the question, you should look for a gray square with a white circle in the center. Answer choice (C) is the correct answer.

14. (C)

     In the first set of figures, you see a sort of crude four-pointed star. After the arrow, a point is added at the top of the first shape, and the crude four-pointed star becomes a nice five-pointed star. In the next set of figures, you are given a square. What should come after the arrow? Following the pattern from the example, a point should be added at the top of the square, and the square should become a pentagon. Answer choice (C) is the correct answer.

15. (B)

     Here, in the example, you have a black "123," and after the arrow you have a white "456." In the question, you are given a black "ABC," so you should be looking for a white "DEF" in the answer choices. This can be found in answer choice (B).

16. (C)

     This is a question in which everything seems to switch places from the first set of shapes to the set of shapes after the arrow. The first and third squares on the right move to the left, the second and fourth squares on the left move to the right, the squares surrounding the smaller shapes become shaded when they move to the right, and the squares surrounding the smaller shapes become white when they move to the left. Following this pattern in the question given to you, you should look for an answer choice that has two white circles on the left, each with a square inside it, and two gray circles on the right, each with a star inside it. The first and third circles should contain squares, and the second and fourth circles should contain stars. Answer choice (C) is correct.

17. (C)

    In the first set of figures, the figure after the arrow is flipped upside down, and black circles replace the black squares from the first figure. The figure in the question is four connected squares with two black circles on top of the squares. Don't get confused that the pattern has been reversed here—just work backward. You know that you're going to have to mentally flip the figure upside down and imagine the two black circles on the bottom of the figure. Then, the black circles just become black squares. Answer choice (C) is the correct answer. You can double-check your answer by following the same pattern as in the example; if you flip your answer choice upside down and replace the black squares with circles, do you get the figure given to you in the question? The answer is yes.

18. (C)

    Your focus in this question should be on the movement of the dots. In the example, the dots in the figure after the arrow move into the inner circle and become arranged horizontally instead of vertically. So, in the question, in the figure after the arrow, the dots should move into the inner circle and become arranged vertically. This is shown in answer choice (C), so it is the correct answer.

19. (C)

    Once again, you should focus on the dots in this question. In the first set of figures, the dots in each half of the circle double after the arrow. Following this pattern in the question you're given, you should look for an answer choice with a figure with eight dots in the top half of the circle and four dots in the bottom half of the circle. Answer choice (C) is correct.

20. (D)

    In this question, you have "1 2" going down diagonally from left to right, and after the arrow you have "3 4" going down diagonally from right to left. In the question you're being asked to solve, the first figure has "5 6" going down diagonally from left to right, and you're supposed to find the correct figure that comes after the arrow. The correct answer will be four squares with a "7 8" going down diagonally from right to left. Answer choice (D) is correct.

21. (D)

    Here's another question in which you should focus on the changes in the dots before and after the arrow. After the arrow, the dots move clockwise from one section of the triangle to the next section. You should also notice that the dots change color after the arrow from black to white. Looking at the question you're being asked to solve, you are looking for a figure that has two black dots in the left section of the square, one black dot in the top section of the square, and one black dot in the bottom section of the square. That figure can be found in answer choice (D).

22. (C)

    In the example given to you, the letters move over one section in a clockwise direction and become numbers. The numbers correspond to the first letters in the alphabet, so "1 2 3" means "a b c." Following this pattern in the question, the "4 5 6" should move over to the upper right, lower right, and lower left quadrants in the circle, and those numbers should become "d e f." Answer choice (C) is correct.

23. (B)

    Here, you are given three different shapes that are similar in size and are lined up vertically. After the arrow, they become enlarged and placed inside each other. The top shape becomes the midsized shape, the middle shape becomes the small shape, and the bottom shape becomes the largest shape. Looking at the question you're being asked to solve, you should notice that you're being asked to reverse this pattern. So, the pentagon is the large shape, which means that it will become the bottom shape, the gray circle is the midsized shape, which means that it will become the top shape, and the square is the small shape, which means that it will be the middle shape. The order of shapes, from top to bottom, should be circle, square, and pentagon. Answer choice (B) is correct.

24. (D)

    Here, the pattern is that, after the arrow, the domino is rotated 90 degrees counterclockwise (to the left) and the dots are doubled. So, among the answer choices, you should be looking for an upright domino with four dots on the top half and six dots on the bottom half. That domino can be found in answer choice (D).

25. (D)

    In the example given to you, one of the four smaller shapes becomes the large shape after the arrow, and the large shape becomes four smaller shapes that are placed where the corners of the large shape used to be. You should also notice that large shape in the second figure keeps the horizontal lines from the circles in the first figure. Looking at the question given to you, you should be looking for a large circle with horizontal lines through it that has five pentagons where the corners of the large pentagon used to be. Answer choice (D) is correct.

26. (B)

    In the first set of figures, the three stacked triangles become a figure with two triangles at the bottom and one triangle on top. The smaller triangles inside each triangle change from black to white. Looking at the question, you should notice that you're going to have to reverse the pattern. So, the three squares are going to become stacked, and the smaller squares inside the squares will become white. This figure can be found in answer choice (B).

OLSAT® Preparation Guide - Levels D, E, and F

Pattern Matrices

OLSAT® Preparation Guide - Levels D, E, and F

Pattern Matrices Strategies

Pattern matrices are one of the Figural Reasoning subtests that you will encounter on the OLSAT®. You will be given a box with a number of drawings inside of it. Somewhere in the bottom row of the matrix, there will be a question mark. Usually, the top row will show a number of changes that are occurring to a drawing or shape. You will need to figure out the pattern of these changes and then apply the pattern to the bottom row in order to determine which drawing among the answer choices belongs in place of the question mark. Sometimes, however, the top row will display a concept that must be applied to the bottom row. You may also encounter pattern matrix questions that have more than two rows. In some of the questions on this subtest, the pattern continues from left to right from the top row to the bottom row. You will have to detect the pattern across the entire matrix in order to determine the figure that belongs in place of the question mark. While these questions may look a bit difficult at first, they get a lot easier if you can learn to see the various types of patterns that are frequently employed on the test.

Beware of opposite reactions. If you notice that the pattern that is occurring in the top row is also occurring in the bottom row, be on the lookout for what is happening to the shape above the question mark. You will probably have to apply that change to the bottom row in order to get the correct answer.

Look out for changing colors/shades. Always be on the lookout when certain shapes or areas in shapes become darkened or lightened in pattern matrices. You will usually have to apply a similar change in order to find the correct figure that belongs in place of the question mark. Be careful, though! Sometimes the pattern is not simply that a shape or area becomes black or gray, but that it *changes* color or shading. For example, the second figure in the top row of a pattern matrix might be black, and the third figure might be white. In the bottom row, if the second figure is white, the third figure must be black, according to the above pattern. To clarify, you might not be looking for an identical color but rather a *change* in color—even one that is not identical.

Recognize disappearing lines/shapes. Take careful notice of when certain lines or shapes disappear or reappear in the top row. Identifying the correct figure may depend upon the disappearance or reappearance of these lines or shapes.

Identify rotational movements. Sometimes drawings or shapes will be rotated around from one figure to the next in a row. You should note whether the rotation is clockwise or counterclockwise as well as how many degrees the drawing or shape appears to rotate. The figure will usually either rotate 45 degrees (ex: from pointing directly up to pointing diagonally upward to the right), 90 degrees (ex: from pointing directly up to pointing directly to the right), or 180 degrees (such as from pointing directly up to pointing directly down).

Beware of mirror images. Sometimes two figures in a row will be mirror images of each other. That is, if you were to draw a horizontal line between the two figures, they would be perfectly symmetrical. You could take one figure and fold it perfectly on the other figure. It's best to think of mirror images as concerning the overall shape of two figures. For example, you might see two figures that are mirror images of each other but that are shaded oppositely in relation to each other. Focus on the mirror image aspect to get the correct shape. Once you have the right shape, you can focus on the correct shading of the figure.

Identify shapes within a shape. You might be given a figure that has a number of shapes within a shape. Sometimes, as you move down the row, the shapes will trade places with one another. For example, the pattern might be that the large shape becomes the midsized shape, the midsized shape becomes the small shape, and the small shape becomes the large shape. Once you have nailed down the pattern, apply it to the last figure in the bottom row in order to determine which answer choice is correct.

Look out for continuous pattern questions. Sometimes a pattern continues on past the first row to the second or even third row. You will need to follow the figures until you discover that the pattern is repeating itself. Once you find out when the pattern repeats itself, identify at what stage in the pattern the question mark shows up. Once you determine the stage, you can determine a certain characteristic of the figure you are looking for. This can help you eliminate some answer choices and uncover the correct figure that belongs in place of the question mark.

Make sure to keep track if there is more than one pattern. There might be multiple patterns occurring in a single matrix. You may have to keep track of all of them in order to figure out the correct answer. You may want to consider writing certain things in shorthand to help you remember what is happening. For example, you could write WGW to mean "white to gray to white," CSC to mean "circle to square to circle," and so on. Create whatever shorthand or other system feels comfortable and helpful. The important thing is that you somehow keep track of the different patterns occurring in the matrix.

Remember that it's not the result that matters; it's the action. If a shape is upright in the first figure and on its side in the second figure, the important thing to remember is that it was rotated 90 degrees in a certain direction. In the bottom row, if the shape is on its side in the first figure, you will need to mentally rotate the figure 90 degrees in the same direction that was employed in the top row.

Pattern Matrices Questions

The figures in the box go together in a certain way. Which figure goes where you see the question mark?

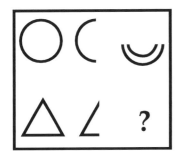

A   B   C   D   E

The figures in the box go together in a certain way. Which figure goes where you see the question mark?

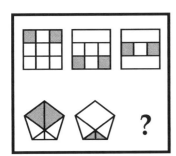

A   B   C   D   E

The figures in the box go together in a certain way. Which figure goes where you see the question mark?

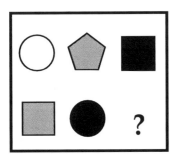

A   B   C   D   E

4.

The drawings in the box go together in a certain way. Which figure goes where you see the question mark?

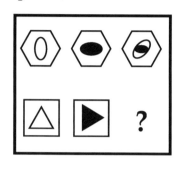

A   B   C   D   E

5.

The drawings in the box go together in a certain way. Which figure goes where you see the question mark?

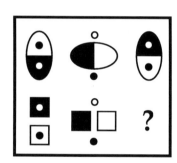

A   B   C   D   E

6.

The drawings in the box go together in a certain way. Which figure goes where you see the question mark?

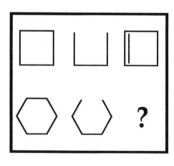

A   B   C   D   E

7.

The drawings in the box go together in a certain way. Which figure goes where you see the question mark?

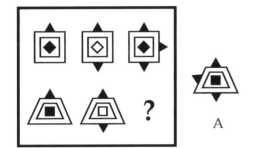

A   B   C   D   E

8.

The drawings in the box go together in a certain way. Which figure goes where you see the question mark?

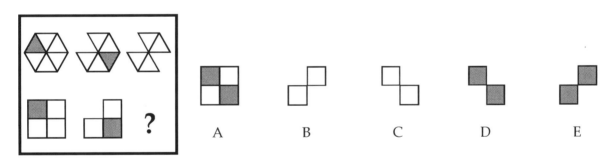

A   B   C   D   E

9.

The drawings in the box go together in a certain way. Which figure goes where you see the question mark?

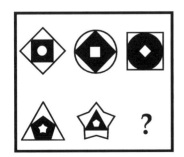

A   B   C   D   E

10.

The figures in the box go together in a certain way. Which figure goes where you see the question mark?

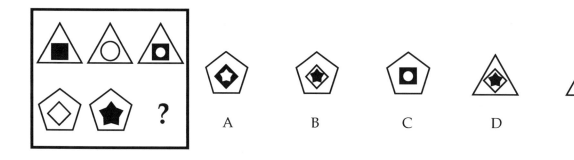

11.

The figures in the box go together in a certain way. Which figure goes where you see the question mark?

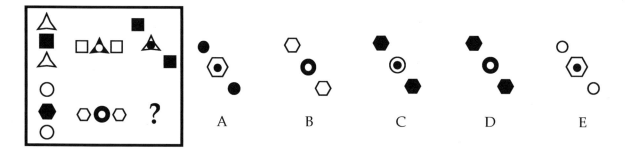

12.

The figures in the box go together in a certain way. Which figure goes where you see the question mark?

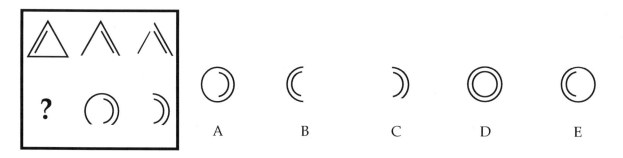

13.

The figures in the box go together in a certain way. Which figure goes where you see the question mark?

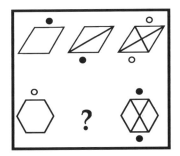

A   B   C   D   E

14.

The figures in the box go together in a certain way. Which figure goes where you see the question mark?

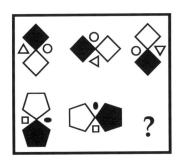

A   B   C   D   E

15.

The figures in the box go together in a certain way. Which figure goes where you see the question mark?

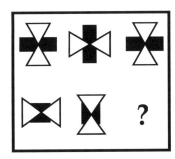

A   B   C   D   E

16.

The figures in the box go together in a certain way. Which figure goes where you see the question mark?

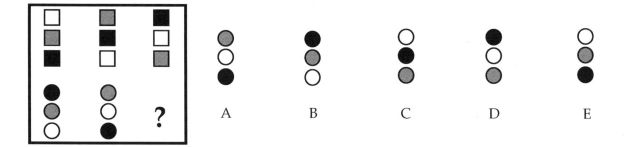

17.

The figures in the box go together in a certain way. Which figure goes where you see the question mark?

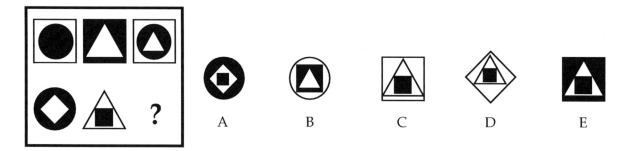

18.

The figures in the box go together in a certain way. Which figure goes where you see the question mark?

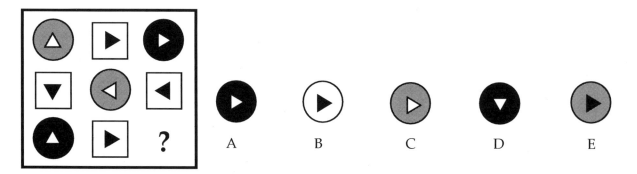

19.

The figures in the box go together in a certain way. Which figure goes where you see the question mark?

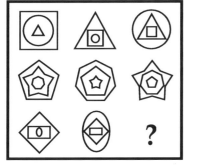

A   B   C   D   E

20.

The figures in the box go together in a certain way. Which figure goes where you see the question mark?

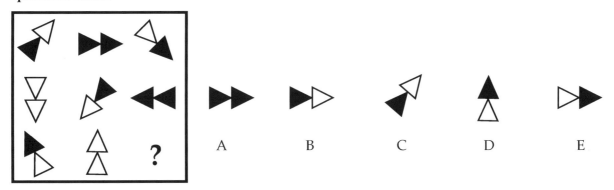

A   B   C   D   E

21.

The figures in the box go together in a certain way. Which figure goes where you see the question mark?

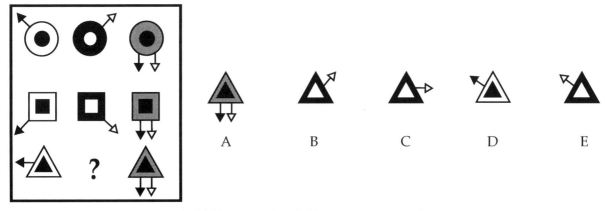

A   B   C   D   E

22.

The figures in the box go together in a certain way. Which figure goes where you see the question mark?

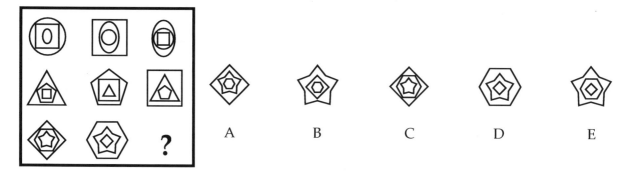

23.

The figures in the box go together in a certain way. Which figure goes where you see the question mark?

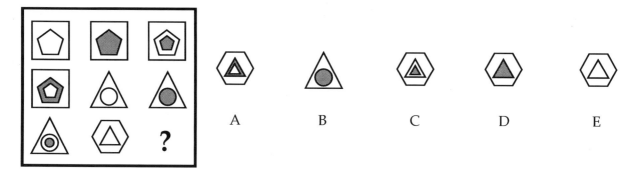

Pattern Matrices Answer Key

1. (B)

The first figure in the series is a shape. The second figure is that shape torn in half. The third figure moves the second figure 90 degrees counterclockwise and adds a smaller version of the other half right above the previous figure. If you follow this pattern with the triangle, you should get answer choice (B) as the next figure in the pattern.

2. (C)

The first figure is a shape with a bunch of lines drawn through it that form three different levels that are divided in three. The outside two squares in the top level in the first figure are shaded. In the second figure, the top level is no longer divided in three, and the bottom level is shaded. In the third figure, the bottom level is no longer divided into three, and the middle level is shaded. If you follow this pattern with the divided pentagon, the third figure in the series is answer choice (C).

3. (A)

Here we have a pattern of a circle, a pentagon, and a square. One of these shapes is white, one is shaded, and one is black. In the second row, you are missing a pentagon. Since the square is shaded and the circle is black, the pentagon must be white. Answer choice (A) is correct.

4. (C)

All of the figures in the first row are inside a hexagon, and all of the figures in the second row are inside a square. The shape inside the square moves 90 degrees clockwise from the first figure to the second figure. It also becomes black. In the third figure, the shape moves 45 degrees counterclockwise and becomes clear. The black shape from the second figure is then reduced in size, tilted a bit clockwise, and placed inside the new shape. If you follow this pattern, you should see that the third figure in the second row is answer choice (C).

5. (A)

In this question, it's best to just focus on the first and third figures in the pattern. It looks as though the first and third figures in each row are mirror images that have opposite shading. So, in the second row, for the third figure in the series, the top box should be white with a black dot in the middle, and the bottom box should be black with a white dot in the middle. Answer choice (A) is correct.

6. (A)

The first figure is a shape. The second figure has the top part of the shape removed. The third figure restores the top part of the shape and adds another line on the side. Following this pattern with the hexagon, you should get answer choice (A) as your answer.

7. **(E)**

With these series of figures, you have a smaller shape inside of two shapes that are the same shape. In the first row, you have a diamond inside two squares. There is also a triangle at the top of the figure. Both the triangle and the diamond are black. In the second figure, the center shape is now white, and a black triangle has been added to the bottom of the figure. In the third figure, a black triangle has been added to the right side of the figure, and the center shape has turned back to black. If you follow this pattern in the second row, you should be looking for a black square inside two trapezoids, with black triangles at the top, bottom, and right sides of the figure. Answer choice (E) shows that, so it is the correct answer.

8. **(B)**

Each shaded part in the shape is disappearing with each new figure. So, in the second row, you should be looking for the figure that will show after the bottom right square is removed from the second figure. The figure in answer choice (B) is what you get once that happens, so it is the correct answer.

9. **(A)**

Here, you have three shapes within each other that take turns becoming the large, middle, and small shapes. Looking at the second figure in the first row, you should see that to get the third figure, the small shape becomes the large shape, the middle shape becomes the small shape, and the large shape becomes the middle shape. If you follow this pattern in the second row, you should get answer choice (A) as the next figure in the series.

10. **(B)**

In this series, different shapes are being placed inside a large shape. In the first row, the shapes are inside a triangle. The third figure in the series takes the smaller shape from the second figure and places it inside the smaller shape from the first figure. So, in the second row, the first figure has a white diamond inside a pentagon, and the second figure has a black star inside a pentagon. The third figure will be a pentagon that has a white diamond with a black star inside of it. Answer choice (B) is correct.

11. **(C)**

It'll be easiest to just focus on the second figure in this series and see how it changes into the third figure. So, in the third figure, the two shapes on the sides become black and move to a slanted angle relative to the center shape. Also, the center shape switches colors; the black in the shape becomes white, and the white becomes black. If you follow this pattern in the second row, you should get the figure in answer choice (C) as the next figure in the series.

12. (E)

    The first figure in the top row is a shape with an extra line inside on the left. The bottom of the shape is taken away in the next figure. Since you are being asked to find the first figure in the series in the bottom row, you should look for a full shape with an extra line inside of it on the left. Answer choice (E) is correct.

13. (A)

    You are being asked to find the second figure in the series in this question. The first figure is a shape with a circle that is either black or white at the top of it. The second figure switches the black or white circle to the bottom of the shape and adds a diagonal line through the shape. So, in the second row, for the second figure, you should be looking for a hexagon with a white circle underneath it and a black line going diagonally upward from left to right through the hexagon. Answer choice (A) is correct.

14. (A)

    The figure is moving 90 degrees counterclockwise each time. Just imagine taking the figure and moving it around with your hand. The third figure in the second row is shown in answer choice (A).

15. (D)

    The figure is moving 90 degrees clockwise each time. Answer choice (D) is correct.

16. (C)

    In this series, imagine the colors moving up with each new figure, with the top colors becoming the bottom colors. So, in the second row, the third figure should be three circles with the top circle being white, the middle circle being black, and the bottom circle being gray. Answer choice (C) is correct.

17. (A)

    In the third figure in this series, the smaller shape from the second figure is placed inside the inner shape from the first figure, and then both of those shapes are placed inside the outer shape in the first figure. Answer choice (A) shows this pattern for the second row, so it is the correct answer.

18. (C)

    This is a tough question. This is also your first continuous pattern question. Here, you have a continuous pattern going from left to right and from row to row. You have a circle always alternating with a square. You also have a color pattern for the circle or square that goes *gray, white, black, white* and then repeats itself. Inside either the circle or square, you have a triangle that alternates between white and black. The triangle also moves every so often. It points upward for one figure, to the right for two figures, downward for one figure, then to the left for two figures, and then begins the pattern all over again. Now, these are a bunch of patterns to try and keep track of, but you just need to take it one step at a time. So, looking at the figure represented by the question mark, you should know that it's going to be a circle since the previous shape was a square. The color scheme was just *gray, white, black, white,* so the next color will have to be gray. Since you're looking for a gray circle, you can narrow down your choices to (C) and (E). What about the direction of the triangle? The previous triangle was pointing to the right, so the next triangle in the pattern must also be pointing to the right. That doesn't help since both (C) and (E) have triangles that point to the right. You're going to have to figure out the color of the pattern. Since you know that the color of the triangle alternates between black and white, the triangle in the next figure will have to be white. Answer choice (C) is correct.

19. (B)

Here we have another pattern in which three shapes are within each other and exchange places in the subsequent figure. Looking at the second and third figures, you can see that the smallest shape becomes the largest shape, the midsized shape becomes the smallest shape, and the largest shape becomes the midsized shape. Following this pattern with the shapes in the third row, you should get answer choice (B) as the correct answer.

20. (C)

This is a continuous pattern question. The two arrows are moving 45 degrees clockwise in these figures. The color pattern is as follows: one triangle is black and one triangle is white, then both triangles are black, then the triangles switch colors from the first arrangement, and then both triangles are white. Every time there is a black and a white triangle, the colors are reversed from the pattern two figures ago. So, looking at the last row, the last figure in the row is going to be two triangles pointing upward and toward the right. Since the previous triangles were both white, you're going to have one black triangle and one white triangle. Looking at the last black and white triangle figure, you're going to need to reverse the colors. So, the lower triangle is going to be black, and the higher triangle is going to be white. This is represented in answer choice (C), which is the correct answer.

21. (C)

If you were to draw a vertical line between the first and second figures, you would see that the second figure in the pattern is the mirror image of the first figure. So, the mirror image of the first figure in the third row must be a white triangle inside a black triangle with an arrow pointing directly to the right. Answer choice (C) is correct.

22. (B)

Here is another question that uses a pattern of shapes within a shape. Looking at the second and third figures, you should be able to see that the large shape becomes the small shape, the midsized shape becomes the large shape, and the small shape becomes the midsized shape. Following this pattern, you should get answer choice (B) as the correct answer.

23. (D)

This is a continuous pattern question. Something is happening to each figure at different stages here. Then, a new figure emerges, and the same stages begin to occur to the new figure. Fortunately, the last figure you see in the box is a new figure. It looks as though the second stage for a new figure is to simply shade the inner shape. Answer choice (D) is correct.

OLSAT® Preparation Guide - Levels D, E, and F

Figural Series

OLSAT® Preparation Guide - Levels D, E, and F

Figural Series Strategies

The figural series questions in the Figural Reasoning section of the OLSAT® involve a series of four figures and a question mark that stands for the fifth figure. You will have to determine what is happening at each step in the series and then apply the appropriate pattern to discover which figure among the answer choices belongs in place of the question mark. Sometimes the series will continue in a certain pattern to the fifth figure, and sometimes the pattern in the series will repeat itself after two, three, or four figures. At other times, there might be two different patterns occurring for different figures in the series; for example, there might be one pattern for the first and third figures and another pattern for the second and fourth figures. Finally, the question mark may not always be in the fifth position in the series; for example, it might be in the third position. Once you discover the correct pattern, it should be relatively easy to choose the correct figure among the answer choices.

The last figure is what matters. Once you've determined the correct pattern, the last known figure involving that pattern is what matters. That figure will be the one to which you will apply the pattern in order to get the correct answer.

Note the stage in the series. It's important to be at the correct stage of whatever pattern you are applying. For example, if the pattern repeats itself after three figures and you're trying to find the fifth figure in the series, you need to remember that you are on the second step of the pattern. Whatever was done to the first figure will also be done to the fourth figure, so looking at the second figure will help you determine what the fifth figure will look like.

Look out for numbers. Numbers might be employed as a pattern in some of the questions. For example, the increasing or decreasing number of shapes in each figure, the increasing or decreasing number of shaded or darkened areas in each figure, and the increasing or decreasing number of dots in each figure might help to indicate a particular pattern in the series.

Visualize the movement. The movement of objects from figure to figure in a series will be important. Sometimes, you might actually be able to visualize an item or a shape moving from one figure to the next. Having a number of figures helps you see the movement of shapes much more easily.

Focus only on the pattern you are trying to solve. If a series has two different patterns, focus on the pattern that involves the figure you're being asked to find. Do not spend your time on the other pattern; it's irrelevant to the question being asked.

Focus on one thing at a time. You might find it easier to focus on one thing at a time when you're trying to determine what happens from one figure to the next. Once you have discovered what is going on with one element, focus on another element and nail that one down. You'll discover that approaching the elements individually can help you break down the different patterns.

Break down patterns involving shapes within shapes. With these questions, you should focus on two sequential figures and write down the changes from one figure to the next. Try to be general in your determination of the pattern—note what size changes to what size and whether there are any color changes from figure to figure. You can use some kind of shorthand if you think it will help you keep track of the changes in size. Once you have figured out the pattern, go to the figure before the question mark and apply it in order to determine the correct answer among the answer choices.

Note the enlargement or reduction of shapes or figures. Some shapes or figures might become larger or smaller from figure to figure in the series. Take care to note this pattern and to apply it appropriately to the last figure in the series.

Think of the figures in the series as stop animation. Sometimes if you look at the figures in these questions from left to right, you can almost see the different shapes or dots moving, growing larger, growing smaller, or jumping from one position to the next. If you're having trouble finding the pattern, take a step back and try to actually see what's occurring from one figure to the next. Imagine that you're looking at crude stop animation and that something must be changing from one frame to the next. This technique may help you to discover the pattern that is occurring in the series of figures.

Figural Series Questions

The figures below form a series. Which figure continues that series and goes where you see the question mark?

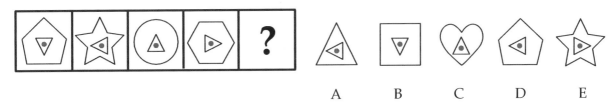

The figures below form a series. Which figure continues that series and goes where you see the question mark?

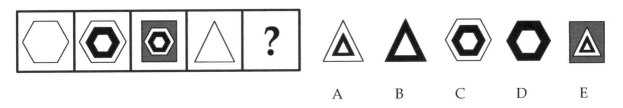

The figures below form a series. Which figure continues that series and goes where you see the question mark?

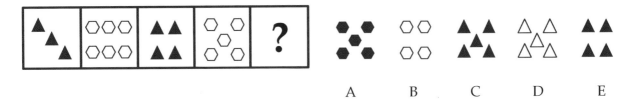

The figures below form a series. Which figure continues that series and goes where you see the question mark?

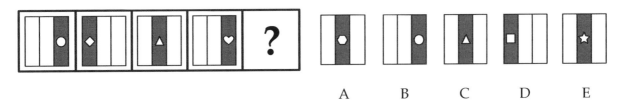

5.

The figures below form a series. Which figure continues that series and goes where you see the question mark?

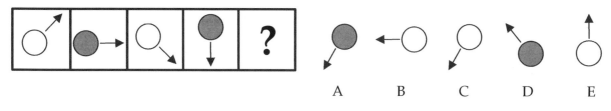

6.

The figures below form a series. Which figure continues that series and goes where you see the question mark?

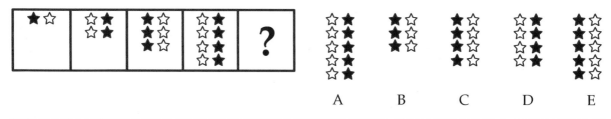

7.

The figures below form a series. Which figure continues that series and goes where you see the question mark?

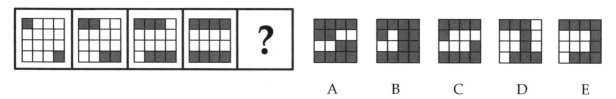

8.

The figures below form a series. Which figure continues that series and goes where you see the question mark?

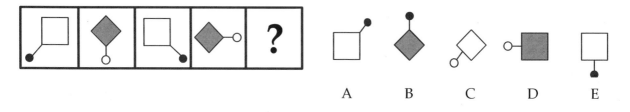

9.

The figures below form a series. Which figure continues that series and goes where you see the question mark?

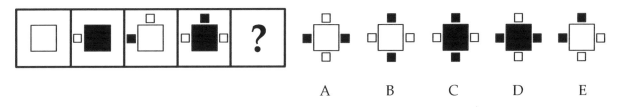

10.

The figures below form a series. Which figure continues that series and goes where you see the question mark?

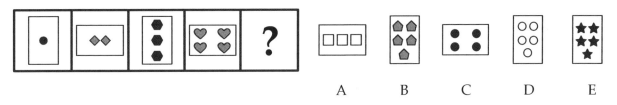

11.

The figures below form a series. Which figure continues that series and goes where you see the question mark?

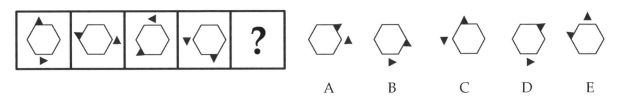

12.

The figures below form a series. Which figure continues that series and goes where you see the question mark?

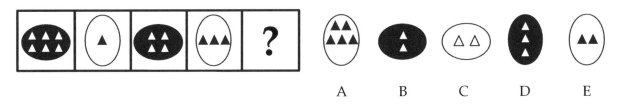

13.

The figures below form a series. Which figure continues that series and goes where you see the question mark?

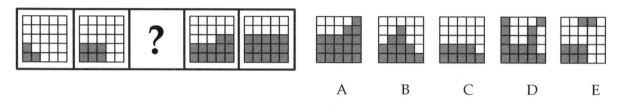

A   B   C   D   E

14.

The figures below form a series. Which figure continues that series and goes where you see the question mark?

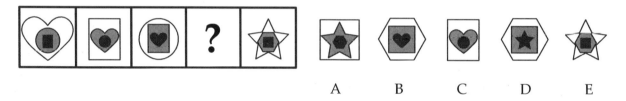

A   B   C   D   E

15.

The figures below form a series. Which figure continues that series and goes where you see the question mark?

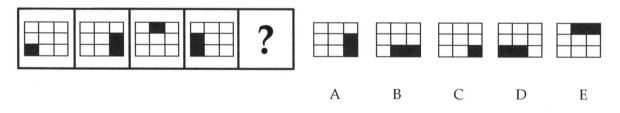

A   B   C   D   E

16.

The figures below form a series. Which figure continues that series and goes where you see the question mark?

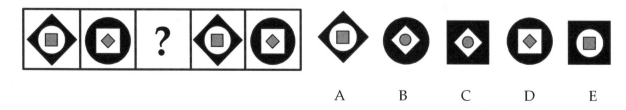

A   B   C   D   E

17.

The figures below form a series. Which figure continues that series and goes where you see the question mark?

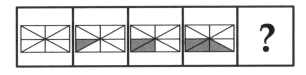

   A   B   C   D   E

18.

The figures below form a series. Which figure continues that series and goes where you see the question mark?

   A   B   C   D   E

19.

The figures below form a series. Which figure continues that series and goes where you see the question mark?

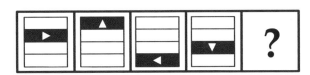

   A   B   C   D   E

20.

The figures below form a series. Which figure continues that series and goes where you see the question mark?

   A   B   C   D   E

21.

The figures below form a series. Which figure continues that series and goes where you see the question mark?

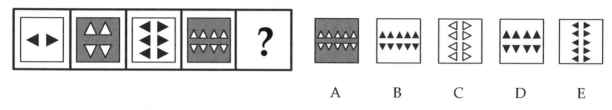

A   B   C   D   E

22.

The figures below form a series. Which figure continues that series and goes where you see the question mark?

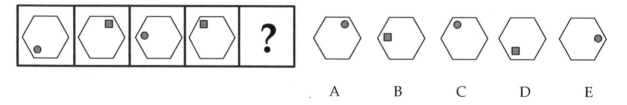

A   B   C   D   E

23.

The figures below form a series. Which figure continues that series and goes where you see the question mark?

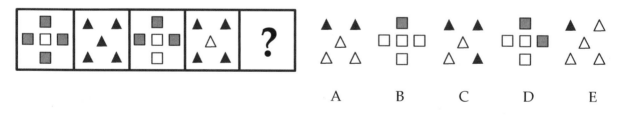

A   B   C   D   E

24.

The figures below form a series. Which figure continues that series and goes where you see the question mark?

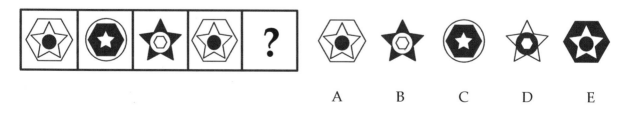

A   B   C   D   E

Figural Series Answer Key

1. (B)

   In this series, you have a triangle with a gray dot inside it moving clockwise 90 degrees in each new shape. It points down, then to the left, then up, and then to the right. Where will it point next? According to our pattern, the triangle should point down in our answer choice. The only answer choice that has a downward-facing triangle with a gray dot inside it is answer choice (B), so it is the correct answer.

2. (A)

   Here, you have a shape that goes through a series of two changes. In the fourth figure, you see a new shape that is about to go through the same series of steps. So, what is going to happen to the triangle? Looking back at the hexagon, in the second step of the series, a black hexagon appears inside the large hexagon, and there is a white hexagon inside the black hexagon. Thus, with the triangle, you can expect a black triangle to appear inside the large triangle, and there should also be a white triangle inside the black triangle. This is the figure in answer choice (A), so it is the correct answer.

3. (C)

   In this series, the figures alternate between triangles and hexagons. The triangles are increasing by one each time, and the hexagons are decreasing by one each time. The next figure in the series is going to be a group of triangles. Since there were four triangles in the last group, there should be five triangles in this group. Answer choice (C) shows this arrangement, so it is the correct answer.

4. (D)

   The gray shade in this series is moving from left to right. When the gray shade reaches the last rectangle, it goes back to the rectangle on the left and begins moving to the right again. Since there is no discernible pattern to the shapes in the gray shading, all you should focus on is the shading itself. In the last figure, the rectangle on the far right is shaded. So, you should be looking for an answer choice in which the rectangle on the far left is shaded. Answer choice (D) is the correct answer.

5. (C)

   The arrows in this series are moving 45 degrees clockwise in each new figure. The arrow points diagonally upward to the right, then straight to the right, then diagonally downward to the right, and then straight down. In the next figure, you would expect the arrow to point diagonally downward to the left. Also, the shading of the circle alternates between white and gray. Since the circle in the last figure is gray, the circle will be white in the next figure. Answer choice (C) shows a white circle with an arrow pointing diagonally downward to the left, so it is the correct answer.

6. (E)

   In this series, one star is being added to each column in each new figure. The stars in each column are also alternating between white and black in each new figure. In the last figure given to us, there are two columns, each with four stars. The left column has only white stars, and the right column has only black stars. Thus, we can expect that the next figure in the series would be a left column with five black stars and a right column with five white stars. This figure can be seen in answer choice (E), which is the correct answer.

7. **(C)**

　　One square is changing to gray in the top and bottom rows in each new figure; the gray squares are showing up from left to right in the top row and from right to left in the bottom row. In the last figure, you can see that the top and bottom rows are now completely gray. The next figure should have two more squares changing to gray: the leftmost square in the second row and the rightmost square in the third row. Answer choice (C) is the correct answer.

8. **(A)**

　　First off, you should notice that the square is alternating between gray and white in each new figure. The last figure in the series has a gray square. So, the correct answer choice will have a white square. You can narrow down your answer choices to (A), (C), and (E). In each new figure, a tiny circle connected to one corner of the square is rotating in a counterclockwise manner. Those tiny circles alternate between black and white, such that one of the two shapes in each figure is always white. Following all of these patterns, the next figure in the series should be a white square with a tiny black circle connected to it that is pointing diagonally up toward the right. Answer choice (A) displays this figure, so it is the correct answer.

9. **(A)**

　　The large squares in this series alternate between white and black, so you should know right away that the fifth figure in the series will be white. That narrows down your answer choices to (A), (B), and (E). Now take a look at the small squares in each figure. The small squares increase by one in each figure, but that doesn't help you because (A), (B), and (E) all have four small squares. You should also notice that the small squares alternate in color between white and black, and they switch colors with each new figure. Thinking about the color patterns of the small squares, you should see that the small squares need to alternate colors, and the one at the bottom needs to be white. Answer choice (A) is correct.

10. **(E)**

　　Since four different shapes are used in the figures in the series, there can be no pattern to the type of shape used. However, there is a pattern to the number of shapes being used and the shading of the shapes. The shapes are increasing by one in each new figure, and the shading alternates between black and gray. The last figure in the series shows four gray hearts. Thus, the next figure must show five black shapes. There are five black stars in answer choice (E), so it must be the correct answer. If you didn't notice the pattern in the shading, you would not have been able to determine whether answer choice (B), (D), or (E) was the next figure in the series.

11. (B)

Here's a series in which you will have to pay attention to the direction and movement of the arrows. One arrow in each figure rests on the hexagon, and one arrow is completely outside of the hexagon. The arrow on the hexagon is moving counterclockwise from corner to corner. The outside arrow is changing direction 90 degrees counterclockwise in each new figure; it points to the right, then up, then to the left, and finally down. The outside arrow also moves 90 degrees counterclockwise around the hexagon in each new figure. In the fifth figure in the series, the arrow on the hexagon should be on the rightmost corner of the hexagon, and the outside arrow should be at the bottom of the hexagon and pointing to the right. Answer choice (B) shows this figure.

12. (B)

The oval is alternating between being black/sideways and white/upright. Just knowing that would lead you to answer choice (B) as being the correct answer. You can double-check your answer by noticing that the triangles in the black ovals are decreasing by two in each new black oval, and the triangles in the white ovals are increasing by two in each new white oval. So, having two white triangles in a black sideways oval would make sense as the next figure in this series. Answer choice (B) is correct.

13. (C)

The first figure in the series has three gray squares, the second figure has six gray squares, the fourth figure has twelve gray squares, and the fifth figure has fifteen gray squares. So, how many squares should the third figure in the series have? Since the gray squares are increasing by three in each new figure, the third figure should have nine gray squares. Answer choice (C) shows a figure with nine gray squares, so it must be the correct answer.

14. (D)

This question is a bit tough. Three shapes in this series alternate between being a small black shape, a midsized gray shape, and a large white shape. Once each shape has been all three, three new shapes appear. Here, in the last figure, you are shown a large white star, a midsized gray hexagon, and a small black square. Since this is the fifth figure in the series, it must be the second in a series of new shapes. So, you need to look back at the second figure in the series and work backward to see how the first figure became the second figure. Going from the second figure to the first figure, the large white shape became the small black shape, the midsized gray shape became the large white shape, and the small black shape became the midsized gray shape. Now it's time to apply this formula to the fifth figure in the series and work backward. The large white star has to become a small black star, the midsized gray hexagon has to become a large white hexagon, and the small black square has to become a midsized gray square. This figure is shown in answer choice (D).

15. (C)

    For this one, you could imagine the black squares as moving counterclockwise around the perimeter of the squares. The black squares alternate between being one square and two squares. Whenever the black squares move counterclockwise, they move over by two squares. So, if there's one black square, it moves over two squares and then adds one more square ahead of it. If there are two black squares, the top square moves over two squares, and the trailing square disappears. Following this pattern, the next figure in the series should have one black square, and it should be in the lower right corner of the square. Answer choice (C) is correct.

16. (C)

    Here's another question that involves keeping track of what sizes of shapes turn into other sizes of shapes in the next figure. Once again, you just need to break it down. So, the large black shape turns into the small gray shape, the midsized white shape turns into the large black shape, and the small gray shape turns into the midsized white shape. Looking at the second figure in order to predict the third one, the large black circle will become a small gray circle, the midsized white square will become a large black square, and the small gray diamond will become a midsized white diamond. This figure can be seen in answer choice (C), which is the correct answer.

17. (D)

    In this series, one gray triangle is being added counterclockwise in each new figure. The fifth figure should have four gray triangles that cover the bottom half of the figure. Answer choice (D) is correct.

18. (A)

    In this series, the shape in the figure alternates between being a triangle and a pentagon. Since the fourth figure is a pentagon, the correct answer is going to be a triangle. So, you can narrow down your answer choices to (A), (D), and (E). The triangle is pointing up in the first figure and to the right in the third figure, so it must point down in the fifth figure. Answer choice (A) must be the correct answer. To double-check, take a look at the number of small black circles in each triangle in the series. The first triangle has three small black circles. The second triangle has six small black circles. There must be nine small black circles in the third triangle. This confirms that answer choice (A) is correct.

19. (C)

    The black bars in this series are moving upward from figure to figure. After the black bar reaches the top, it drops to the bottom and begins to move upward again. Each new figure has a white arrow that changes direction; the arrow is moving counterclockwise and points to the right, then up, then to the left, and finally down. Applying these patterns, the next figure in the series should have a black bar in the second row with a white arrow pointing to the right. Answer choice (C) is correct.

20. (A)

    The pattern in this series is that the small shape becomes the large shape in the next figure, and the arrow on the new small shape moves 90 degrees counterclockwise. So, for the next figure in the series, you should expect to see a large star with a new small shape inside it that has an arrow pointing upward. This figure can be seen in answer choice (A

21. (E)

    Here, the squares are alternating between white and gray. According to this pattern, the next figure in the series will be a white square. The triangles also alternate in color between black and white, so the next figure also must have black triangles. You can narrow down your possible answer choices to (B), (D), and (E). In the white squares, the black triangles are always pointing to the left and right sides. The only answer choice with triangles pointing to the left and right is answer choice (E). The triangles are also increasing by two on each side in each new white square. Thus, there should be five black triangles pointing to the left and five black triangles pointing to the right in the next figure. Answer choice (E) is correct.

22. (C)

    Here, in every other figure, you have either a small gray circle moving clockwise from corner to corner around the hexagon or a small gray square moving counterclockwise from corner to corner around the hexagon. Since the fourth figure contains a small gray square, the next figure must contain a small gray circle. In the third figure, the small gray circle was at the leftmost point of the hexagon. In the fifth figure, the small gray circle should be in the upper left-hand corner of the hexagon. The figure in answer choice (C) shows this, so it is the correct answer.

23. (D)

    In every other figure, you have either five squares or five triangles. Since the fourth figure has five triangles, the next figure in the series will have five squares. The number of gray squares in each new figure is being reduced by one. There are three gray squares in the third figure, so there should only be two gray squares in the fifth figure. Answer choice (D) is the correct answer.

24. (C)

    In this question, you're given a repeating pattern in the first three figures, and the fourth figure looks just like the first figure. That must mean that the fifth figure has to look just like the second figure. Answer choice (C) looks just like the second figure, so it must be the correct answer.

OLSAT® Preparation Guide - Levels D, E, and F

Number Series

OLSAT® Preparation Guide - Levels D, E, and F

Number Series Strategies

The number series questions in the Quantitative Reasoning section of the OLSAT® are all about finding patterns. That is the entire key to answering these questions correctly. As with analogies, if you can discover the correct relationship or pattern, it will become easier for you to find the correct answer.

The questions on this test are just like the example below. Each question has a series of numbers. Find out the rule associated with each series, and then find out what number must come next by applying the same rule.

Example: 1   2   3   4   5   ?

A. 6   B. 7   C. 8   D. 9   E. 5

Looking at the series above, you can tell that 1 is being added to each number in order to get the next number in the series. Thus, the next number after 5 will be 6, or answer choice (A).

Approach these problems in a systematic way. With each of these questions, you will want to go through each number in the series in order until you have found a definite pattern. So, look at the first number and determine what you need to do to get the second number. Then, look at the second number and see what you need to do to get the third number. Keep doing this until you have discovered the pattern.

Mark between the numbers. Write a math symbol like +3 or –2 between the numbers to help you determine the pattern.

Realize that there may be more than one pattern. Sometimes there will be two different patterns in a number series. These different patterns will usually affect only certain places in the series. For example, you may have one pattern that affects the first, third, and fifth places in the numbers series. That is, some math operation is happening to the number in the first position that creates the number in the third position. There might also be a different pattern that is affecting the numbers in the second, fourth, and sixth places in the number series.

Watch out for a mix of numbers and letters. In a similar vein, there might be numbers *and* letters in a series. Usually, there will be different patterns for the numbers and letters.

Look out for overall patterns. Sometimes you might have to find the overall pattern of the numbers and letters in a series. For example, you might have a series that has a number followed by two letters, then a number followed by two letters. At this point, you should look at the last item in the series to determine whether the correct answer is going to be a number or a letter. Whichever one it is, you should only focus on determining the pattern of the answer you are looking for. You may also be able to eliminate some answer choices by determining the overall pattern.

OLSAT® Preparation Guide - Levels D, E, and F　　　Bright Kids NYC Inc. ©

Number Series Questions

1.

What comes next in the series?

| 5 | 7 | 9 | 11 | 13 | 15 | ? |

A. 17   B. 20   C. 21   D. 18   E. 12

2.

What comes next in the series?

| 3 | 5 | 7 | 9 | 11 | 13 | ? |

A. 17   B. 14   C. 15   D. 16   E. 12

3.

What comes next in the series?

| 0 | 4 | 8 | 12 | 16 | 20 | ? |

A. 17   B. 22   C. 21   D. 18   E. 24

4.

What comes next in the series?

| 9 | 11 | 13 | 15 | 17 | 19 | ? |

A. 23   B. 22   C. 21   D. 18   E. 20

5.

What comes next in the series?

| 2 | 4 | 6 | 8 | 10 | 12 | ? |

A. 10   B. 14   C. 16   D. 18   E. 4

6.

What comes next in the series?

| 5 | 10 | 15 | 20 | 25 | 30 | ? |

A. 15   B. 30   C. 40   D. 25   E. 35

7.

What comes next in the series?

| 13 | 18 | 16 | 21 | 19 | 24 | ? |

A. 29   B. 22   C. 25   D. 21   E. 19

8.

What comes next in the series?

2	8	13	17	20	22	?

A. 23   B. 22   C. 17   D. 20   E. 19

9.

What comes next in the series?

5	7	4	6	3	5	?

A. 4   B. 5   C. 2   D. 10   E. 8

10.

What comes next in the series?

11	14	12	15	13	16	?

A. 19   B. 14   C. 13   D. 17   E. 18

11.

What comes next in the series?

3	4	7	12	19	28	?

A. 40   B. 35   C. 34   D. 37   E. 39

12.

What comes next in the series?

1	4	2	6	4	9	?

A. 4   B. 5   C. 8   D. 7   E. 9

13.

What number is missing in the series?

7	12	17	22	?	32	37

A. 24   B. 25   C. 28   D. 27   E. 30

14.

What number is missing in the series?

9	13	?	21	25	29	33

A. 17   B. 20   C. 24   D. 28   E. 32

15.

What number is missing in the series?

| 9 | 19 | ? | 39 | 49 | 59 |

A. 17   B. 29   C. 24   D. 28   E. 28

16.

What number is missing in the series?

| 0 | ? | 14 | 21 | 28 | 35 | 42 |

A. 7   B. 29   C. 8   D. 10   E. 6

17.

What comes next in the series?

| 10 | 9 | 13 | 12 | 16 | 15 | 19 | ? |

A. 17   B. 22   C. 18   D. 10   E. 21

18.

What comes next in the series?

| 25 | 20 | 30 | 25 | 35 | 30 | 40 | ? |

A. 30   B. 20   C. 25   D. 35   E. 45

19.

What comes next in the series?

| A | C | E | G | I | K | ? |

A. L   B. M   C. N   D. O   E. P

20.

What comes next in the series?

| Z | A | X | C | V | E | ? |

A. D   B. M   C. S   D. U   E. T

21.

What comes next in the series?

| 1 | A | 2 | B | 3 | C | 4 | D | 5 | ? |

A. F   B. E   C. 6   D. 4

22.

What comes next in the series?

| B | C | 3 | C | D | 4 | D | E | 5 | E | F | 6 | ? |

A. F   B. E   C. 6   D. 7

23.

What comes next in the series?

| 1 | A | B | 2 | B | C | 3 | C | D | ? |

A. 5   B. E   C. D   D. 4

24.

What comes next in the series?

| 1 | 5 | A | B | 2 | 6 | C | D | 3 | ? |

A. E   B. 9   C. 7   D. F

25.

What comes next in the series?

| 1 | 2 | 2A1 | 3 | 4 | 4A3 | 5 | 6 | ? |

A. 7A6   B. 6A5   C. 7   D. 5A6   E. 6A7

26.

What comes next in the series?

| K | 24 | L | 22 | M | 20 | N | ? |

A. 18   B. 16   C. 0   D. P   E. 22

27.

What comes next in the series?

| 12 | Z | 10 | X | 14 | V | 16 | ? |

A. S   B. 12   C. 18   D. T   E. U

28.

What comes next in the series?

| F | 24 | H | 29 | J | 24 | L | ? |

A. 18   B. 16   C. 29   D. P   E. 22

29.

What comes next in the series?

| 32 | D | 27 | G | 22 | J | 17 | ? |

A. N   B. M   C. O   D. 19   E. 18

30.

What comes next in the series?

| 2 | 4 | 5 | 10 | 11 | 22 | ? |

A. 26   B. 24   C. 18   D. 21   E. 23

31.

What comes next in the series?

| 1 | 3 | 6 | 8 | 11 | 13 | ? |

A. 15   B. 20   C. 16   D. 18   E. 22

32.

What comes next in the series?

| 12 | 11 | 13 | 10 | 14 | 9 | ? |

A. 14   B. 15   C. 10   D. 11   E. 14

33.

What comes next in the series?

| 30 | 23 | 28 | 21 | 26 | 19 | ? |

A. 11   B. 15   C. 24   D. 20   E. 18

34.

What comes next in the series?

| 32 | 24 | 31 | 37 | 32 | 36 | ? |

A. 32   B. 34   C. 35   D. 28   E. 39

35.

What comes next in the series?

| 20 | 23 | 21 | 25 | 22 | 27 | ? |

A. 11   B. 15   C. 23   D. 20   E. 18

36.

What comes next in the series?

| 40 | 20 | 24 | 12 | 16 | 8 | ? |

A. 24   B. 10   C. 12   D. 20   E. 18

Number Series Answer Key

1. (A) 17

Remember that the main focus with these types of questions is finding the pattern of the operation or operations being used with the numbers. So, look at each number and see what you can do to each number in order to get the next number. Here, you add 2 to the previous number in order to get the next number in the sequence. The last number given is 15, so the next number in the series is 17 (choice A).

2. (C) 15

This question has the same pattern as the previous question. That is, you need to add 2 to the previous number to get the next number in the series. The correct answer is 15 (choice C).

3. (E) 24

Here, every number has 4 added to it in order to get the next number in the sequence. The last number in the series is 20, so the answer must be 20 + 4 = 24 (choice E).

4. (C) 21

Here's another sequence in which you just have to add 2 to the previous number. These should be quite easy for you. The correct answer is 21 (choice C).

5. (B) 14

This is another easy one in which you just need to add 2 to the last number to get 14—answer choice (B)—as the next number in the series.

6. (E) 35

The pattern here is 5 being added to every number to get the next number in the series. Looking at the last number, which is 30, we know that the next number has to be 35 (choice E).

7. (B) 22

With this question, you're now encountering a pattern that changes from number to number. You're going to want to focus to see if you can detect a pattern in the equations being used on each number in the series. So, to get from 13 to 18, you need to add 5 to 13. Put a +5 between the two numbers. To get from 18 to 16, you need to subtract 2. Put a −2 between the next numbers. To get from 16 to 21, you need to add 5 to 16. It looks as though the pattern is +5 to one number and then −2 to the next number. Following that pattern, you should subtract 2 from 24 to get 22 (choice B) as your answer.

8. (A) 23

This is another changing pattern question. So, let's start with the first number and work our way through the series. To get from 2 to 8, you need to add 6 to 2. Put a +6 between the two numbers. To get from 8 to 13, you need to add 5 to 8. Put a +5 between the numbers 8 and 13 in the number series. To get from 13 to 17, you need to add 4 to 13. Put a +4 between the two numbers. It looks as though our pattern is +6, +5, +4, +3, and so on. Following this pattern, you will have to add 1 to 22 in order to get 23 (choice A) as the next number in the series.

9. (C) 2

Use the method mentioned above to find the pattern in the equations in this number series. You should find that the pattern is +2 and then –3. Write down this pattern between the numbers, and after the last number in the series you should get –3. So, in order to get the next number, you need to subtract 3 from 5. The correct answer is (C) 2.

10. (B) 14

The correct pattern for this question is +3 and then –2. Writing out the pattern, you should end up with 16 – 2 = 14, so 14 is the next number in the series.

11. (E) 39

Using your usual method, you should get a pattern of +1, +3, and +5. The pattern seems to be that you add 2 to your adding pattern every time. So, put +7 between the 12 and 19, and +9 between the 19 and 28. In order to find the next number in the series, you will need to add 11 to 28. That yields a sum of 39, so answer choice (E) is correct.

12. (D) 7

With this question, you may need to write out all of the equations in order to find the correct pattern. If you do this, your pattern should be +3, –2 , +4, –2 , +5. It seems that the pattern is that the added numbers are increasing by 1 after each subtraction of 2. If the pattern were to continue, it would be –2, +6, –2, +7, –2, +8, and so on. However, we only need to subtract 2 in order to get the next number in the series. 9 – 2 = 7, so answer choice (D) is correct.

13. (D) 27

This question is a bit easier. We can see that the pattern is just adding 5 to the previous number, so adding 5 to 22 will yield 27. The correct answer is (D).

14. (A) 17

Here is where things can get a little trickier since the missing number (represented by the first question mark) is in the middle of the number sequence instead of at the end. Looking at the first number, you know that you can add 4 to 9 to get 13. So, you can place +4 between those two numbers. However, the next number is not given, so you have no idea what number is added or subtracted to 13 to get the mystery number. You also have no idea what is added or subtracted to the mystery number to get 21. But, if you look at the other numbers in the series, you can see that the +4 pattern can be placed in the next two spaces. Thus, +4 must be the pattern for every number. 13 + 4 = 17, so answer choice (A) is correct.

15. (B) 29

This question presents a similar situation. Calculating all the spaces between the numbers you are given, you should find that the pattern is +10. 19 + 10 = 29, so the correct answer is (B).

16. (A) 7

Employing the same method that you used in the previous two questions, you should get a pattern of +7 in all of the spaces. 0 + 7 = 7, which makes (A) the correct answer.

17. (C) 18

The pattern in this number series is –1, +4, –1, +4. So, you're just subtracting 1 from a number to get a new number, adding 4 to a number to get the next number, and so on. Writing out the pattern between the numbers, you should get 19 – 1 = 18. The next number in the series is 18. The correct answer is (C).

18. (D) 35

The pattern in this number series is –5, +10, –5, +10. Continuing the pattern out to the last number, you should get 40 – 5 = 35, which is answer choice (D).

19. (B) M

Here, you have a series of letters instead of numbers. Don't worry, though—in many ways, the method is the same for determining the pattern. The first letter in the sequence is A, the second letter is C, and the third letter is E. Can you see a relationship here? The next letter in the sequence always moves ahead 2 letters in the alphabet from the previous letter. So, after E comes G, and so on. The last letter is K, so moving ahead 2 letters takes you to M. The correct answer is (B).

20. (E) T

This is a bit of a tougher question. There are actually two patterns going on here. On the 1st, 3rd, 5th, etc., letters in the sequence, you are moving 2 letters back from Z. So, that pattern is Z, X, V. And on the 2nd, 4th, 6th, etc., letters in the sequence, you are moving 2 letters forward from A. That pattern is A, C, E. Because you are looking for the 7th letter in the sequence, you are using the first pattern. What letter is two letters behind V? The answer is T (choice E).

21. (B) E

This question employs the same type of concept as the previous question. There are two different patterns here, one involving numbers and the other involving letters. The 1st, 3rd, 5th, 7th, and 9th places are numbers, and the 2nd, 4th, 6th, and 8th places are letters. Since you are looking for the 10th place in the sequence, you are looking for a letter. Every letter in that sequence only moves up by 1 letter. So, after D, the next letter is E (choice B).

22. (A) F

The pattern here is 2 letters followed by a number, a repetition of the last letter, then the next letter in the alphabet, and then adding 1 to the previous number in the sequence. If you follow this pattern, the next letter in the sequence will be F (choice A).

23. (D) 4

The pattern here is a number followed by 2 letters, which are then followed by another number. The numbers are increasing by 1 every time, and the letters are moving up alphabetically, but the last letter is repeated when you come to the next two-letter sequence. So, after CD, you're going to have a number. The previous number in the series was 3, so the next number must be 4. Answer choice (D) is correct.

24. (C) 7

Here you have 2 numbers, then 2 letters, then 2 numbers, and so on. For the numbers, 4 is added to the previous number in order to get the next number. After the letter, 3 is subtracted from the previous number in the series to get the next number. This pattern repeats. The letters just go up alphabetically. Since the last item we see in the series is a number, we know that the next item in the series must be a number. To get that number, we will have to add 4 to 3. The next number is 7 (choice C).

25. (B) 6A5

The pattern here is that there are 2 numbers, then a number/letter combination, followed by 2 numbers, and so on. The numbers are just increasing by 1 every time. The number/letter combinations always have an A in the middle. The numbers to the left and right of the A are identical to the pair of numbers that precede that number/letter combination, but they're in reverse order. So, the first number/letter combination is 2A1, and the second number/letter combination is 4A3. Looking at the overall pattern, we know that the next item is the series is going to be a number/letter combination. Using our pattern, that combination should be 6A5, which is answer choice (B).

26. (A) 18

The overall pattern is a letter, a number, a letter, a number, and so on. The pattern of the letters is that they are going up 1 letter each time. The pattern of the numbers is that they are subtracting 2 from the previous number each time. Based on the overall pattern, the next item in the series will be a number. The previous number was 20, so the next number has to be 18. Answer choice (A) is correct.

27. (D) T

The overall pattern is a number, a letter, a number, a letter, and so on. Thus, you should only focus on the pattern of the letters because the next item in the series has to be a letter. If you were to look at the numbers, you'd actually have a hard time finding out the pattern. Don't waste your time. Looking at the letters, you can see that they are going back 2 letters each time, starting from Z. The last letter in the series is V, so the next number has to be T (choice D).

28. (C) 29

The overall pattern is a letter followed by a number, then a letter followed by a number, and so on. Since the last item in the series is a letter, you are looking for a number. The numbers seem to alternate between 24 and 29. Since 29 is one of the answer choices, this must be the correct answer.

29. (B) M

The overall pattern is number, letter, number, letter, and so on. The last item in the series is a number, so you're looking for a letter. The first letter is D, the second letter is G, and the third letter is J. The pattern is that the next letter is 3 letters ahead of the previous letter. So, the next letter in the series should be M (choice B).

30. (E) 23

Here's a pattern that involves both addition and multiplication. Looking at the first number, you can see that you either add 2 or multiply by 2 to get from 2 to 4. The third number in the sequence is 5, so you had to add 1 there. The fourth number in the sequence is 10. Now you know that multiplying by 2 was the first operation in this series. The pattern is x2, +1, x2, +1. Following this pattern, you're going to have to add 1 to the last number in the series to get your answer. The correct answer is 23 (choice E).

31. (C) 16

The pattern here is +2, +3, +2, +3. Continue out this pattern and your answer will be 16 (choice C).

32. (B) 15

The pattern in this question is a bit tricky to discover. But, if you do the operations to see what you need to do to get each number, you should discover a pattern of –1, +2, –3, +4, –5. So, the numbers are increasing by one each time and alternating between addition and subtraction. The next operation should be +6, so 9 + 6 = 15, which is answer choice (B).

33. (C) 24

The pattern in this question is –7, +5, –7, +5. Continue out this pattern and you should get 19 + 5 = 24, which is answer choice (C).

34. (E) 39

The pattern is –8, +7, +6, –5, +4. So, the numbers are going down sequentially, and the pattern of the signs is –, +, +, –, +, +. The next number in the pattern is going to be +3, so 36 + 3 = 39, which is answer choice (E).

35. (C) 23

This pattern is a bit tricky. If you try to identify a single pattern from one number to the next, you will quickly see that there isn't one. Instead, there are two different patterns in this number series. There is a pattern for the 1st, 3rd, and 5th numbers and a different pattern for the 2nd, 4th, and 6th numbers. Although you should not waste time finding the pattern of the 2nd, 4th, and 6th numbers, for your information, it is +2. For the 1st, 3rd, and 5th numbers, it is +1. Since we want to find the 7th number in this series, we need to add 1 to the 5th number. 22 + 1 = 23, which is answer choice (C).

36. (C) 12

The pattern in this number series is a combination of division and addition. The pattern is ÷2, +4, ÷2, +4. Following this pattern, you will need to add 4 to the last number in the series. Your answer will be 12 (choice C).

OLSAT® Preparation Guide - Levels D, E, and F

Numeric Inferences

Numeric Inferences Strategies

Patterns are once again the name of the game for the numeric inference questions in the Quantitative Reasoning section of the OLSAT®. You're probably even seeing a pattern in how the OLSAT® loves to test you on whether you can find patterns or relationships between different words or numbers. The more adept you become at detecting patterns, the better you will score on the various sections of the OLSAT®. For the questions in this section, there will be three boxes, and each box will contain either two or three numbers. The numbers in each box will be related to each other in some way; that is, some mathematic operation will be performed on the first number in the box to get the second number in the box, and so on. This mathematic operation is the same for each box. There will be a missing number in one or two of the boxes. Your task will be to find the missing number or numbers. Below is an example of a numeric inference question:

| 5, 15 | | 20, 60 | | 30, ? |

Looking at the numbers in the boxes, you are supposed to determine the relationship between the pairs or trios of numbers, which will allow you to find the missing number(s) in the box(es). In the above example, what is being done to the first number to get the second number in each box? For the first box, the first number is being multiplied by 3 to get the second number. This pattern recurs in the second box. To find the missing number in the third box, you will have to multiply the first number by 3. 30 x 3 = 90. The missing number is 90.

Determine what is being done to the first number to get the second number. Ask yourself this question every time you encounter a numeric inference question. Determining the answer to this question will give you the pattern of the operation being used in the boxes. This is the key to discovering the correct answer.

Use both mental and written computation. You may find that you're able to mentally figure out what is being done to the first number to get the second number. That's the easiest way to solve these problems. However, if you find that you cannot picture the operation in your head, there are easy ways to write out this process as an equation.

<u>Second number is larger than first number</u>

Either addition or multiplication is being used. If addition is being used, you need to subtract the first number from the second number to find out the pattern. If multiplication is being used, you need to divide the second number by the first number to find out the pattern. Examples are shown below ("P" represents the pattern number you are trying to find):

Addition: | 9, 17 |

What is being done to 9 to get 17? The equation is $9 + P = 17$. You can subtract 9 from both sides and get: $P = 17 - 9 = 8$. 8 is being added to 9 to get 17.

Multiplication: 8, 32

What is being done to 8 to get 32? The equation is 8 x P = 32. You can divide both sides by 8 to isolate the P. Now, your equation is: P = 32/8 = 4. 8 is being multiplied by 4 to get 32.

<u>Second number is smaller than first number</u>

Either subtraction or division is being used. If subtraction is being used, you need to subtract the second number from the first number to find out the pattern. If division is being used, you need to divide the first number by the second number to figure out the pattern. Examples are shown below (P once again represents the pattern number you are trying to find):

Subtraction: 24, 10

What is being done to 24 to get 10? The equation is 24 – P = 10. Whenever you have a subtraction operation occurring in these questions, your final equation will be P = First number – Second number.

Division: 100, 25

What is being done to 100 to get 25? The equation is 100/P = 25. If you bring the P to the other side of the equation, you now have P x 25 = 100. You can isolate the P by dividing both sides by 25. Now, you have P = 100/25 = 4, so 100 is being divided by 4 to get 25. Whenever you have a division operation occurring in a numeric inference question, your final equation will be P = First number/Second number.

Watch out for nonconstant patterns. Sometimes, the pattern that is occurring in one box will not be the same as the pattern that is occurring in another box. At this point, you need to look at both patterns and try to determine whether you can see any relationship between the pair. For example, the pattern for one box may be adding 5 to the first number to get the second number. We can represent this pattern with +5. The pattern for the second box may be adding 7 to the first number to get the second number. We can represent this pattern with +7. So, our two patterns are +5 and +7. It looks as though the pattern is increasing by 2 every time. Therefore, the pattern for the third box is going to be +9, or adding 9 to the first number in the box.

Be careful with your arithmetic. Once you figure out the pattern, all you need to do is apply the pattern to the first number in the third box to get your answer. Be careful with your arithmetic on this part!

Numeric Inferences Questions

The numbers in each box go together using the same rule. Apply this rule to find which answer choice goes where you see the question mark.

| 0, 0 | | 1, 1 | | 2, ? |

A. 2   B. 0   C. 1   D. 3

The numbers in each box go together using the same rule. Apply this rule to find which answer choice goes where you see the question mark.

| 2, 1 | | 3, 2 | | 4, ? |

A. 4   B. 3   C. 1   D. 6

The numbers in each box go together using the same rule. Apply this rule to find which answer choice goes where you see the question mark.

| 1, 2 | | 3, 4 | | 5, ? |

A. 5   B. 6   C. 4   D. 7

The numbers in each box go together using the same rule. Apply this rule to find which answer choice goes where you see the question mark.

| 1, 3 | | 2, 4 | | 3, ? |

A. 6   B. 7   C. 5   D. 4

The numbers in each box go together using the same rule. Apply this rule to find which answer choice goes where you see the question mark.

| 1, 3 | | 2, 6 | | 3, ? |

A. 8   B. 9   C. 10   D. 12

The numbers in each box go together using the same rule. Apply this rule to find which answer choice goes where you see the question mark.

| 3, 6 | | 5, 8 | | 7, ? |

A. 12   B. 10   C. 14   D. 16

7.

The numbers in each box go together using the same rule. Apply this rule to find which answer choice goes where you see the question mark.

| 2, 4 | | 4, 8 | | 6, ? | A. 12 B. 14 C. 16 D. 18

8.

The numbers in each box go together using the same rule. Apply this rule to find which answer choice goes where you see the question mark.

| 6, 2 | | 9, 3 | | 12, ? | A. 5 B. 4 C. 9 D. 6

9.

The numbers in each box go together using the same rule. Apply this rule to find which answer choice goes where you see the question mark.

| 18, 9 | | 16, 8 | | 14, ? | A. 9 B. 7 C. 4 D. 3

10.

The numbers in each box go together using the same rule. Apply this rule to find which answer choice goes where you see the question mark.

| 12, 6 | | 8, 4 | | 4, ? | A. 2 B. 5 C. 1 D. 6

11.

The numbers in each box go together using the same rule. Apply this rule to find which answer choice goes where you see the question mark.

| 5, 11 | | 7, 15 | | 9, ? | A. 20 B. 21 C. 18 D. 15 E. 19

12.

The numbers in each box go together using the same rule. Apply this rule to find which answer choice goes where you see the question mark.

| 2, 4 | | 8, 16 | | 14, ? | A. 20 B. 22 C. 18 D. 29 E. 28

13.

The numbers in each box go together using the same rule. Apply this rule to find which answer choice goes where you see the question mark.

| 5, 10 | | 10, 20 | | 15, ? | A. 40 | B. 30 | C. 50 | D. 20 | E. 10 |

14.

The numbers in each box go together using the same rule. Apply this rule to find which answer choice goes where you see the question mark.

| 4, 12 | | 5, 15 | | 6, ? | A. 18 | B. 12 | C. 14 | D. 24 | E. 30 |

15.

The numbers in each box go together using the same rule. Apply this rule to find which answer choice goes where you see the question mark.

| 2, 20 | | 3, 30 | | 4, ? | A. 20 | B. 30 | C. 40 | D. 50 | E. 60 |

16.

The numbers in each box go together using the same rule. Apply this rule to find which answer choice goes where you see the question mark.

| 1, 4 | | 5, 20 | | 10, ? | A. 40 | B. 25 | C. 20 | D. 15 | E. 30 |

17.

The numbers in each box go together using the same rule. Apply this rule to find which answer choice goes where you see the question mark.

| 40, 20 | | 30, 15 | | 20, ? | A. 10 | B. 5 | C. 25 | D. 30 | E. 40 |

18.

The numbers in each box go together using the same rule. Apply this rule to find which answer choice goes where you see the question mark.

| 2, 12 | | 3, 18 | | 4, ? | A. 20 | B. 24 | C. 28 | D. 36 | E. 32 |

19.

The numbers in each box go together using the same rule. Apply this rule to find which answer choice goes where you see the question mark.

| 12, 10 | | 8, 6 | | 6, ? | A. 4 | B. 2 | C. 6 | D. 8 | E. 12 |

20.

The numbers in each box go together using the same rule. Apply this rule to find which answer choice goes where you see the question mark.

| 100, 50 | | 80, 40 | | 60, ? | A. 30 | B. 25 | C. 20 | D. 15 | E. 10 |

21.

The numbers in each box go together using the same rule. Apply this rule to find which answer choices goes where you see the question marks.

| 3, 9 | | ?, 18 | | 9, ? | A. 9, 24 | B. 9, 27 | C. 7, 21 | D. 3, 18 | E. 6, 27 |

22.

The numbers in each box go together using the same rule. Apply this rule to find which answer choices goes where you see the question marks.

| 4, 20 | | ?, 25 | | 6, ? | A. 5, 24 | B. 4, 40 | C. 4, 30 | D. 5, 25 | E. 5, 30 |

23.

The numbers in each box go together using the same rule. Apply this rule to find which answer choice goes where you see the question mark.

| 8, 14 | | 10, 18 | | 12, ? |

A. 20   B. 22   C. 24   D. 18   E. 28

24.

The numbers in each box go together using the same rule. Apply this rule to find which answer choice goes where you see the question mark.

| 10, 6 | | 20, 14 | | 30, ? |

A. 21   B. 22   C. 17   D. 15   E. 20

25.

The numbers in each box go together using the same rule. Apply this rule to find which answer choices goes where you see the question marks.

| 1, 3, 5 | | 7, ?, 11 | | 13, ?, 17 |

A. 9, 15   B. 7, 15   C. 5, 22   D. 1, 11   E. 9, 12

OLSAT® Preparation Guide - Levels D, E, and F

Bright Kids NYC Inc. ©

Numeric Inferences Answer Key

1. (A) 2

The pattern is that the first number in each box is being repeated to get the second number. Since the first number in the third box is 2, the missing number has to be 2 as well. The correct answer is (A).

2. (B) 3

In this question, the pattern is that the first number is being decreased by 1 to get the second number. In the third box, the first number is 4, so the second number must be 3. Answer choice (B) is correct.

3. (B) 6

The first number in each box is being increased by 1. The first number in the third box is 5, so the missing number must be 6, which is answer choice (B).

4. (C) 5

The pattern for this question is that 2 is being added to the first number to get the second number. 3 + 2 = 5, so answer choice (C) is correct.

5. (B) 9

Here's our first question in this section that deals with multiplication. The first number is being multiplied by 3 to get the second number. The first number in the third box is 3, so the missing number can be found by multiplying 3 by 3 to get 9. Answer choice (B) is correct.

6. (B) 10

In this question, the first number is being increased by 3 to get the second number. 7 + 3 = 10, so answer choice (B) is correct.

7. (A) 12

Looking at the first box, you might think that the first number is being increased by 2. The second box, however, doesn't fit that pattern, so now we know that multiplication is at work here. One way you could think of the equation to get the second number in the second box is $4 \times P = 8$, where P stands for the pattern number that you are trying to identify. How will you figure out what P is? You can think of what could be multiplied by 4 in order to get 8. You can also change the equation above to a division equation. You can divide both sides of the equation by 4 and cancel out the 4 on the left-hand side of the equation. Now, your equation is $P = 8/4$. So, you could just divide 8 by 4 to get your answer. Either equation or way of thinking is correct. The pattern is that the first number in each box is being multiplied by 2 to get the second number. So, for the third box, $6 \times 2 = 12$. The missing number is 12, so (A) is the correct answer.

8. **(B) 4**

Because the numbers are decreasing in each box, the pattern has to involve either subtraction or division. For the first box, it seems as though 4 could be the number being subtracted from the first number to get the second number. However, this pattern doesn't hold for the second box. This must be our first division problem. What can 6 be divided by that would give you 2 (6/P = 2)? Or, in other words, what is 6 divided by 2 (P = 6/2)? You can also turn this around to a multiplication problem and ask yourself, what can 2 be multiplied by to get 6 (2 x P = 6)? What is 6 divided by 2? The answer is 3, so our pattern involves dividing the first number by 3 in order to get the second number. Now it's time to look at the third box. What is 12 divided by 3? The correct answer is 4, which is answer choice (B).

9. **(B) 7**

What is happening to the first number in each box that could get you the second number in each box? It looks like a division operation since there isn't a constant number being subtracted from the first number in both boxes. The answer is that you need to divide the first number by 2 in order to get the second number. If you had trouble figuring this out in your head, you could write out the equation as 18/P = 9, where P stands for the pattern number that you are trying to find. If you want to find out what P is in this type of equation, all you need to do is divide 18 by 9 to get 2. If you have an equation like this and you don't like division, try imagining what could be multiplied by 9 to get 18. Since you're dividing by 2, your equation for the third box is 14/2 = 7. The missing number is 7, so answer choice (B) is correct.

10. **(A) 2**

The first number is being divided by 2 in each box to get the second number. 4/2 = 2, so answer choice (A) is correct.

11. **(E) 19**

Here's our first example of an operation that changes from one box to the next. The key here will be to find a pattern in the changes. In the first box, you can see that 6 is being added to the first number to get the second number. In the second box, you can see that 8 is being added to the first number to get the second number. So, the pattern is +6, +8, and then another number. It seems as though +10 would be the next logical choice since the pattern numbers are increasing by 2 after each box. 9 + 10 = 19. Answer choice (E) is correct.

12. **(E) 28**

The first number is being multiplied by 2 to get the second number. To find the missing number, we need to multiply 14 by 2. 14 x 2 = 28, which makes answer choice (E) the correct answer.

13. **(B) 30**

The pattern here is that the first number is being multiplied by 2 to get the second number. 15 x 2 = 30, so answer choice (B) is correct.

14. (A) 18

Multiply the first number by 3 to get the second number. The missing number is 18, so the correct answer choice is (A).

15. (C) 40

Looking at the large increase from the first number to the second number in each of the boxes, it's safe to assume that multiplication is at work here. What can 2 be multiplied by to get 20? How about 10? Turning to the second box, since 3 x 10 = 30, you know that 10 must be the number being multiplied by the first number to get the second number. 4 x 10 = 40, which makes answer choice (C) correct.

16. (A) 40

Here, you need to multiply the first number by 4 to get the second number. Looking at the third box, you need to multiply the equation 10 x 4 to get the missing number. Answer choice (A), 40, is correct.

17. (A) 10

Division is at work here. The first number is being divided by 2 to get the second number in the box. In the third box, the first number is 20, so the missing number must be 10. Answer choice (A) is correct.

18. (B) 24

An equation you could set up to help you find the pattern would be 2 x P = 12. What could 2 be multiplied by in order to get the product 12? You could also move the 2 over to the other side of the equation by dividing both sides by 2. Now, your equation is P = 12/2 = 6. So, you need to multiply the first number by 6 to get the second number. Looking at the third box, to find your missing number, you will need to multiply 4 by 6. The missing number is 24, which is answer choice (B).

19. (A) 4

Subtract 2 from the first number to get the second number. 6 – 2 = 4, so answer choice (A) is correct.

20. (A) 30

What can you divide 100 by in order to get 50? Or, what can you multiply 50 by if you want to get 100? Your equation can be 100/ P = 50. You can bring the P over to the other side of the equation by multiplying both sides of the equation by P. Now, the P is canceled out from the left-hand side of the equation, so your new equation is 100 = 50 x P. What can 50 be multiplied by to get the product 100? If you don't know, you can isolate the P by dividing both sides of the equation by 50. Now, your equation is P = 100/50. Your pattern number is 2, which means that the first number in each box needs to be divided by 2 in order to get the second number in the box. One shortcut for all of this is to remember that the equation 100/P = 50 is exactly the same as 100/50 = P. So, whenever you ask yourself, "What can 100 be divided by in order to get 50?" you can just divide 100 by 50 to get your answer. Now you just need to plug your pattern into the third box by using the equation 60/2 = 30. Answer choice (A) is correct.

21. (E) 6, 27

This is our first multiple missing number question in the numeric inference section. Looking at the first box, it would seem that the first number is being multiplied by 3 to get the second number. So, turning to the second box, you are going to have to find a number that, when multiplied by 3, will equal 18. If you were to write out this equation, it would be 3 x ? = 18, where ? is the missing number. To figure out the missing number, you need to divide 18 by 3, so ? = 18/3 = 6. Our missing number in the second box is 6. The only answer choice with 6 as the first missing number is (E), so (E) should be correct. Let's see if the other missing number in the answer choice works, though. According to our pattern, the second number in the third box should be 9 x 3 = 27. Answer choice (E) is correct.

22. (E) 5, 30

Looking at the first box, a possible pattern between the first and second numbers might be to multiply the first number by 5 in order to get the second number. Moving on to the second box, what would you have to multiply by 5 in order to get 25? So, 5 x ? = 25, which can be changed to ? = 25/5 = 5. 5 can be multiplied by 5 to get 25. How about the second missing number? 6 x 5 = 30. Is there an answer choice listed for 5 and 30 as the missing numbers in the boxes? There sure is. So, answer choice (E) is correct.

23. (B) 22

Since the second number in each of the boxes isn't a multiple of the first number, you can assume that addition is going to be used to find the patterns in the boxes. In the first box, 6 is added to the first number to get the second number. In the second box, 8 is added to the first number to get the second number. Following this pattern, it looks as though 10 will be added to the first number to get the second number in the third box. So, 12 + 10 = 22, which means that answer choice (B) is correct.

24. (B) 22

The pattern for the first box is to subtract 4 from the first number to get the second number. The pattern for the second box is to subtract 6 from the first number to get the second number. The pattern for the third box might be to subtract 8 from the first number to get the second number. 30 – 8 = 22. Answer choice (B) is correct.

25. (A) 9, 15

We have three numbers in each box in this question. In the first box, 2 is being added to each number to get the next number in the box. That would mean that the missing number in the second box is 9, and the missing number in the third box is 15. Answer choice (A) is correct.

Number Matrices

Number Matrices Strategies

The number matrices questions in the Quantitative Reasoning section of the OLSAT® is another section that is mainly concerned with patterns. In this section, you are going to be shown a group of numbers that are inside a matrix. In mathematics, a matrix is an array of numbers in a rectangular box. The placement of the numbers in the box is often important. The numbers are placed in rows and columns inside the box. In the number matrices on the OLSAT®, there will be a missing number that will be represented by a question mark. You will be asked to find the missing number. Here is an example of a matrix:

2	4	8
4	8	?

The number matrices that you will be given in this section of the OLSAT® will all have some kind of number pattern in both their rows and their columns. This pattern will be some sort of mathematic operation that can be used to determine the next number in either a row or column. In the above example, the pattern for the rows is that the first number in the row is being multiplied by 2 to get the second number in the row. If you want to find the third number in the row, you need to multiply the second number by 2. The pattern for the columns is the same; the top numbers are being multiplied by 2 to get the bottom numbers in the columns. To find the missing number, you need to calculate the equation 8 x 2. The missing number is 16.

Understand that this section is similar to the number series section of the OLSAT®. Just like the number series section, you are trying to find a pattern in a string of numbers. Here, there are multiple rows instead of a single row. But the same pattern will be used in each row, so it's still the same concept—figure out the pattern and then apply it. In a similar vein, each column can be considered a number series that is vertical instead of horizontal.

Realize that you can identify patterns by looking at both rows and columns. Every matrix will have a pattern for the numbers in the rows and a pattern for the numbers in the columns. Sometimes, these patterns will be the same, but at other times the patterns will be different from one another. It is completely up to you to decide which pattern you feel more comfortable looking for. If you find it easier to look at the numbers from left to right in order to determine a pattern, look for a pattern in the rows. If you find it easier to look at the numbers from top to bottom in order to determine a pattern, look for a pattern in the columns.

Watch out for different operations in a row/column. Sometimes the math operation in a row will not be the same for the second and third numbers in the row. However, the pattern of the math operations in the entire row will be the same for each row. If this occurs, the pattern will be different for each set of columns. However, in each column, the pattern will be the same.

Identify the correct pattern. The key to answering these questions successfully will always come down to determining the correct pattern of the operation or operations being applied to the numbers in the rows/columns. Get in the habit of immediately recognizing what could be done to one number in order to get the next number in the row/column. Once you find the pattern, determining the answer should be a piece of cake.

Form a plan of attack. The best way to approach number matrix problems is to have a clear method for solving them. So, before you take this test, you should know whether you want to find patterns in rows or columns. You should also get in the habit of writing in your booklet the operation that is occurring from one number to the next. In the answer booklet, notations like +6 and –8 are occasionally used as shorthand to describe what is occurring to the first number to get the second number in the row/column. You should use whatever kind of shorthand is easiest for you.

Use process of elimination. If a question has multiple missing numbers, you are probably going to have to find one missing number in order to figure out the other missing number. Once you discover one of the missing numbers, use process of elimination to narrow down your choices. You will actually only be able to use this strategy on these types of questions.

Be careful with your arithmetic. The operations you will need to calculate in order to find the missing number in the matrix will be relatively simple. Be careful of having a mental hiccup and miscalculate an equation like 5 x 5 or 9 + 8. After all your hard work to get the answer, a silly mistake like that can be quite costly.

Number Matrices Questions

1.

The numbers in the box go together in a certain way. Choose the number that goes where you see the question mark.

1	5	9
5	9	13
9	13	?

A. 20   B. 17   C. 15   D. 18

2.

The numbers in the box go together in a certain way. Choose the number that goes where you see the question mark.

6	4	2
8	6	4
10	8	?

A. 2   B. 4   C. 6   D. 8

3.

The numbers in the box go together in a certain way. Choose the number that goes where you see the question mark.

0	1	2
2	3	4
4	5	?

A. 5   B. 4   C. 6   D. 7

4.

The numbers in the box go together in a certain way. Choose the number that goes where you see the question mark.

3	7	11
5	9	13
7	11	?

A. 14   B. 15   C. 18   D. 12

5.

The numbers in the box go together in a certain way. Choose the number that goes where you see the question mark.

1	7	13
3	9	15
5	11	?

A. 18　　　　B. 19　　　　C. 15　　　　D. 17

6.

The numbers in the box go together in a certain way. Choose the number that goes where you see the question mark.

4	2	0
6	4	2
8	6	?

A. 4　　　　B. 3　　　　C. 5　　　　D. 7

7.

The numbers in the box go together in a certain way. Choose the number that goes where you see the question mark.

18	12	6
26	20	?

A. 15　　　B. 18　　　C. 14　　　D. 12　　　E. 16

8.

The numbers in the box go together in a certain way. Choose the number that goes where you see the question mark.

30	20	10
45	35	?

A. 20　　　B. 25　　　C. 15　　　D. 35　　　E. 30

9.

The numbers in the box go together in a certain way. Choose the number that goes where you see the question mark.

22	18	12
30	26	?

A. 24   B. 22   C. 16   D. 20   E. 32

10.

The numbers in the box go together in a certain way. Choose the number that goes where you see the question mark.

40	33	26
45	38	?

A. 30   B. 31   C. 32   D. 33   E. 35

11.

The numbers in the box go together in a certain way. Choose the number that goes where you see the question mark.

1	2	4
2	4	?

A. 8   B. 15   C. 12   D. 10   E. 2

12.

The numbers in the box go together in a certain way. Choose the number that goes where you see the question mark.

2	4	8
3	6	?

A. 18   B. 10   C. 14   D. 12   E. 15

13.

The numbers in the box go together in a certain way. Choose the number that goes where you see the question mark.

1	5	25
2	10	?

A. 40   B. 30   C. 25   D. 45   E. 50

14.

The numbers in the box go together in a certain way. Choose the number that goes where you see the question mark.

3	6	12
5	10	?

A. 12   B. 16   C. 20   D. 30   E. 15

15.

The numbers in the box go together in a certain way. Choose the number that goes where you see the question mark.

3	9	27
5	15	?

A. 45   B. 55   C. 40   D. 51   E. 54

16.

The numbers in the box go together in a certain way. Choose the number that goes where you see the question mark.

12	6	3
24	12	?

A. 9   B. 6   C. 8   D. 24   E. 18

17.

The numbers in the box go together in a certain way. Choose the number that goes where you see the question mark.

6	10	14
8	14	20
10	18	?

A. 22   B. 26   C. 28   D. 20   E. 18

18.

The numbers in the box go together in a certain way. Choose the number that goes where you see the question mark.

1	3	9
2	6	18
3	9	?

A. 36   B. 27   C. 36   D. 18   E. 45

19.

The numbers in the box go together in a certain way. Choose the number that goes where you see the question mark.

1	2	4
3	6	12
5	10	?

A. 20   B. 15   C. 10   D. 18   E. 50

20.

The numbers in the box go together in a certain way. Choose the number that goes where you see the question mark.

18	24	30
21	27	?

A. 31   B. 30   C. 33   D. 36   E. 28

21.

The numbers in the box go together in a certain way. Choose the number that goes where you see the question mark.

8	15	22
13	20	?

A. 28   B. 27   C. 30   D. 35   E. 26

22.

The numbers in the box go together in a certain way. Choose the number that goes where you see the question mark.

8	4	12
10	5	15
12	?	18

A. 15   B. 18   C. 6   D. 8   E. 24

23.

The numbers in the box go together in a certain way. Choose the numbers that goes where you see the question marks.

5	10	12
7	?	16
9	18	?

A. 12, 20   B. 14, 20   C. 14, 22   D. 18, 22   E. 10, 36

24.

The numbers in the box go together in a certain way. Choose the number that goes where you see the question mark.

7	10	13
16	19	22
?	28	31

A. 24   B. 27   C. 20   D. 18   E. 25

25.

The numbers in the box go together in a certain way. Choose the numbers that goes where you see the question marks.

2	4	16
3	?	24
4	8	?

A. 5, 16   B. 6, 18   C. 6, 32   D. 8, 32   E. 6, 24

Number Matrices Answer Key

1. **(B) 17**
    Looking at the top row in the matrix, you can see that every number has 4 added to it to get the next number. Going down one of the columns, you can see the same pattern. So, the only number that makes sense for the answer is the sum of 13 and 4. The correct answer is (B), which is 17.

2. **(C) 6**
    A subtraction operation is occurring in the different rows of numbers; 2 is being subtracted from each number in order to get the next number in the row. There is also an addition operation occurring in the different columns; 2 is being added to each number in order to get the next number in the column. The only number that can work in the matrix and fulfill both of these operations is 6 since 8 – 2 = 6 and 4 + 2 = 6. The correct answer is (C).

3. **(C) 6**
    In this matrix, the numbers in the rows are increasing sequentially (in other words, 1 is being added to each number to get the next number). The addition operation for the columns involves the addition of 2 to each number as you move vertically down the column. The only number for ? that can fulfill both operations is 6 (answer choice C).

4. **(B) 15**
    Looking at the rows first, you should see that 4 is being added to each previous number. Going down the columns, you should see that 2 is being added to each number. 11 + 4 = 15 and 13 + 2 = 15. The correct answer is (B).

5. **(D) 17**
    The pattern in the rows is +6 to each previous number. The pattern for the columns is +2 to each number as you move down vertically. 11 + 6 = 17 and 15 + 2 = 17. The correct answer is (D).

6. **(A) 4**
    The pattern in the rows is –2 to each previous number. The pattern in the columns is +2 to each number as you move down vertically. 6 – 2 = 4 and 2 + 2 = 4. The correct answer is (A).

7. **(C) 14**
    In this matrix, the pattern for the rows is –6, and the pattern for the columns is +8. In order to find out what ? is, we need to solve the equation 20 – 6 or the equation 6 + 8. Both equations give us 14 (answer choice C), which must be the missing number in the matrix

8. **(B) 25**
    The pattern for the rows is –10, and the pattern for the columns is +15. 35 – 10 = 25 and 10 + 15 = 25. The correct answer is (B).

9. **(D) 20**
    In this matrix, you can see that there are two different patterns in the rows; 4 is being subtracted from the first number to get the second number; then, in the top row, 6 is subtracted from the second number to get the third number. Looking at the columns,

there is a definite pattern of adding 8 to the top number in order to get the bottom number. If we add 8 to 12, our answer is 20. The number 20 is also 6 less than the previous number in the row, which matches the pattern of the top row. The correct answer is (D).

10. (B) 31

What number is subtracted from 40 to get 33? Or, what number is added to 33 to get 40? The answer for both of those questions is 7, so the pattern for the rows is the subtraction of 7 from the previous number. How about the columns? What number is added to 40 to get 45? The answer is 5. So, 5 is being added to each top number in order to get the number below it. What does 38 – 7 equal? And what does 26 + 5 equal? The answer for both of those equations is 31, so 31 (answer choice B) must be the missing number in the matrix.

11. (A) 8

Looking at this matrix, you should notice that there is no addition or subtraction pattern that can fit for either the rows or the columns. What other operation could it be? Since the numbers are getting larger, it's best to try multiplication. It looks as though every number is being multiplied by 2 to get the next number in the row. The top numbers in the columns are also being multiplied by 2 to get the bottom numbers. To find the missing number, multiply 4 by 2 to get 8. The correct answer is (A).

12. (D) 12

Once again, you should notice that there is no addition or subtraction pattern that can be used in the rows or columns. The correct pattern must involve multiplication. Looking at the numbers in the rows, the common multiplier is 2; so, the previous number in the row is being multiplied by 2 to get the next number in the row. That would mean that the ? has to be 12 since 6 x 2 = 12. When you have a multiplication pattern in a matrix, finding the pattern in either the rows or the columns should be enough to convince you that you have found the correct answer. Here, the pattern for the columns is a bit tricky and more difficult to find than the pattern in the rows. For example, using the top number in the second column, 4/2 = 2, and then you add 2 to 4 in order to get the bottom number, which is 6.

13. (E) 50

Multiplication is the name of the game for this matrix. The numbers in the rows are being multiplied by 5 to get the next number in the row, and the numbers at the tops of the columns are being multiplied by 2 to get the bottom numbers. So, to find the missing number, you need to solve either 10 x 5 or 25 x 2. In either case, your answer will be 50, which is answer choice (E).

14. (C) 20

Here's another multiplication pattern matrix. In the rows, you can see an easy pattern of multiplying the previous number by 2 to get the next number. That should be enough to get the equation 10 x 2 and figure out that the missing number must be 20. Since the pattern in the columns is tougher to find, you should be content with this answer. But, for your information, the pattern in the columns is to find the difference between the two numbers in the previous column, multiply that difference by 2, and then add the product to the top number to find the bottom number.

15. (A) 45

Looking at the rows, you should see a pattern of multiplying the previous number by 3 in order to get the next number in the row. To find the missing number, we need to multiply 15 by 3. Our answer is 45, which is answer choice (A). Once again, the rows pattern is pretty simple, and finding it is the quickest way to solve this problem. The pattern for the columns is to take the difference between the numbers in the previous column, multiply that difference by 3, and then add that product to the top number in order to find the bottom number.

16. (B) 6

This matrix involves both multiplication and division in its pattern. For the rows, each previous number is being divided by 2 in order to get the next number in the row. For the columns, the top number is being multiplied by 2 in order to get the bottom number in the matrix. You can use the equation 12/2 or the equation 3 x 2 to get 6 as your missing number. Answer choice (B) is correct.

17. (B) 26

Here's another example of a matrix in which you don't have a constant number to add or subtract for all of the rows and columns. The best way to approach this problem is to take it one row at a time. In the first row, you can see that 4 is being added to each number to get the next number in the row. In the second row, the pattern is +6. In the last row, the pattern is +8. For each new row, it looks as though the next multiple of 2 is being added to the numbers in the row. So, if there were another row, the pattern would be +10. A similar pattern is going on with the columns. The pattern for the first column is +2, the pattern for the second column is +4, and the pattern for the third column is +6. If there were another column, you would be adding 8 to every number in order to find the number below it. To find the missing number, you can solve the equation 18 + 8 or 20 + 6 to get 26, which is answer choice (B).

18. (B) 27

In this matrix, the pattern for the rows involves multiplication; every previous number in the row is being multiplied by 3 to get the next number in the row. 9 x 3 = 27, which is our missing number. The pattern for the columns is that each number is the next multiple of the top number in each column. The multiples of 3 are 3, 6, 9, 12, 15, and so on, so the first three numbers in the second column are 3, 6, and 9. The multiples of 9 are 9, 18, 27, 36, 45, and so on, so 27 must be our missing number since it is the third multiple of 9. The correct answer is (B).

19. (A) 20

The pattern for the rows is to multiply the previous number by 2; 10 x 2 = 20, so answer choice (A) must be correct. The pattern for the columns is to take the difference between the numbers in the previous column, multiply the difference by 2, and then add this product to each number as you move down the column. The pattern for the rows is much easier to find and use.

20. (C) 33

Looking at the rows, you should see that 6 is being added to each previous number to get the next number in the row. Following this pattern, the missing number can be found by solving the equation 27 + 6. The pattern for the columns is to add 3 to the top number in order to get the bottom number, so our equation is 30 + 3. The missing number is 33, so answer choice (C) is correct.

21. (B) 27

Here, the pattern for the rows is +7, and the pattern for the columns is +5. You can use either 20 + 7 or 22 + 5 to get 27 as your missing number. Answer choice (B) is correct.

22. (C) 6

Here's a matrix that doesn't have a constant pattern within its rows. In order to get the second number in the row, you need to divide the first number by 2. However, if you want to get the third number in the row, you need to multiply the second number in the row by 3. Since we are only looking at the second number in the third row, we just need to divide the first number in the third row by 2. 12/2 = 6. The pattern for the columns seems to be that they go up by a constant number as you move down a column; however, every column has its own constant number. The numbers in the first column have a +2 pattern, the numbers in the second column have a +1 pattern, and the numbers in the third column have a +3 pattern. For the third number in the second column, the equation is 5 + 1 = 6. Our missing number is 6, which is answer choice (C).

23. (B) 14, 20

You will need to find two missing numbers in this matrix. Once again, it's best to focus on a pattern row by row or column by column. In the top row, it looks as though 5 is either being multiplied by 2 or having 5 added to it to get 10. Because of the missing number in the second row, we need to look at the third row to see which operation is right. Since 9 x 2 = 18, we know that in order to get the second number in the row, we need to multiply the first number by 2. So, our first missing number in the second row should be 14. We can narrow our answer choices down to (B) and (C). Now that we have figured out the missing number in the second row, it seems as though there's a different operation to get the third number in the rows of this matrix; you need to add 2 to the second number in order to get the third number. Looking at the third row, you can add 2 to 18 to get 20. The patterns for the columns are +2 for the first column and +4 for the second and third columns, or 10 + 4 = 14 for the second number in the second column and 16 + 4 = 20 for the third number in the third column. Answer choice (B) is correct.

24. (E) 25

The pattern for the rows is +3 to each previous number in order to get the next number. However, since the missing number is the first number in the third row, you will actually need to subtract 3 from second number in the third row. 28 – 3 = 25, which is the missing number. The pattern for the columns is to add 9 to each number in order to get the number below it. So, 16 + 9 = 25. The correct answer is (E).

25. (C) 6, 32

 Here's another question with two missing numbers, so you'll probably need to find one missing number in order to figure out the other missing number. Let's try to find the missing number in the second row. For the first row, 2 is either being added or multiplied by 2 to get 4. Looking at the third row, it's clear that the first number in the row is being multiplied by 2 to get the second number. Since 3 x 2 = 6, the missing number in the second row must be 6. We can narrow down our answer choices to (B), (C), and (E). It looks as though there's a different operation to get the third number in the row; we need to multiply the second number by 4 to get the third number. 8 x 4 = 32, so answer choice (C) must be correct. The pattern for the columns is +1 for the first column, +2 for the second column, and +8 for the third column. 4 + 2 = 6 for the missing number in the second column, and 24 + 8 = 32 for the missing number in the third column.

OLSAT® Preparation Guide - Levels D, E, and F

Bright Kids NYC Inc. ©

STUDENT NAME			
DATE OF BIRTH	GRADE	TEST SECTION	TEST DATE (Month/Year)

1. (A) (B) (C) (D) (E)
2. (A) (B) (C) (D) (E)
3. (A) (B) (C) (D) (E)
4. (A) (B) (C) (D) (E)
5. (A) (B) (C) (D) (E)
6. (A) (B) (C) (D) (E)
7. (A) (B) (C) (D) (E)
8. (A) (B) (C) (D) (E)
9. (A) (B) (C) (D) (E)
10. (A) (B) (C) (D) (E)
11. (A) (B) (C) (D) (E)
12. (A) (B) (C) (D) (E)
13. (A) (B) (C) (D) (E)
14. (A) (B) (C) (D) (E)
15. (A) (B) (C) (D) (E)
16. (A) (B) (C) (D) (E)
17. (A) (B) (C) (D) (E)
18. (A) (B) (C) (D) (E)
19. (A) (B) (C) (D) (E)
20. (A) (B) (C) (D) (E)
21. (A) (B) (C) (D) (E)
22. (A) (B) (C) (D) (E)
23. (A) (B) (C) (D) (E)
24. (A) (B) (C) (D) (E)
25. (A) (B) (C) (D) (E)

26. (A) (B) (C) (D) (E)
27. (A) (B) (C) (D) (E)
28. (A) (B) (C) (D) (E)
29. (A) (B) (C) (D) (E)
30. (A) (B) (C) (D) (E)
31. (A) (B) (C) (D) (E)
32. (A) (B) (C) (D) (E)
33. (A) (B) (C) (D) (E)
34. (A) (B) (C) (D) (E)
35. (A) (B) (C) (D) (E)
36. (A) (B) (C) (D) (E)
37. (A) (B) (C) (D) (E)
38. (A) (B) (C) (D) (E)
39. (A) (B) (C) (D) (E)
40. (A) (B) (C) (D) (E)
41. (A) (B) (C) (D) (E)
42. (A) (B) (C) (D) (E)
43. (A) (B) (C) (D) (E)
44. (A) (B) (C) (D) (E)
45. (A) (B) (C) (D) (E)
46. (A) (B) (C) (D) (E)
47. (A) (B) (C) (D) (E)
48. (A) (B) (C) (D) (E)
49. (A) (B) (C) (D) (E)
50. (A) (B) (C) (D) (E)

OLSAT® Preparation Guide - Levels D, E, and F

STUDENT NAME			
DATE OF BIRTH	GRADE	TEST SECTION	TEST DATE (Month/Year)

1. Ⓐ Ⓑ Ⓒ Ⓓ Ⓔ
2. Ⓐ Ⓑ Ⓒ Ⓓ Ⓔ
3. Ⓐ Ⓑ Ⓒ Ⓓ Ⓔ
4. Ⓐ Ⓑ Ⓒ Ⓓ Ⓔ
5. Ⓐ Ⓑ Ⓒ Ⓓ Ⓔ
6. Ⓐ Ⓑ Ⓒ Ⓓ Ⓔ
7. Ⓐ Ⓑ Ⓒ Ⓓ Ⓔ
8. Ⓐ Ⓑ Ⓒ Ⓓ Ⓔ
9. Ⓐ Ⓑ Ⓒ Ⓓ Ⓔ
10. Ⓐ Ⓑ Ⓒ Ⓓ Ⓔ
11. Ⓐ Ⓑ Ⓒ Ⓓ Ⓔ
12. Ⓐ Ⓑ Ⓒ Ⓓ Ⓔ
13. Ⓐ Ⓑ Ⓒ Ⓓ Ⓔ
14. Ⓐ Ⓑ Ⓒ Ⓓ Ⓔ
15. Ⓐ Ⓑ Ⓒ Ⓓ Ⓔ
16. Ⓐ Ⓑ Ⓒ Ⓓ Ⓔ
17. Ⓐ Ⓑ Ⓒ Ⓓ Ⓔ
18. Ⓐ Ⓑ Ⓒ Ⓓ Ⓔ
19. Ⓐ Ⓑ Ⓒ Ⓓ Ⓔ
20. Ⓐ Ⓑ Ⓒ Ⓓ Ⓔ
21. Ⓐ Ⓑ Ⓒ Ⓓ Ⓔ
22. Ⓐ Ⓑ Ⓒ Ⓓ Ⓔ
23. Ⓐ Ⓑ Ⓒ Ⓓ Ⓔ
24. Ⓐ Ⓑ Ⓒ Ⓓ Ⓔ
25. Ⓐ Ⓑ Ⓒ Ⓓ Ⓔ

26. Ⓐ Ⓑ Ⓒ Ⓓ Ⓔ
27. Ⓐ Ⓑ Ⓒ Ⓓ Ⓔ
28. Ⓐ Ⓑ Ⓒ Ⓓ Ⓔ
29. Ⓐ Ⓑ Ⓒ Ⓓ Ⓔ
30. Ⓐ Ⓑ Ⓒ Ⓓ Ⓔ
31. Ⓐ Ⓑ Ⓒ Ⓓ Ⓔ
32. Ⓐ Ⓑ Ⓒ Ⓓ Ⓔ
33. Ⓐ Ⓑ Ⓒ Ⓓ Ⓔ
34. Ⓐ Ⓑ Ⓒ Ⓓ Ⓔ
35. Ⓐ Ⓑ Ⓒ Ⓓ Ⓔ
36. Ⓐ Ⓑ Ⓒ Ⓓ Ⓔ
37. Ⓐ Ⓑ Ⓒ Ⓓ Ⓔ
38. Ⓐ Ⓑ Ⓒ Ⓓ Ⓔ
39. Ⓐ Ⓑ Ⓒ Ⓓ Ⓔ
40. Ⓐ Ⓑ Ⓒ Ⓓ Ⓔ
41. Ⓐ Ⓑ Ⓒ Ⓓ Ⓔ
42. Ⓐ Ⓑ Ⓒ Ⓓ Ⓔ
43. Ⓐ Ⓑ Ⓒ Ⓓ Ⓔ
44. Ⓐ Ⓑ Ⓒ Ⓓ Ⓔ
45. Ⓐ Ⓑ Ⓒ Ⓓ Ⓔ
46. Ⓐ Ⓑ Ⓒ Ⓓ Ⓔ
47. Ⓐ Ⓑ Ⓒ Ⓓ Ⓔ
48. Ⓐ Ⓑ Ⓒ Ⓓ Ⓔ
49. Ⓐ Ⓑ Ⓒ Ⓓ Ⓔ
50. Ⓐ Ⓑ Ⓒ Ⓓ Ⓔ

OLSAT® Preparation Guide - Levels D, E, and F

STUDENT NAME			
DATE OF BIRTH	GRADE	TEST SECTION	TEST DATE (Month/Year)

1. Ⓐ Ⓑ Ⓒ Ⓓ Ⓔ
2. Ⓐ Ⓑ Ⓒ Ⓓ Ⓔ
3. Ⓐ Ⓑ Ⓒ Ⓓ Ⓔ
4. Ⓐ Ⓑ Ⓒ Ⓓ Ⓔ
5. Ⓐ Ⓑ Ⓒ Ⓓ Ⓔ
6. Ⓐ Ⓑ Ⓒ Ⓓ Ⓔ
7. Ⓐ Ⓑ Ⓒ Ⓓ Ⓔ
8. Ⓐ Ⓑ Ⓒ Ⓓ Ⓔ
9. Ⓐ Ⓑ Ⓒ Ⓓ Ⓔ
10. Ⓐ Ⓑ Ⓒ Ⓓ Ⓔ
11. Ⓐ Ⓑ Ⓒ Ⓓ Ⓔ
12. Ⓐ Ⓑ Ⓒ Ⓓ Ⓔ
13. Ⓐ Ⓑ Ⓒ Ⓓ Ⓔ
14. Ⓐ Ⓑ Ⓒ Ⓓ Ⓔ
15. Ⓐ Ⓑ Ⓒ Ⓓ Ⓔ
16. Ⓐ Ⓑ Ⓒ Ⓓ Ⓔ
17. Ⓐ Ⓑ Ⓒ Ⓓ Ⓔ
18. Ⓐ Ⓑ Ⓒ Ⓓ Ⓔ
19. Ⓐ Ⓑ Ⓒ Ⓓ Ⓔ
20. Ⓐ Ⓑ Ⓒ Ⓓ Ⓔ
21. Ⓐ Ⓑ Ⓒ Ⓓ Ⓔ
22. Ⓐ Ⓑ Ⓒ Ⓓ Ⓔ
23. Ⓐ Ⓑ Ⓒ Ⓓ Ⓔ
24. Ⓐ Ⓑ Ⓒ Ⓓ Ⓔ
25. Ⓐ Ⓑ Ⓒ Ⓓ Ⓔ

26. Ⓐ Ⓑ Ⓒ Ⓓ Ⓔ
27. Ⓐ Ⓑ Ⓒ Ⓓ Ⓔ
28. Ⓐ Ⓑ Ⓒ Ⓓ Ⓔ
29. Ⓐ Ⓑ Ⓒ Ⓓ Ⓔ
30. Ⓐ Ⓑ Ⓒ Ⓓ Ⓔ
31. Ⓐ Ⓑ Ⓒ Ⓓ Ⓔ
32. Ⓐ Ⓑ Ⓒ Ⓓ Ⓔ
33. Ⓐ Ⓑ Ⓒ Ⓓ Ⓔ
34. Ⓐ Ⓑ Ⓒ Ⓓ Ⓔ
35. Ⓐ Ⓑ Ⓒ Ⓓ Ⓔ
36. Ⓐ Ⓑ Ⓒ Ⓓ Ⓔ
37. Ⓐ Ⓑ Ⓒ Ⓓ Ⓔ
38. Ⓐ Ⓑ Ⓒ Ⓓ Ⓔ
39. Ⓐ Ⓑ Ⓒ Ⓓ Ⓔ
40. Ⓐ Ⓑ Ⓒ Ⓓ Ⓔ
41. Ⓐ Ⓑ Ⓒ Ⓓ Ⓔ
42. Ⓐ Ⓑ Ⓒ Ⓓ Ⓔ
43. Ⓐ Ⓑ Ⓒ Ⓓ Ⓔ
44. Ⓐ Ⓑ Ⓒ Ⓓ Ⓔ
45. Ⓐ Ⓑ Ⓒ Ⓓ Ⓔ
46. Ⓐ Ⓑ Ⓒ Ⓓ Ⓔ
47. Ⓐ Ⓑ Ⓒ Ⓓ Ⓔ
48. Ⓐ Ⓑ Ⓒ Ⓓ Ⓔ
49. Ⓐ Ⓑ Ⓒ Ⓓ Ⓔ
50. Ⓐ Ⓑ Ⓒ Ⓓ Ⓔ

OLSAT® Preparation Guide - Levels D, E, and F

STUDENT NAME			
DATE OF BIRTH	GRADE	TEST SECTION	TEST DATE (Month/Year)

1. (A) (B) (C) (D) (E)
2. (A) (B) (C) (D) (E)
3. (A) (B) (C) (D) (E)
4. (A) (B) (C) (D) (E)
5. (A) (B) (C) (D) (E)
6. (A) (B) (C) (D) (E)
7. (A) (B) (C) (D) (E)
8. (A) (B) (C) (D) (E)
9. (A) (B) (C) (D) (E)
10. (A) (B) (C) (D) (E)
11. (A) (B) (C) (D) (E)
12. (A) (B) (C) (D) (E)
13. (A) (B) (C) (D) (E)
14. (A) (B) (C) (D) (E)
15. (A) (B) (C) (D) (E)
16. (A) (B) (C) (D) (E)
17. (A) (B) (C) (D) (E)
18. (A) (B) (C) (D) (E)
19. (A) (B) (C) (D) (E)
20. (A) (B) (C) (D) (E)
21. (A) (B) (C) (D) (E)
22. (A) (B) (C) (D) (E)
23. (A) (B) (C) (D) (E)
24. (A) (B) (C) (D) (E)
25. (A) (B) (C) (D) (E)

26. (A) (B) (C) (D) (E)
27. (A) (B) (C) (D) (E)
28. (A) (B) (C) (D) (E)
29. (A) (B) (C) (D) (E)
30. (A) (B) (C) (D) (E)
31. (A) (B) (C) (D) (E)
32. (A) (B) (C) (D) (E)
33. (A) (B) (C) (D) (E)
34. (A) (B) (C) (D) (E)
35. (A) (B) (C) (D) (E)
36. (A) (B) (C) (D) (E)
37. (A) (B) (C) (D) (E)
38. (A) (B) (C) (D) (E)
39. (A) (B) (C) (D) (E)
40. (A) (B) (C) (D) (E)
41. (A) (B) (C) (D) (E)
42. (A) (B) (C) (D) (E)
43. (A) (B) (C) (D) (E)
44. (A) (B) (C) (D) (E)
45. (A) (B) (C) (D) (E)
46. (A) (B) (C) (D) (E)
47. (A) (B) (C) (D) (E)
48. (A) (B) (C) (D) (E)
49. (A) (B) (C) (D) (E)
50. (A) (B) (C) (D) (E)

OLSAT® Preparation Guide - Levels D, E, and F   Bright Kids NYC Inc. ©

STUDENT NAME			
DATE OF BIRTH	GRADE	TEST SECTION	TEST DATE (Month/Year)

1. (A) (B) (C) (D) (E)
2. (A) (B) (C) (D) (E)
3. (A) (B) (C) (D) (E)
4. (A) (B) (C) (D) (E)
5. (A) (B) (C) (D) (E)
6. (A) (B) (C) (D) (E)
7. (A) (B) (C) (D) (E)
8. (A) (B) (C) (D) (E)
9. (A) (B) (C) (D) (E)
10. (A) (B) (C) (D) (E)
11. (A) (B) (C) (D) (E)
12. (A) (B) (C) (D) (E)
13. (A) (B) (C) (D) (E)
14. (A) (B) (C) (D) (E)
15. (A) (B) (C) (D) (E)
16. (A) (B) (C) (D) (E)
17. (A) (B) (C) (D) (E)
18. (A) (B) (C) (D) (E)
19. (A) (B) (C) (D) (E)
20. (A) (B) (C) (D) (E)
21. (A) (B) (C) (D) (E)
22. (A) (B) (C) (D) (E)
23. (A) (B) (C) (D) (E)
24. (A) (B) (C) (D) (E)
25. (A) (B) (C) (D) (E)

26. (A) (B) (C) (D) (E)
27. (A) (B) (C) (D) (E)
28. (A) (B) (C) (D) (E)
29. (A) (B) (C) (D) (E)
30. (A) (B) (C) (D) (E)
31. (A) (B) (C) (D) (E)
32. (A) (B) (C) (D) (E)
33. (A) (B) (C) (D) (E)
34. (A) (B) (C) (D) (E)
35. (A) (B) (C) (D) (E)
36. (A) (B) (C) (D) (E)
37. (A) (B) (C) (D) (E)
38. (A) (B) (C) (D) (E)
39. (A) (B) (C) (D) (E)
40. (A) (B) (C) (D) (E)
41. (A) (B) (C) (D) (E)
42. (A) (B) (C) (D) (E)
43. (A) (B) (C) (D) (E)
44. (A) (B) (C) (D) (E)
45. (A) (B) (C) (D) (E)
46. (A) (B) (C) (D) (E)
47. (A) (B) (C) (D) (E)
48. (A) (B) (C) (D) (E)
49. (A) (B) (C) (D) (E)
50. (A) (B) (C) (D) (E)

OLSAT® Preparation Guide - Levels D, E, and F

STUDENT NAME			
DATE OF BIRTH	**GRADE**	**TEST SECTION**	**TEST DATE** (Month/Year)

1. Ⓐ Ⓑ Ⓒ Ⓓ Ⓔ
2. Ⓐ Ⓑ Ⓒ Ⓓ Ⓔ
3. Ⓐ Ⓑ Ⓒ Ⓓ Ⓔ
4. Ⓐ Ⓑ Ⓒ Ⓓ Ⓔ
5. Ⓐ Ⓑ Ⓒ Ⓓ Ⓔ
6. Ⓐ Ⓑ Ⓒ Ⓓ Ⓔ
7. Ⓐ Ⓑ Ⓒ Ⓓ Ⓔ
8. Ⓐ Ⓑ Ⓒ Ⓓ Ⓔ
9. Ⓐ Ⓑ Ⓒ Ⓓ Ⓔ
10. Ⓐ Ⓑ Ⓒ Ⓓ Ⓔ
11. Ⓐ Ⓑ Ⓒ Ⓓ Ⓔ
12. Ⓐ Ⓑ Ⓒ Ⓓ Ⓔ
13. Ⓐ Ⓑ Ⓒ Ⓓ Ⓔ
14. Ⓐ Ⓑ Ⓒ Ⓓ Ⓔ
15. Ⓐ Ⓑ Ⓒ Ⓓ Ⓔ
16. Ⓐ Ⓑ Ⓒ Ⓓ Ⓔ
17. Ⓐ Ⓑ Ⓒ Ⓓ Ⓔ
18. Ⓐ Ⓑ Ⓒ Ⓓ Ⓔ
19. Ⓐ Ⓑ Ⓒ Ⓓ Ⓔ
20. Ⓐ Ⓑ Ⓒ Ⓓ Ⓔ
21. Ⓐ Ⓑ Ⓒ Ⓓ Ⓔ
22. Ⓐ Ⓑ Ⓒ Ⓓ Ⓔ
23. Ⓐ Ⓑ Ⓒ Ⓓ Ⓔ
24. Ⓐ Ⓑ Ⓒ Ⓓ Ⓔ
25. Ⓐ Ⓑ Ⓒ Ⓓ Ⓔ

26. Ⓐ Ⓑ Ⓒ Ⓓ Ⓔ
27. Ⓐ Ⓑ Ⓒ Ⓓ Ⓔ
28. Ⓐ Ⓑ Ⓒ Ⓓ Ⓔ
29. Ⓐ Ⓑ Ⓒ Ⓓ Ⓔ
30. Ⓐ Ⓑ Ⓒ Ⓓ Ⓔ
31. Ⓐ Ⓑ Ⓒ Ⓓ Ⓔ
32. Ⓐ Ⓑ Ⓒ Ⓓ Ⓔ
33. Ⓐ Ⓑ Ⓒ Ⓓ Ⓔ
34. Ⓐ Ⓑ Ⓒ Ⓓ Ⓔ
35. Ⓐ Ⓑ Ⓒ Ⓓ Ⓔ
36. Ⓐ Ⓑ Ⓒ Ⓓ Ⓔ
37. Ⓐ Ⓑ Ⓒ Ⓓ Ⓔ
38. Ⓐ Ⓑ Ⓒ Ⓓ Ⓔ
39. Ⓐ Ⓑ Ⓒ Ⓓ Ⓔ
40. Ⓐ Ⓑ Ⓒ Ⓓ Ⓔ
41. Ⓐ Ⓑ Ⓒ Ⓓ Ⓔ
42. Ⓐ Ⓑ Ⓒ Ⓓ Ⓔ
43. Ⓐ Ⓑ Ⓒ Ⓓ Ⓔ
44. Ⓐ Ⓑ Ⓒ Ⓓ Ⓔ
45. Ⓐ Ⓑ Ⓒ Ⓓ Ⓔ
46. Ⓐ Ⓑ Ⓒ Ⓓ Ⓔ
47. Ⓐ Ⓑ Ⓒ Ⓓ Ⓔ
48. Ⓐ Ⓑ Ⓒ Ⓓ Ⓔ
49. Ⓐ Ⓑ Ⓒ Ⓓ Ⓔ
50. Ⓐ Ⓑ Ⓒ Ⓓ Ⓔ

OLSAT® Preparation Guide - Levels D, E, and F

STUDENT NAME			
DATE OF BIRTH	GRADE	TEST SECTION	TEST DATE (Month/Year)

1. Ⓐ Ⓑ Ⓒ Ⓓ Ⓔ
2. Ⓐ Ⓑ Ⓒ Ⓓ Ⓔ
3. Ⓐ Ⓑ Ⓒ Ⓓ Ⓔ
4. Ⓐ Ⓑ Ⓒ Ⓓ Ⓔ
5. Ⓐ Ⓑ Ⓒ Ⓓ Ⓔ
6. Ⓐ Ⓑ Ⓒ Ⓓ Ⓔ
7. Ⓐ Ⓑ Ⓒ Ⓓ Ⓔ
8. Ⓐ Ⓑ Ⓒ Ⓓ Ⓔ
9. Ⓐ Ⓑ Ⓒ Ⓓ Ⓔ
10. Ⓐ Ⓑ Ⓒ Ⓓ Ⓔ
11. Ⓐ Ⓑ Ⓒ Ⓓ Ⓔ
12. Ⓐ Ⓑ Ⓒ Ⓓ Ⓔ
13. Ⓐ Ⓑ Ⓒ Ⓓ Ⓔ
14. Ⓐ Ⓑ Ⓒ Ⓓ Ⓔ
15. Ⓐ Ⓑ Ⓒ Ⓓ Ⓔ
16. Ⓐ Ⓑ Ⓒ Ⓓ Ⓔ
17. Ⓐ Ⓑ Ⓒ Ⓓ Ⓔ
18. Ⓐ Ⓑ Ⓒ Ⓓ Ⓔ
19. Ⓐ Ⓑ Ⓒ Ⓓ Ⓔ
20. Ⓐ Ⓑ Ⓒ Ⓓ Ⓔ
21. Ⓐ Ⓑ Ⓒ Ⓓ Ⓔ
22. Ⓐ Ⓑ Ⓒ Ⓓ Ⓔ
23. Ⓐ Ⓑ Ⓒ Ⓓ Ⓔ
24. Ⓐ Ⓑ Ⓒ Ⓓ Ⓔ
25. Ⓐ Ⓑ Ⓒ Ⓓ Ⓔ

26. Ⓐ Ⓑ Ⓒ Ⓓ Ⓔ
27. Ⓐ Ⓑ Ⓒ Ⓓ Ⓔ
28. Ⓐ Ⓑ Ⓒ Ⓓ Ⓔ
29. Ⓐ Ⓑ Ⓒ Ⓓ Ⓔ
30. Ⓐ Ⓑ Ⓒ Ⓓ Ⓔ
31. Ⓐ Ⓑ Ⓒ Ⓓ Ⓔ
32. Ⓐ Ⓑ Ⓒ Ⓓ Ⓔ
33. Ⓐ Ⓑ Ⓒ Ⓓ Ⓔ
34. Ⓐ Ⓑ Ⓒ Ⓓ Ⓔ
35. Ⓐ Ⓑ Ⓒ Ⓓ Ⓔ
36. Ⓐ Ⓑ Ⓒ Ⓓ Ⓔ
37. Ⓐ Ⓑ Ⓒ Ⓓ Ⓔ
38. Ⓐ Ⓑ Ⓒ Ⓓ Ⓔ
39. Ⓐ Ⓑ Ⓒ Ⓓ Ⓔ
40. Ⓐ Ⓑ Ⓒ Ⓓ Ⓔ
41. Ⓐ Ⓑ Ⓒ Ⓓ Ⓔ
42. Ⓐ Ⓑ Ⓒ Ⓓ Ⓔ
43. Ⓐ Ⓑ Ⓒ Ⓓ Ⓔ
44. Ⓐ Ⓑ Ⓒ Ⓓ Ⓔ
45. Ⓐ Ⓑ Ⓒ Ⓓ Ⓔ
46. Ⓐ Ⓑ Ⓒ Ⓓ Ⓔ
47. Ⓐ Ⓑ Ⓒ Ⓓ Ⓔ
48. Ⓐ Ⓑ Ⓒ Ⓓ Ⓔ
49. Ⓐ Ⓑ Ⓒ Ⓓ Ⓔ
50. Ⓐ Ⓑ Ⓒ Ⓓ Ⓔ

OLSAT® Preparation Guide - Levels D, E, and F

STUDENT NAME			
DATE OF BIRTH	GRADE	TEST SECTION	TEST DATE (Month/Year)

DIRECTIONS:

- Use a #2 black lead pencil only.
- Do not use ink or colored pencil.
- Completely fill in one oval per question.
- Erase clearly any answer you wish to change.
- Make no stray marks on this answer sheet.

1. Ⓐ Ⓑ Ⓒ Ⓓ Ⓔ
2. Ⓐ Ⓑ Ⓒ Ⓓ Ⓔ
3. Ⓐ Ⓑ Ⓒ Ⓓ Ⓔ
4. Ⓐ Ⓑ Ⓒ Ⓓ Ⓔ
5. Ⓐ Ⓑ Ⓒ Ⓓ Ⓔ
6. Ⓐ Ⓑ Ⓒ Ⓓ Ⓔ
7. Ⓐ Ⓑ Ⓒ Ⓓ Ⓔ
8. Ⓐ Ⓑ Ⓒ Ⓓ Ⓔ
9. Ⓐ Ⓑ Ⓒ Ⓓ Ⓔ
10. Ⓐ Ⓑ Ⓒ Ⓓ Ⓔ
11. Ⓐ Ⓑ Ⓒ Ⓓ Ⓔ
12. Ⓐ Ⓑ Ⓒ Ⓓ Ⓔ
13. Ⓐ Ⓑ Ⓒ Ⓓ Ⓔ
14. Ⓐ Ⓑ Ⓒ Ⓓ Ⓔ
15. Ⓐ Ⓑ Ⓒ Ⓓ Ⓔ
16. Ⓐ Ⓑ Ⓒ Ⓓ Ⓔ
17. Ⓐ Ⓑ Ⓒ Ⓓ Ⓔ
18. Ⓐ Ⓑ Ⓒ Ⓓ Ⓔ
19. Ⓐ Ⓑ Ⓒ Ⓓ Ⓔ
20. Ⓐ Ⓑ Ⓒ Ⓓ Ⓔ
21. Ⓐ Ⓑ Ⓒ Ⓓ Ⓔ
22. Ⓐ Ⓑ Ⓒ Ⓓ Ⓔ
23. Ⓐ Ⓑ Ⓒ Ⓓ Ⓔ
24. Ⓐ Ⓑ Ⓒ Ⓓ Ⓔ
25. Ⓐ Ⓑ Ⓒ Ⓓ Ⓔ

26. Ⓐ Ⓑ Ⓒ Ⓓ Ⓔ
27. Ⓐ Ⓑ Ⓒ Ⓓ Ⓔ
28. Ⓐ Ⓑ Ⓒ Ⓓ Ⓔ
29. Ⓐ Ⓑ Ⓒ Ⓓ Ⓔ
30. Ⓐ Ⓑ Ⓒ Ⓓ Ⓔ
31. Ⓐ Ⓑ Ⓒ Ⓓ Ⓔ
32. Ⓐ Ⓑ Ⓒ Ⓓ Ⓔ
33. Ⓐ Ⓑ Ⓒ Ⓓ Ⓔ
34. Ⓐ Ⓑ Ⓒ Ⓓ Ⓔ
35. Ⓐ Ⓑ Ⓒ Ⓓ Ⓔ
36. Ⓐ Ⓑ Ⓒ Ⓓ Ⓔ
37. Ⓐ Ⓑ Ⓒ Ⓓ Ⓔ
38. Ⓐ Ⓑ Ⓒ Ⓓ Ⓔ
39. Ⓐ Ⓑ Ⓒ Ⓓ Ⓔ
40. Ⓐ Ⓑ Ⓒ Ⓓ Ⓔ
41. Ⓐ Ⓑ Ⓒ Ⓓ Ⓔ
42. Ⓐ Ⓑ Ⓒ Ⓓ Ⓔ
43. Ⓐ Ⓑ Ⓒ Ⓓ Ⓔ
44. Ⓐ Ⓑ Ⓒ Ⓓ Ⓔ
45. Ⓐ Ⓑ Ⓒ Ⓓ Ⓔ
46. Ⓐ Ⓑ Ⓒ Ⓓ Ⓔ
47. Ⓐ Ⓑ Ⓒ Ⓓ Ⓔ
48. Ⓐ Ⓑ Ⓒ Ⓓ Ⓔ
49. Ⓐ Ⓑ Ⓒ Ⓓ Ⓔ
50. Ⓐ Ⓑ Ⓒ Ⓓ Ⓔ

OLSAT® Preparation Guide - Levels D, E, and F

STUDENT NAME			
DATE OF BIRTH	GRADE	TEST SECTION	TEST DATE (Month/Year)

EXAMPLE

1 Ⓐ ⊗ Ⓒ Ⓓ WRONG
2 ☑ Ⓑ Ⓒ Ⓓ WRONG
3 Ⓐ Ⓑ ◓ Ⓓ WRONG
4 Ⓐ Ⓑ Ⓒ ● CORRECT

DIRECTIONS:

- Use a #2 black lead pencil only.
- Do not use ink or colored pencil.
- Completely fill in one oval per question.
- Erase clearly any answer you wish to change.
- Make no stray marks on this answer sheet.

1. Ⓐ Ⓑ Ⓒ Ⓓ Ⓔ
2. Ⓐ Ⓑ Ⓒ Ⓓ Ⓔ
3. Ⓐ Ⓑ Ⓒ Ⓓ Ⓔ
4. Ⓐ Ⓑ Ⓒ Ⓓ Ⓔ
5. Ⓐ Ⓑ Ⓒ Ⓓ Ⓔ
6. Ⓐ Ⓑ Ⓒ Ⓓ Ⓔ
7. Ⓐ Ⓑ Ⓒ Ⓓ Ⓔ
8. Ⓐ Ⓑ Ⓒ Ⓓ Ⓔ
9. Ⓐ Ⓑ Ⓒ Ⓓ Ⓔ
10. Ⓐ Ⓑ Ⓒ Ⓓ Ⓔ
11. Ⓐ Ⓑ Ⓒ Ⓓ Ⓔ
12. Ⓐ Ⓑ Ⓒ Ⓓ Ⓔ
13. Ⓐ Ⓑ Ⓒ Ⓓ Ⓔ
14. Ⓐ Ⓑ Ⓒ Ⓓ Ⓔ
15. Ⓐ Ⓑ Ⓒ Ⓓ Ⓔ
16. Ⓐ Ⓑ Ⓒ Ⓓ Ⓔ
17. Ⓐ Ⓑ Ⓒ Ⓓ Ⓔ
18. Ⓐ Ⓑ Ⓒ Ⓓ Ⓔ
19. Ⓐ Ⓑ Ⓒ Ⓓ Ⓔ
20. Ⓐ Ⓑ Ⓒ Ⓓ Ⓔ
21. Ⓐ Ⓑ Ⓒ Ⓓ Ⓔ
22. Ⓐ Ⓑ Ⓒ Ⓓ Ⓔ
23. Ⓐ Ⓑ Ⓒ Ⓓ Ⓔ
24. Ⓐ Ⓑ Ⓒ Ⓓ Ⓔ
25. Ⓐ Ⓑ Ⓒ Ⓓ Ⓔ

26. Ⓐ Ⓑ Ⓒ Ⓓ Ⓔ
27. Ⓐ Ⓑ Ⓒ Ⓓ Ⓔ
28. Ⓐ Ⓑ Ⓒ Ⓓ Ⓔ
29. Ⓐ Ⓑ Ⓒ Ⓓ Ⓔ
30. Ⓐ Ⓑ Ⓒ Ⓓ Ⓔ
31. Ⓐ Ⓑ Ⓒ Ⓓ Ⓔ
32. Ⓐ Ⓑ Ⓒ Ⓓ Ⓔ
33. Ⓐ Ⓑ Ⓒ Ⓓ Ⓔ
34. Ⓐ Ⓑ Ⓒ Ⓓ Ⓔ
35. Ⓐ Ⓑ Ⓒ Ⓓ Ⓔ
36. Ⓐ Ⓑ Ⓒ Ⓓ Ⓔ
37. Ⓐ Ⓑ Ⓒ Ⓓ Ⓔ
38. Ⓐ Ⓑ Ⓒ Ⓓ Ⓔ
39. Ⓐ Ⓑ Ⓒ Ⓓ Ⓔ
40. Ⓐ Ⓑ Ⓒ Ⓓ Ⓔ
41. Ⓐ Ⓑ Ⓒ Ⓓ Ⓔ
42. Ⓐ Ⓑ Ⓒ Ⓓ Ⓔ
43. Ⓐ Ⓑ Ⓒ Ⓓ Ⓔ
44. Ⓐ Ⓑ Ⓒ Ⓓ Ⓔ
45. Ⓐ Ⓑ Ⓒ Ⓓ Ⓔ
46. Ⓐ Ⓑ Ⓒ Ⓓ Ⓔ
47. Ⓐ Ⓑ Ⓒ Ⓓ Ⓔ
48. Ⓐ Ⓑ Ⓒ Ⓓ Ⓔ
49. Ⓐ Ⓑ Ⓒ Ⓓ Ⓔ
50. Ⓐ Ⓑ Ⓒ Ⓓ Ⓔ

STUDENT NAME			
DATE OF BIRTH	GRADE	TEST SECTION	TEST DATE (Month/Year)

EXAMPLE

1 Ⓐ Ⓧ Ⓒ Ⓓ   WRONG
2 ✓ Ⓑ Ⓒ Ⓓ   WRONG
3 Ⓐ Ⓑ ◖ Ⓓ   WRONG
4 Ⓐ Ⓑ Ⓒ ●   CORRECT

DIRECTIONS:

- Use a #2 black lead pencil only.
- Do not use ink or colored pencil.
- Completely fill in one oval per question.
- Erase clearly any answer you wish to change.
- Make no stray marks on this answer sheet.

1. Ⓐ Ⓑ Ⓒ Ⓓ Ⓔ
2. Ⓐ Ⓑ Ⓒ Ⓓ Ⓔ
3. Ⓐ Ⓑ Ⓒ Ⓓ Ⓔ
4. Ⓐ Ⓑ Ⓒ Ⓓ Ⓔ
5. Ⓐ Ⓑ Ⓒ Ⓓ Ⓔ
6. Ⓐ Ⓑ Ⓒ Ⓓ Ⓔ
7. Ⓐ Ⓑ Ⓒ Ⓓ Ⓔ
8. Ⓐ Ⓑ Ⓒ Ⓓ Ⓔ
9. Ⓐ Ⓑ Ⓒ Ⓓ Ⓔ
10. Ⓐ Ⓑ Ⓒ Ⓓ Ⓔ
11. Ⓐ Ⓑ Ⓒ Ⓓ Ⓔ
12. Ⓐ Ⓑ Ⓒ Ⓓ Ⓔ
13. Ⓐ Ⓑ Ⓒ Ⓓ Ⓔ
14. Ⓐ Ⓑ Ⓒ Ⓓ Ⓔ
15. Ⓐ Ⓑ Ⓒ Ⓓ Ⓔ
16. Ⓐ Ⓑ Ⓒ Ⓓ Ⓔ
17. Ⓐ Ⓑ Ⓒ Ⓓ Ⓔ
18. Ⓐ Ⓑ Ⓒ Ⓓ Ⓔ
19. Ⓐ Ⓑ Ⓒ Ⓓ Ⓔ
20. Ⓐ Ⓑ Ⓒ Ⓓ Ⓔ
21. Ⓐ Ⓑ Ⓒ Ⓓ Ⓔ
22. Ⓐ Ⓑ Ⓒ Ⓓ Ⓔ
23. Ⓐ Ⓑ Ⓒ Ⓓ Ⓔ
24. Ⓐ Ⓑ Ⓒ Ⓓ Ⓔ
25. Ⓐ Ⓑ Ⓒ Ⓓ Ⓔ

26. Ⓐ Ⓑ Ⓒ Ⓓ Ⓔ
27. Ⓐ Ⓑ Ⓒ Ⓓ Ⓔ
28. Ⓐ Ⓑ Ⓒ Ⓓ Ⓔ
29. Ⓐ Ⓑ Ⓒ Ⓓ Ⓔ
30. Ⓐ Ⓑ Ⓒ Ⓓ Ⓔ
31. Ⓐ Ⓑ Ⓒ Ⓓ Ⓔ
32. Ⓐ Ⓑ Ⓒ Ⓓ Ⓔ
33. Ⓐ Ⓑ Ⓒ Ⓓ Ⓔ
34. Ⓐ Ⓑ Ⓒ Ⓓ Ⓔ
35. Ⓐ Ⓑ Ⓒ Ⓓ Ⓔ
36. Ⓐ Ⓑ Ⓒ Ⓓ Ⓔ
37. Ⓐ Ⓑ Ⓒ Ⓓ Ⓔ
38. Ⓐ Ⓑ Ⓒ Ⓓ Ⓔ
39. Ⓐ Ⓑ Ⓒ Ⓓ Ⓔ
40. Ⓐ Ⓑ Ⓒ Ⓓ Ⓔ
41. Ⓐ Ⓑ Ⓒ Ⓓ Ⓔ
42. Ⓐ Ⓑ Ⓒ Ⓓ Ⓔ
43. Ⓐ Ⓑ Ⓒ Ⓓ Ⓔ
44. Ⓐ Ⓑ Ⓒ Ⓓ Ⓔ
45. Ⓐ Ⓑ Ⓒ Ⓓ Ⓔ
46. Ⓐ Ⓑ Ⓒ Ⓓ Ⓔ
47. Ⓐ Ⓑ Ⓒ Ⓓ Ⓔ
48. Ⓐ Ⓑ Ⓒ Ⓓ Ⓔ
49. Ⓐ Ⓑ Ⓒ Ⓓ Ⓔ
50. Ⓐ Ⓑ Ⓒ Ⓓ Ⓔ

OLSAT® Preparation Guide - Levels D, E, and F

STUDENT NAME

DATE OF BIRTH	GRADE	TEST SECTION	TEST DATE (Month/Year)

EXAMPLE	DIRECTIONS:
1 Ⓐ ⊗ Ⓒ Ⓓ WRONG 2 ✓ Ⓑ Ⓒ Ⓓ WRONG 3 Ⓐ Ⓑ ◕ Ⓓ WRONG 4 Ⓐ Ⓑ Ⓒ ● CORRECT	• Use a #2 black lead pencil only. • Do not use ink or colored pencil. • Completely fill in one oval per question. • Erase clearly any answer you wish to change. • Make no stray marks on this answer sheet.

1. Ⓐ Ⓑ Ⓒ Ⓓ Ⓔ
2. Ⓐ Ⓑ Ⓒ Ⓓ Ⓔ
3. Ⓐ Ⓑ Ⓒ Ⓓ Ⓔ
4. Ⓐ Ⓑ Ⓒ Ⓓ Ⓔ
5. Ⓐ Ⓑ Ⓒ Ⓓ Ⓔ
6. Ⓐ Ⓑ Ⓒ Ⓓ Ⓔ
7. Ⓐ Ⓑ Ⓒ Ⓓ Ⓔ
8. Ⓐ Ⓑ Ⓒ Ⓓ Ⓔ
9. Ⓐ Ⓑ Ⓒ Ⓓ Ⓔ
10. Ⓐ Ⓑ Ⓒ Ⓓ Ⓔ
11. Ⓐ Ⓑ Ⓒ Ⓓ Ⓔ
12. Ⓐ Ⓑ Ⓒ Ⓓ Ⓔ
13. Ⓐ Ⓑ Ⓒ Ⓓ Ⓔ
14. Ⓐ Ⓑ Ⓒ Ⓓ Ⓔ
15. Ⓐ Ⓑ Ⓒ Ⓓ Ⓔ
16. Ⓐ Ⓑ Ⓒ Ⓓ Ⓔ
17. Ⓐ Ⓑ Ⓒ Ⓓ Ⓔ
18. Ⓐ Ⓑ Ⓒ Ⓓ Ⓔ
19. Ⓐ Ⓑ Ⓒ Ⓓ Ⓔ
20. Ⓐ Ⓑ Ⓒ Ⓓ Ⓔ
21. Ⓐ Ⓑ Ⓒ Ⓓ Ⓔ
22. Ⓐ Ⓑ Ⓒ Ⓓ Ⓔ
23. Ⓐ Ⓑ Ⓒ Ⓓ Ⓔ
24. Ⓐ Ⓑ Ⓒ Ⓓ Ⓔ
25. Ⓐ Ⓑ Ⓒ Ⓓ Ⓔ

26. Ⓐ Ⓑ Ⓒ Ⓓ Ⓔ
27. Ⓐ Ⓑ Ⓒ Ⓓ Ⓔ
28. Ⓐ Ⓑ Ⓒ Ⓓ Ⓔ
29. Ⓐ Ⓑ Ⓒ Ⓓ Ⓔ
30. Ⓐ Ⓑ Ⓒ Ⓓ Ⓔ
31. Ⓐ Ⓑ Ⓒ Ⓓ Ⓔ
32. Ⓐ Ⓑ Ⓒ Ⓓ Ⓔ
33. Ⓐ Ⓑ Ⓒ Ⓓ Ⓔ
34. Ⓐ Ⓑ Ⓒ Ⓓ Ⓔ
35. Ⓐ Ⓑ Ⓒ Ⓓ Ⓔ
36. Ⓐ Ⓑ Ⓒ Ⓓ Ⓔ
37. Ⓐ Ⓑ Ⓒ Ⓓ Ⓔ
38. Ⓐ Ⓑ Ⓒ Ⓓ Ⓔ
39. Ⓐ Ⓑ Ⓒ Ⓓ Ⓔ
40. Ⓐ Ⓑ Ⓒ Ⓓ Ⓔ
41. Ⓐ Ⓑ Ⓒ Ⓓ Ⓔ
42. Ⓐ Ⓑ Ⓒ Ⓓ Ⓔ
43. Ⓐ Ⓑ Ⓒ Ⓓ Ⓔ
44. Ⓐ Ⓑ Ⓒ Ⓓ Ⓔ
45. Ⓐ Ⓑ Ⓒ Ⓓ Ⓔ
46. Ⓐ Ⓑ Ⓒ Ⓓ Ⓔ
47. Ⓐ Ⓑ Ⓒ Ⓓ Ⓔ
48. Ⓐ Ⓑ Ⓒ Ⓓ Ⓔ
49. Ⓐ Ⓑ Ⓒ Ⓓ Ⓔ
50. Ⓐ Ⓑ Ⓒ Ⓓ Ⓔ

OLSAT® Preparation Guide - Levels D, E, and F

Bright Kids NYC Inc. ©

STUDENT NAME			
DATE OF BIRTH	GRADE	TEST SECTION	TEST DATE (Month/Year)

1. Ⓐ Ⓑ Ⓒ Ⓓ Ⓔ
2. Ⓐ Ⓑ Ⓒ Ⓓ Ⓔ
3. Ⓐ Ⓑ Ⓒ Ⓓ Ⓔ
4. Ⓐ Ⓑ Ⓒ Ⓓ Ⓔ
5. Ⓐ Ⓑ Ⓒ Ⓓ Ⓔ
6. Ⓐ Ⓑ Ⓒ Ⓓ Ⓔ
7. Ⓐ Ⓑ Ⓒ Ⓓ Ⓔ
8. Ⓐ Ⓑ Ⓒ Ⓓ Ⓔ
9. Ⓐ Ⓑ Ⓒ Ⓓ Ⓔ
10. Ⓐ Ⓑ Ⓒ Ⓓ Ⓔ
11. Ⓐ Ⓑ Ⓒ Ⓓ Ⓔ
12. Ⓐ Ⓑ Ⓒ Ⓓ Ⓔ
13. Ⓐ Ⓑ Ⓒ Ⓓ Ⓔ
14. Ⓐ Ⓑ Ⓒ Ⓓ Ⓔ
15. Ⓐ Ⓑ Ⓒ Ⓓ Ⓔ
16. Ⓐ Ⓑ Ⓒ Ⓓ Ⓔ
17. Ⓐ Ⓑ Ⓒ Ⓓ Ⓔ
18. Ⓐ Ⓑ Ⓒ Ⓓ Ⓔ
19. Ⓐ Ⓑ Ⓒ Ⓓ Ⓔ
20. Ⓐ Ⓑ Ⓒ Ⓓ Ⓔ
21. Ⓐ Ⓑ Ⓒ Ⓓ Ⓔ
22. Ⓐ Ⓑ Ⓒ Ⓓ Ⓔ
23. Ⓐ Ⓑ Ⓒ Ⓓ Ⓔ
24. Ⓐ Ⓑ Ⓒ Ⓓ Ⓔ
25. Ⓐ Ⓑ Ⓒ Ⓓ Ⓔ

26. Ⓐ Ⓑ Ⓒ Ⓓ Ⓔ
27. Ⓐ Ⓑ Ⓒ Ⓓ Ⓔ
28. Ⓐ Ⓑ Ⓒ Ⓓ Ⓔ
29. Ⓐ Ⓑ Ⓒ Ⓓ Ⓔ
30. Ⓐ Ⓑ Ⓒ Ⓓ Ⓔ
31. Ⓐ Ⓑ Ⓒ Ⓓ Ⓔ
32. Ⓐ Ⓑ Ⓒ Ⓓ Ⓔ
33. Ⓐ Ⓑ Ⓒ Ⓓ Ⓔ
34. Ⓐ Ⓑ Ⓒ Ⓓ Ⓔ
35. Ⓐ Ⓑ Ⓒ Ⓓ Ⓔ
36. Ⓐ Ⓑ Ⓒ Ⓓ Ⓔ
37. Ⓐ Ⓑ Ⓒ Ⓓ Ⓔ
38. Ⓐ Ⓑ Ⓒ Ⓓ Ⓔ
39. Ⓐ Ⓑ Ⓒ Ⓓ Ⓔ
40. Ⓐ Ⓑ Ⓒ Ⓓ Ⓔ
41. Ⓐ Ⓑ Ⓒ Ⓓ Ⓔ
42. Ⓐ Ⓑ Ⓒ Ⓓ Ⓔ
43. Ⓐ Ⓑ Ⓒ Ⓓ Ⓔ
44. Ⓐ Ⓑ Ⓒ Ⓓ Ⓔ
45. Ⓐ Ⓑ Ⓒ Ⓓ Ⓔ
46. Ⓐ Ⓑ Ⓒ Ⓓ Ⓔ
47. Ⓐ Ⓑ Ⓒ Ⓓ Ⓔ
48. Ⓐ Ⓑ Ⓒ Ⓓ Ⓔ
49. Ⓐ Ⓑ Ⓒ Ⓓ Ⓔ
50. Ⓐ Ⓑ Ⓒ Ⓓ Ⓔ

OLSAT® Preparation Guide - Levels D, E, and F

STUDENT NAME			
DATE OF BIRTH	GRADE	TEST SECTION	TEST DATE (Month/Year)

DIRECTIONS:

- Use a #2 black lead pencil only.
- Do not use ink or colored pencil.
- Completely fill in one oval per question.
- Erase clearly any answer you wish to change.
- Make no stray marks on this answer sheet.

1. Ⓐ Ⓑ Ⓒ Ⓓ Ⓔ
2. Ⓐ Ⓑ Ⓒ Ⓓ Ⓔ
3. Ⓐ Ⓑ Ⓒ Ⓓ Ⓔ
4. Ⓐ Ⓑ Ⓒ Ⓓ Ⓔ
5. Ⓐ Ⓑ Ⓒ Ⓓ Ⓔ
6. Ⓐ Ⓑ Ⓒ Ⓓ Ⓔ
7. Ⓐ Ⓑ Ⓒ Ⓓ Ⓔ
8. Ⓐ Ⓑ Ⓒ Ⓓ Ⓔ
9. Ⓐ Ⓑ Ⓒ Ⓓ Ⓔ
10. Ⓐ Ⓑ Ⓒ Ⓓ Ⓔ
11. Ⓐ Ⓑ Ⓒ Ⓓ Ⓔ
12. Ⓐ Ⓑ Ⓒ Ⓓ Ⓔ
13. Ⓐ Ⓑ Ⓒ Ⓓ Ⓔ
14. Ⓐ Ⓑ Ⓒ Ⓓ Ⓔ
15. Ⓐ Ⓑ Ⓒ Ⓓ Ⓔ
16. Ⓐ Ⓑ Ⓒ Ⓓ Ⓔ
17. Ⓐ Ⓑ Ⓒ Ⓓ Ⓔ
18. Ⓐ Ⓑ Ⓒ Ⓓ Ⓔ
19. Ⓐ Ⓑ Ⓒ Ⓓ Ⓔ
20. Ⓐ Ⓑ Ⓒ Ⓓ Ⓔ
21. Ⓐ Ⓑ Ⓒ Ⓓ Ⓔ
22. Ⓐ Ⓑ Ⓒ Ⓓ Ⓔ
23. Ⓐ Ⓑ Ⓒ Ⓓ Ⓔ
24. Ⓐ Ⓑ Ⓒ Ⓓ Ⓔ
25. Ⓐ Ⓑ Ⓒ Ⓓ Ⓔ

26. Ⓐ Ⓑ Ⓒ Ⓓ Ⓔ
27. Ⓐ Ⓑ Ⓒ Ⓓ Ⓔ
28. Ⓐ Ⓑ Ⓒ Ⓓ Ⓔ
29. Ⓐ Ⓑ Ⓒ Ⓓ Ⓔ
30. Ⓐ Ⓑ Ⓒ Ⓓ Ⓔ
31. Ⓐ Ⓑ Ⓒ Ⓓ Ⓔ
32. Ⓐ Ⓑ Ⓒ Ⓓ Ⓔ
33. Ⓐ Ⓑ Ⓒ Ⓓ Ⓔ
34. Ⓐ Ⓑ Ⓒ Ⓓ Ⓔ
35. Ⓐ Ⓑ Ⓒ Ⓓ Ⓔ
36. Ⓐ Ⓑ Ⓒ Ⓓ Ⓔ
37. Ⓐ Ⓑ Ⓒ Ⓓ Ⓔ
38. Ⓐ Ⓑ Ⓒ Ⓓ Ⓔ
39. Ⓐ Ⓑ Ⓒ Ⓓ Ⓔ
40. Ⓐ Ⓑ Ⓒ Ⓓ Ⓔ
41. Ⓐ Ⓑ Ⓒ Ⓓ Ⓔ
42. Ⓐ Ⓑ Ⓒ Ⓓ Ⓔ
43. Ⓐ Ⓑ Ⓒ Ⓓ Ⓔ
44. Ⓐ Ⓑ Ⓒ Ⓓ Ⓔ
45. Ⓐ Ⓑ Ⓒ Ⓓ Ⓔ
46. Ⓐ Ⓑ Ⓒ Ⓓ Ⓔ
47. Ⓐ Ⓑ Ⓒ Ⓓ Ⓔ
48. Ⓐ Ⓑ Ⓒ Ⓓ Ⓔ
49. Ⓐ Ⓑ Ⓒ Ⓓ Ⓔ
50. Ⓐ Ⓑ Ⓒ Ⓓ Ⓔ

OLSAT® Preparation Guide - Levels D, E, and F

STUDENT NAME			
DATE OF BIRTH	GRADE	TEST SECTION	TEST DATE (Month/Year)

1. Ⓐ Ⓑ Ⓒ Ⓓ Ⓔ
2. Ⓐ Ⓑ Ⓒ Ⓓ Ⓔ
3. Ⓐ Ⓑ Ⓒ Ⓓ Ⓔ
4. Ⓐ Ⓑ Ⓒ Ⓓ Ⓔ
5. Ⓐ Ⓑ Ⓒ Ⓓ Ⓔ
6. Ⓐ Ⓑ Ⓒ Ⓓ Ⓔ
7. Ⓐ Ⓑ Ⓒ Ⓓ Ⓔ
8. Ⓐ Ⓑ Ⓒ Ⓓ Ⓔ
9. Ⓐ Ⓑ Ⓒ Ⓓ Ⓔ
10. Ⓐ Ⓑ Ⓒ Ⓓ Ⓔ
11. Ⓐ Ⓑ Ⓒ Ⓓ Ⓔ
12. Ⓐ Ⓑ Ⓒ Ⓓ Ⓔ
13. Ⓐ Ⓑ Ⓒ Ⓓ Ⓔ
14. Ⓐ Ⓑ Ⓒ Ⓓ Ⓔ
15. Ⓐ Ⓑ Ⓒ Ⓓ Ⓔ
16. Ⓐ Ⓑ Ⓒ Ⓓ Ⓔ
17. Ⓐ Ⓑ Ⓒ Ⓓ Ⓔ
18. Ⓐ Ⓑ Ⓒ Ⓓ Ⓔ
19. Ⓐ Ⓑ Ⓒ Ⓓ Ⓔ
20. Ⓐ Ⓑ Ⓒ Ⓓ Ⓔ
21. Ⓐ Ⓑ Ⓒ Ⓓ Ⓔ
22. Ⓐ Ⓑ Ⓒ Ⓓ Ⓔ
23. Ⓐ Ⓑ Ⓒ Ⓓ Ⓔ
24. Ⓐ Ⓑ Ⓒ Ⓓ Ⓔ
25. Ⓐ Ⓑ Ⓒ Ⓓ Ⓔ

26. Ⓐ Ⓑ Ⓒ Ⓓ Ⓔ
27. Ⓐ Ⓑ Ⓒ Ⓓ Ⓔ
28. Ⓐ Ⓑ Ⓒ Ⓓ Ⓔ
29. Ⓐ Ⓑ Ⓒ Ⓓ Ⓔ
30. Ⓐ Ⓑ Ⓒ Ⓓ Ⓔ
31. Ⓐ Ⓑ Ⓒ Ⓓ Ⓔ
32. Ⓐ Ⓑ Ⓒ Ⓓ Ⓔ
33. Ⓐ Ⓑ Ⓒ Ⓓ Ⓔ
34. Ⓐ Ⓑ Ⓒ Ⓓ Ⓔ
35. Ⓐ Ⓑ Ⓒ Ⓓ Ⓔ
36. Ⓐ Ⓑ Ⓒ Ⓓ Ⓔ
37. Ⓐ Ⓑ Ⓒ Ⓓ Ⓔ
38. Ⓐ Ⓑ Ⓒ Ⓓ Ⓔ
39. Ⓐ Ⓑ Ⓒ Ⓓ Ⓔ
40. Ⓐ Ⓑ Ⓒ Ⓓ Ⓔ
41. Ⓐ Ⓑ Ⓒ Ⓓ Ⓔ
42. Ⓐ Ⓑ Ⓒ Ⓓ Ⓔ
43. Ⓐ Ⓑ Ⓒ Ⓓ Ⓔ
44. Ⓐ Ⓑ Ⓒ Ⓓ Ⓔ
45. Ⓐ Ⓑ Ⓒ Ⓓ Ⓔ
46. Ⓐ Ⓑ Ⓒ Ⓓ Ⓔ
47. Ⓐ Ⓑ Ⓒ Ⓓ Ⓔ
48. Ⓐ Ⓑ Ⓒ Ⓓ Ⓔ
49. Ⓐ Ⓑ Ⓒ Ⓓ Ⓔ
50. Ⓐ Ⓑ Ⓒ Ⓓ Ⓔ

OLSAT® Preparation Guide - Levels D, E, and F

STUDENT NAME			
DATE OF BIRTH	GRADE	TEST SECTION	TEST DATE (Month/Year)

1. (A) (B) (C) (D) (E)
2. (A) (B) (C) (D) (E)
3. (A) (B) (C) (D) (E)
4. (A) (B) (C) (D) (E)
5. (A) (B) (C) (D) (E)
6. (A) (B) (C) (D) (E)
7. (A) (B) (C) (D) (E)
8. (A) (B) (C) (D) (E)
9. (A) (B) (C) (D) (E)
10. (A) (B) (C) (D) (E)
11. (A) (B) (C) (D) (E)
12. (A) (B) (C) (D) (E)
13. (A) (B) (C) (D) (E)
14. (A) (B) (C) (D) (E)
15. (A) (B) (C) (D) (E)
16. (A) (B) (C) (D) (E)
17. (A) (B) (C) (D) (E)
18. (A) (B) (C) (D) (E)
19. (A) (B) (C) (D) (E)
20. (A) (B) (C) (D) (E)
21. (A) (B) (C) (D) (E)
22. (A) (B) (C) (D) (E)
23. (A) (B) (C) (D) (E)
24. (A) (B) (C) (D) (E)
25. (A) (B) (C) (D) (E)

26. (A) (B) (C) (D) (E)
27. (A) (B) (C) (D) (E)
28. (A) (B) (C) (D) (E)
29. (A) (B) (C) (D) (E)
30. (A) (B) (C) (D) (E)
31. (A) (B) (C) (D) (E)
32. (A) (B) (C) (D) (E)
33. (A) (B) (C) (D) (E)
34. (A) (B) (C) (D) (E)
35. (A) (B) (C) (D) (E)
36. (A) (B) (C) (D) (E)
37. (A) (B) (C) (D) (E)
38. (A) (B) (C) (D) (E)
39. (A) (B) (C) (D) (E)
40. (A) (B) (C) (D) (E)
41. (A) (B) (C) (D) (E)
42. (A) (B) (C) (D) (E)
43. (A) (B) (C) (D) (E)
44. (A) (B) (C) (D) (E)
45. (A) (B) (C) (D) (E)
46. (A) (B) (C) (D) (E)
47. (A) (B) (C) (D) (E)
48. (A) (B) (C) (D) (E)
49. (A) (B) (C) (D) (E)
50. (A) (B) (C) (D) (E)

OLSAT® Preparation Guide - Levels D, E, and F

STUDENT NAME			
DATE OF BIRTH	GRADE	TEST SECTION	TEST DATE (Month/Year)

EXAMPLE

1 Ⓐ Ⓧ Ⓒ Ⓓ   WRONG
2 ✓Ⓐ Ⓑ Ⓒ Ⓓ   WRONG
3 Ⓐ Ⓑ ● Ⓓ   WRONG
4 Ⓐ Ⓑ Ⓒ ●   CORRECT

DIRECTIONS:

- Use a #2 black lead pencil only.
- Do not use ink or colored pencil.
- Completely fill in one oval per question.
- Erase clearly any answer you wish to change.
- Make no stray marks on this answer sheet.

1. Ⓐ Ⓑ Ⓒ Ⓓ Ⓔ
2. Ⓐ Ⓑ Ⓒ Ⓓ Ⓔ
3. Ⓐ Ⓑ Ⓒ Ⓓ Ⓔ
4. Ⓐ Ⓑ Ⓒ Ⓓ Ⓔ
5. Ⓐ Ⓑ Ⓒ Ⓓ Ⓔ
6. Ⓐ Ⓑ Ⓒ Ⓓ Ⓔ
7. Ⓐ Ⓑ Ⓒ Ⓓ Ⓔ
8. Ⓐ Ⓑ Ⓒ Ⓓ Ⓔ
9. Ⓐ Ⓑ Ⓒ Ⓓ Ⓔ
10. Ⓐ Ⓑ Ⓒ Ⓓ Ⓔ
11. Ⓐ Ⓑ Ⓒ Ⓓ Ⓔ
12. Ⓐ Ⓑ Ⓒ Ⓓ Ⓔ
13. Ⓐ Ⓑ Ⓒ Ⓓ Ⓔ
14. Ⓐ Ⓑ Ⓒ Ⓓ Ⓔ
15. Ⓐ Ⓑ Ⓒ Ⓓ Ⓔ
16. Ⓐ Ⓑ Ⓒ Ⓓ Ⓔ
17. Ⓐ Ⓑ Ⓒ Ⓓ Ⓔ
18. Ⓐ Ⓑ Ⓒ Ⓓ Ⓔ
19. Ⓐ Ⓑ Ⓒ Ⓓ Ⓔ
20. Ⓐ Ⓑ Ⓒ Ⓓ Ⓔ
21. Ⓐ Ⓑ Ⓒ Ⓓ Ⓔ
22. Ⓐ Ⓑ Ⓒ Ⓓ Ⓔ
23. Ⓐ Ⓑ Ⓒ Ⓓ Ⓔ
24. Ⓐ Ⓑ Ⓒ Ⓓ Ⓔ
25. Ⓐ Ⓑ Ⓒ Ⓓ Ⓔ

26. Ⓐ Ⓑ Ⓒ Ⓓ Ⓔ
27. Ⓐ Ⓑ Ⓒ Ⓓ Ⓔ
28. Ⓐ Ⓑ Ⓒ Ⓓ Ⓔ
29. Ⓐ Ⓑ Ⓒ Ⓓ Ⓔ
30. Ⓐ Ⓑ Ⓒ Ⓓ Ⓔ
31. Ⓐ Ⓑ Ⓒ Ⓓ Ⓔ
32. Ⓐ Ⓑ Ⓒ Ⓓ Ⓔ
33. Ⓐ Ⓑ Ⓒ Ⓓ Ⓔ
34. Ⓐ Ⓑ Ⓒ Ⓓ Ⓔ
35. Ⓐ Ⓑ Ⓒ Ⓓ Ⓔ
36. Ⓐ Ⓑ Ⓒ Ⓓ Ⓔ
37. Ⓐ Ⓑ Ⓒ Ⓓ Ⓔ
38. Ⓐ Ⓑ Ⓒ Ⓓ Ⓔ
39. Ⓐ Ⓑ Ⓒ Ⓓ Ⓔ
40. Ⓐ Ⓑ Ⓒ Ⓓ Ⓔ
41. Ⓐ Ⓑ Ⓒ Ⓓ Ⓔ
42. Ⓐ Ⓑ Ⓒ Ⓓ Ⓔ
43. Ⓐ Ⓑ Ⓒ Ⓓ Ⓔ
44. Ⓐ Ⓑ Ⓒ Ⓓ Ⓔ
45. Ⓐ Ⓑ Ⓒ Ⓓ Ⓔ
46. Ⓐ Ⓑ Ⓒ Ⓓ Ⓔ
47. Ⓐ Ⓑ Ⓒ Ⓓ Ⓔ
48. Ⓐ Ⓑ Ⓒ Ⓓ Ⓔ
49. Ⓐ Ⓑ Ⓒ Ⓓ Ⓔ
50. Ⓐ Ⓑ Ⓒ Ⓓ Ⓔ

OLSAT® Preparation Guide - Levels D, E, and F Bright Kids NYC Inc. ©